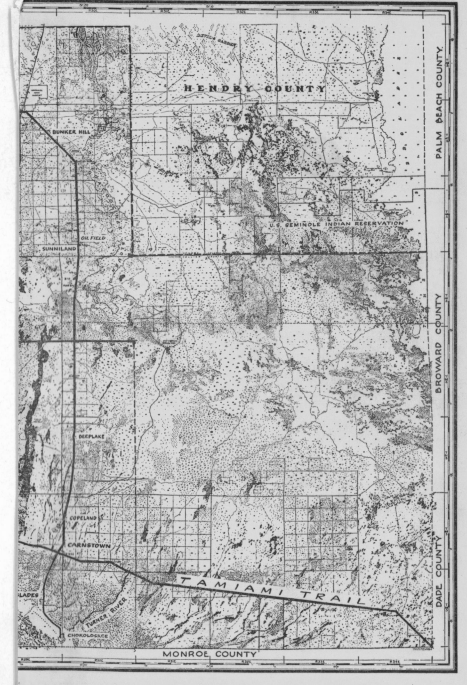

FLORIDA'S
Last
FRONTIER

Mark
Chard

1963

FLORIDA'S
Last
FRONTIER

THE HISTORY OF
COLLIER COUNTY

by

Charlton W. Tebeau

Copeland Studies in Florida History

UNIVERSITY OF MIAMI PRESS

1957

PRINTED BY PARKER, CORAL GABLES, FLORIDA, U.S.A.

Dedicated

TO THE

Three Generations

OF

MEN *and* WOMEN

who have pioneered

on

FLORIDA'S LAST
FRONTIER

Contents

LIST OF ILLUSTRATIONS

FOREWORD

NATURE made Collier County a part of America's last frontier. It did not become a separate political unit until 1923. Even then it was the promise of development rather than that already accomplished which justified the creation of a new county. Few counties in modern times have been created with smaller population and less developed resources in so large an area.

The region had been occupied by Calusa Indians for nearly two thousand years, but they had been gone for a century or more. Spaniards had appeared early in the sixteenth century, but after three hundred years they had left scarcely a place name. Seminole Indians came into southern Florida during and after the War of Indian Removal (1835-1842). Only two or three hundred in number, they were living in the interior around and south of Lake Okeechobee and had not yet been crowded into the lower peninsula.

In 1923 there were tiny white settlements on the southwest coast at Naples, on Marco Island, on Chokoloskee Island, at Everglades, and a few families living near the mouths of rivers and there was one settlement in the interior at Immokalee. Together they numbered scarcely a thousand souls.

These settlements, all on the fringe of the county, had their economic and legal and political connections with places not now in Collier County. Immokalee was in many respects an outpost of Fort Myers and had little or no dealings with the coastal communities. These last had contact with each other and with the outside world only by water and they looked southward to Key West or northward to Fort Myers and Tampa.

The whole interior of the South Florida peninsula had to wait for drainage and highway and railroad before it could be opened up, and before its great potentialities could be recognized and begin to be developed. These did not come to pass until the nineteen twenties and even then events beyond the new county's limits and control hampered its development for another generation.

Stirrings of new activity that would eventually reach the remote and isolated southwest coast of the Florida peninsula began around the turn of the century. The great freeze in the winter of 1894-1895 sent men further south seeking more nearly frost free areas. A direct result was the discovery and development of Deep Lake Hammock which was later to bring Barron G. Collier's attention to the region.

The railroad reached Fort Myers in 1904 and stimulated activity all down the coast. Fort Myers was the county seat of Lee County, created in 1887 and including all of present Hendry and Collier Counties. It had been incorporated in 1885. Since 1884 it had had a weekly newspaper, the *Fort Myers Press,* which in 1911 became a daily. The administration of Governor Napoleon Bonaparte Broward (1905-1909) made the first all-out attack on the drainage problem. If it did not immediately drain the Everglades, it aroused interest and raised hopes.

Two new communities appeared on the coast just north of what was to be the new county. The Koreshans founded Estero in 1894, and in 1906 began to publish the *American Eagle,* a weekly devoted to the promotion of the interests of the entire southwest coast. Bonita Springs was large enough for a school and a post office in 1901.

Over on the East coast Henry M. Flagler's Florida East Coast Railroad reached Miami in 1896 and started that community—with a history to that time much like that of what was to be Collier County —on its way to rapid growth. Soon he was extending the railroad southward to Homestead and Florida City and over the sea to Key West which it reached in 1912. There was talk of a similar railroad development on the western side of the peninsula; and the possibility of a cross-state canal, highway and railroad sometimes seemed near realization.

But a series of state, national and international events seemed to conspire to hold up the development of what Karl Bickel so aptly called the "Mangrove Coast." In 1914 the First World War broke out and three years later the United States was involved. Then came the booming early twenties that seemed to promise so much for southern Florida. The new county was born on the eve of the boom, and for better or worse, had only begun to share in it, when in 1926 it broke and the Florida depression had to be weathered.

Before that was accomplished the national stockmarket crash in 1929 added to the economic woes of Floridians, and slowed, if indeed it did not stop, growth, thus prolonging the waiting period. One more such hurdle must be cleared. The second World War came and at the end of 1941 the United States was in it. This absorbed all the energies and resources of the country for some years.

ACKNOWLEDGMENTS

MANY INDIVIDUALS have had a part in the writing of this history of Collier County. The author takes this means to express his indebtedness and appreciation for their assistance without which it could not have been written. His only regret is that time and circumstance did not make it possible to talk with all the members of every pioneer family for each would have added some bit of information or understanding that would have made the story more complete.

The research for the study was made possible by a grant to the University of Miami in 1950 by the sons of the late Barron G. Collier to underwrite publications in the history of southwestern Florida. David Graham Copeland, for many years resident manager of the Collier properties, and chairman of the board of County Commissioners for twenty years, was collecting material for a history of the region and was beginning to write when he died. He did leave some volumes of maps and notes which have been at the writer's disposal. It is in his honor that the grant was made and the series of studies to be published under it named "The Copeland Studies in Florida History," of which this is the second.

One or more chapters have been read by each of the following persons whose professional knowledge has saved the author from error and has added much useful information. It must suffice here merely to list them. They are, Dr. Taylor R. Alexander of the University of Miami Botany Department; Deaconess Harriet M. Bedell of Glade Cross Mission, Everglades; Dr. James W. Covington, History Department, University of Tampa; Dr. John H. Davis, Jr., Botany Department, University of Florida; Dr. John M. Goggin, Anthropology Department, University of Florida; and Dr. William C. Sturtevant, Smithsonian Institution. Julien C. Yonge, editor emeritus of the *Florida Historical Quarterly,* gave the author much encouragement and read the manuscript in an early draft.

The chapters on the communities and the county at large have been written with the aid of pioneers and sons and daughters of pioneers whose family names are made familiar in this story, as well as many adopted sons and daughters who have become a part of the county's history. Deserving special mention are Charles T. Boggess of Everglades; Mrs. Dewey Brown of Immokalee; Mr. and Mrs. Frank Brown, Immokalee; O. L. Carson, Naples; Michael Chance of the *Collier County News*; Mrs. Fanny Santini Chefneux of Miami; Mr. and Mrs. Hugh N. Davis, Jr., Miami; Mrs. Winnie D. Frederick, Naples; Mr. and Mrs. Robert A. Griffis, Marco; Norman A. Herren, Everglades; George Huntoon, Everglades; Winford Janes, Copeland; D. W. McLeod, Everglades; Kenneth Marmon, Indian Agent, Dania; D. W. Reynolds, County Superintendent of Public Instruction; Mr. and Mrs. Ed Scott, Everglades;

Mr. and Mrs. Ted Smallwood, Everglades; Miss Thelma Smallwood, Chokoloskee; Mr. and Mrs. Claude M. Storter, Naples; Mrs. R. B. Storter, Naples; Mr. and Mrs. Graham Whidden, Immokalee; Mr. and Mrs. Sam Whidden, Corkscrew.

Another equally important group have given information and the use of their treasured pictures saved from early days. Among them are: Mrs. Frank K. Ashworth, Ventura, California; Sam Bonard, Everglades; Miss Florence Brigham, Miami; Mrs. N. Ernest Carroll, Naples; Mrs. M. K. Carson, Immokalee; Clyde L. Clifton, Deep Lake; J. Harvey Doxsee, Marco; Mr. and Mrs. A. C. Hancock, Chokoloskee; Frank Heath, Naples; Mr. and Mrs. Dan House, Sr., Naples; Mrs. Bertie Storter Ison, Bonita Springs; Major Edward T. Keenan, Frostproof; Mrs. Rose Brown Kennon, Immokalee; Mr. and Mrs. Arthur P. "Bud" Kirk, Goodland; Mrs. Jessie Walker Kirkland, Naples; Joel Kuperberg, Naples; John Ludlow, Goodland; Don Lander, County Agricultural Agent; Albert Manly, Coconut Grove; Mrs. Bonnie C. Moore, Everglades; Hiram Newell, Marco; Mrs. Roy V. Ott, Oklawaha; Mr. and Mrs. Chester Pettit, Caxambas; Charles Rawls, Goodland; Mr. and Mrs. Bob Roberts and D. W. Roberts, Immokalee; John Henry Thompson, Chokoloskee; Mr. and Mrs. Sam H. Thompson, Immokalee; W. H. Turner, Everglades; Mr. and Mrs. Ken Vogstad, Goodland; Forrest Walker and J. Lorenzo Walker, Naples; Alfred Weeks and Andrew Weeks, Naples.

Three Newspapers have been used and quoted extensively: *The American Eagle,* published at Estero by the Koreshans from 1906 to 1946, of which the Historical Association of Southern Florida possesses a complete file; the *Collier County News,* born like the county in 1923; and the *Fort Myers Press,* (now *News Press*) published since 1884. For these last two the author thanks the publishers. The library facilities of the University of Miami and the City of Miami as well have been made available and the personnel have been most helpful.

Credit is given in each case for illustrations. John Childers of the Parker Art Company, Coral Gables, made the map which appears on the cover. Bland Bowers of the same company designed the book.

The author is also especially grateful to Mrs. Madeleine Van Slaars who did the typing of the various forms through which the manuscript has passed; to Miss Helen Wilson, who typed a part of the final draft; and to Miss Nedra McNamara of the University of Miami Press for editorial work on the manuscript. William J. Schellings, at that time a student, gave valuable and interested aid in searching early newspapers.

His wife, Violet, has been patient while he neglected his home chores to go history hunting in Collier County, and has convinced him with her confidence and encouragement that he should write the book.

CHARLTON W. TEBEAU

University of Miami
Summer of 1957

Physical Features and
Natural Endowment

NATURE was lavish in supplying Collier County with many unusual physical characteristics and natural resources, but so much of the county was remote and inaccessible that some of it was completely unknown until very recently.

Exploration, surveying and mapping occurred mostly within the last one hundred years and systematic efforts to identify and classify the plant and animal life are scarcely a half century old. Classified as "swamp and overflowed," almost all of the Collier County land was transferred to the State of Florida by the United States Government, under an act of 1850. This was a liberal application of the terms swamp and overflowed, for these suggested that drainage and reclamation would be necessary before the land could be utilized. Though this is true of much of the land, not all of it belongs in that category.

In the final stages of the Seminole wars the military expeditions provided the first accounts of the interior in a systematic fashion. These records were often done by men without any special skills and few if any instruments, and the maps are sketchy and inaccurate. Moreover their reports had only a limited purpose because their makers saw natural features chiefly as those that aided the Seminoles to escape and hide and make it difficult to follow them. Although some reports contained useful data they were not published and did little more than excite the curiosity of the few persons through whose hands they passed. Adequate surveys had to await the day of the aerial photograph and better transportation.

Township and section lines south of the Caloosahatchee River on the west coast were not surveyed until after 1870, and then only about one-half of the county was surveyed. The whole interior back from the coast was considered inaccessible and of no interest. The field notes of the surveyors sometimes describe physical features, comment upon the plant and animal life and suggest the possible agricultural usefulness or lack of it.

Surveyor Apthorp in 1872 made this entry in his field notes that shows graphically why much of the area was left untouched: "a pond, surrounded by bay and cypress swamp, impracticable. Pond full of monstrous alligators. Counted fifty and stopped. Relinquish line." And in another instance, this entry: "Impracticable—deep water, dense swamp, water just ahead four feet deep and getting deeper. Sent a man up a tree—see nothing ahead but cypress, apparently, growing deeper, relinquish line."

Sometimes useful historical data is included in the surveyors' notes. For example, in one we find: "nearly all prairie with numerous grass ponds and a few fertile hammocks. Two Indian families living in this township in sections 10 and 23 in live oak and maple hammocks and cultivating small fields of corn, pumpkin, melons and other vegetables which yield bountifully . . . the old military road runs through this township from Fort Myers to Fort Shackleford."

Even now the casual observer driving along the highways of Collier County may never guess the great variety of the county's natural features back from the roads. He may easily conclude only that it is uniformly low and flat and sometimes wet. The only difference he sees may be in the natural vegetation that changes as he moves from area to area where mangroves or cypresses or palmettoes and pines predominate. He may miss entirely the presence of rich and varied natural assets of which some are unique and many are relatively unspoiled by the hand of man.

The naturalist, whether amateur or scientist, has found in the plants and animals an amazing variety and abundance. Here where the temperate zone begins to merge with the tropic to form a sub-tropical climate he has found life that is unique in the United States. Presence of this abundance and variety of life is the reason that some parts of this last frontier must be preserved unspoiled in the Everglades National Park for all to see and appreciate.

Hunters, particularly those seeking alligators and plume birds, explored the interior earlier and more thoroughly than did anyone else. They followed the wild animals and fowl into the most remote places, but they rarely reported what they had observed.

In 1943, the Florida Geological Survey published *The Natural Features of South Florida,* by John H. Davis, Jr., who made studies of his own and collected data from historical sources. His non-technical but sound study makes good reading and provides much scientific data. Collier County is only a part of the area described in the bulletin but is in many respects typical of the whole area. Much of the information in the remainder of this chapter is from this source.

The county may be roughly divided into the Big Cypress Region, the Western Flat Lands, and the Ten Thousand Islands. The Florida Everglades touches Collier County only in the extreme northeast corner. But it runs along the eastern boundary and effectively separated the west coast from travel contact by land with the east coast until 1928 when the Tamiami Trail "bridged" that obstacle.

Until the Everglades was drained, water from this vast "River of Grass" sometimes overflowed to the west coast in seasons of heavy rainfall. The Everglades was also used as a great highway of canoe travel for Indians and early explorers. Starting from "landings" like Boat or Brown's Landing near Immokalee, or from the mouths of one of the rivers flowing into the Gulf of Mexico, travellers easily made their way across the Everglades to Lake Okeechobee or to the east coast by such waterways as the New River at Fort Lauderdale or the Miami River to Biscayne Bay. To them this great marsh was a great waterway, and by no means a barrier to travel.

Before drainage, when the water level varied greatly between wet and dry seasons or years, a difference of two feet in water level meant the difference between shallow lake and dry land for many square miles. A. W. Dimock described a canoe trip in 1908: "We began the trip in canoes, but ended it in an oxcart. We paddled and wallowed through two hundred miles of flower clad lakes and boggy, moccasin-infested trails, zigzagging from border to border of the Florida Everglades, and were hauled for five days on pine covered stretches of sand, across submerged prairies, and through sloughs of the Big Cypress Country, but we failed to reach the big lake by twenty-five miles . . ."

By contrast, he added: "Last year we crossed the 'Glades from west to east, in a power boat, over the deepest water known for a

Photo by Jack Holmes, Coral Gables.

In the Big Cypress Swamp.

decade. This year from Cape Sable to Lake Okeechobee, we could seldom find water to float a canoe."

The Big Cypress Region, or simply the Big Cypress, is 1200 square miles in extent and lies mostly in western Collier County. The Florida Seminoles call it "Atseenahoofa" and two-thirds of them have at times lived there.

The term Big Cypress is somewhat misleading. Though it once held one of the largest areas of old growth virgin cypress in the United States, by no means all of the cypress is big. Growing along the Tamiami Trail one sees mainly the dwarfed scrub cypresses and occasional cypress domes, so called because the increasing tallness of the trees toward the center gives the cluster a dome shape. There is usually an open pond of water in the center of the dome. There are also cypress strands in long depressions or swamps, in which grew large cypress trees of great commercial importance. Cypress forests do not cover the whole area however; there are also pine forests and marl soil prairies.

Most of the Big Cypress is less than fifteen feet in elevation. The soils are sandy marls and are often thin, large areas being rocklands with little or no soil. Small depressions with no surface drainage are common. Most of the creeks, rivers, sloughs and swamps that drain the region in general trend in a north-south direction even though the drainage on the eastern edge is toward the Everglades on which it borders.

Many of the rivers in Collier County have their origin in the Big Cypress and are short. The longer and better known rivers below Collier County rise in and drain the Everglades. These streams in seasons of high water may carry a great volume of fresh water, but in dry seasons their fresh water sources may dry up and they become little more than tidal inlets. Upstream these water courses gradually lose their character and become mere ill-defined shallow drains for the swamps. At the other extreme their lower parts are lagoons dotted with mangrove islands, and with usually a shallow bar at the mouth.

The Big Cypress is also characterized by hammock forests on the higher lands which are relatively fertile. These have a dense growth of trees and underbrush and are usually not large enough for clearing and cultivation by anyone but Indians. There is, however, one notable exception at Deep Lake hammock where fifty years ago two hundred acres of grapefruit were growing.

Solution holes or sink holes of varied size and depth are also com-

Courtesy of the Collier Development Corporation.

Deep Lake scene, early twenties.

17

mon in the Big Cypress, and there is some evidence of underground drainage. Rainwater percolating downward through the soluble limestone that underlies much of the region has dissolved vertical chimney-like holes in it into which the surface cover collapsed, producing the steep walled open holes. The largest of these in the county is Deep Lake, only about three hundred feet across. Once considered to be bottomless, it is now known to be ninety-five feet deep.

The area along the coast, west and north of the Big Cypress and as far south as Gordon's Pass, is part of the Western Flat Lands. The elevation here is somewhat higher than the Big Cypress. Except around Immokalee the land is generally less than twenty-five feet above sea level. It is a part of the Pamlico Terrace formed on the sea bottom when in geologic time the peninsula was inundated to a depth of twenty-five feet above present sea level. The higher land around Immokalee was at that time an island. The marine sands left on this and other terraces account for the generally sandy nature of much of the soil.

The area is also characterized by a great number of marshes, swamps and open water depressions. More prominent of these are Lake Trafford and the Corkscrew Marsh near it and the Okaloacoochee Slough. Lake Trafford is a shallow depression, 1880 acres in extent, nowhere more than eight feet deep and with no good drainage out of it.

Southwestern Collier County, from Gordon's Pass at Naples, southward to Cape Sable, is another distinctive region with its own physical features. Davis named it "The Southwest Coast and the Ten Thousand Islands." He described it as a "low lying coastal region of many tidal rivers, bays, sounds and lakes with thousands of shoal water islands..." The maze of water courses has connection by bays that are inland from the Gulf of Mexico, and the numerous islands and the mangrove swamps make the whole complex region unique in the United States, if not in the world. The land surfaces in this area are nearly all below five feet elevation except where shell islands and sand dunes rise higher.

Much of the region is flooded, partly due to submergence by a rise in the sea level rather than by a sinking of the land. Before this submergence began the coast and islands were probably much more regular in shape. Evidence of the rise of the sea exists in Indian sites, now under water, which were inhabited when the sea level was lower than it now is. The shore may be gradually extending outward, mainly by the coalescence of the islands aided by the growth of mangrove trees in the shoal waters. However, a number of islands and parts of the mainland from Naples to Cape Romano are built up by sea currents and the movement of sediments. On Marco Island the sand dunes on the south end that were built up by this process are above fifty feet elevation, the highest coastal area in southern Florida.

The Ten Thousand Islands can be adequately viewed or mapped only from the air. Most of the small mangrove clad islands seem stretched out end to end in somewhat parallel rows, nearly all trending in a southeasterly direction. They are mainly shell-fish bars on which mangrove trees have taken root and grown. They vary in size from a tiny cluster of mangrove bushes to Marco Island with its six thousand acres. As there may be as much as four feet difference between low tide and high tide, some islands may at high tide be completely covered by water except for the mangrove tree tops, and at low tide may be half land-half water kind of islands.

A singular feature of great importance in the coastal area is the long sandy beaches which extend northward along the west coast for a distance of 180 miles. The beach at Naples stretches seven miles north of Gordon's Pass, and on Marco Island on the Gulf side there are six miles, all of which yield many multicolored sea shells. Somewhat more inaccessible are the sand and shell beaches of Cape Romano which is separated from Marco by Caxambas Pass, not yet bridged. Now being developed, Cape Romano is destined to be of greater importance in the future.

The plant life of Collier County as in all of southern Florida is unusually varied. This is due partly to the overlapping of species of the south temperate zone with those of subtropical lands, the tropical plants being at or near the northern limit of their range and seldom attaining the large size to which they grow further south. It is due also to local variations in the depth and type of soil, water level and rainfall.

An incomplete count shows that over 850 plants are native to the region, a larger number than may be found in any other comparable area in the United States. Another unusual feature is the great number of woody plants, over ninety of which may be considered trees. There are also 125 woody plants classified as small trees and shrubs. Only the Great Smoky Mountains have more species of woody plants in a comparable area.

Except for pine, cypress and mangrove, the trees do not form large

Photo by Taylor R. Alexander, Miami.

Air plants growing on cypress trees along the Tamiami Trail.

area forests of pure or nearly pure stands, but many of the forests, even on small areas, have a great variety of trees. This is particularly true of the hammocks in which are found many plants rarely if ever found elsewhere in the United States. Over thirty-five species of trees and twice that many shrubs are to be found in the hammocks. Also characteristic of the hammocks is a great abundance of vines, ferns and epiphytes. The epiphytes are principally bromeliads, commonly called air plants which resemble pineapple plants growing on trees; and orchids, more numerous here than in any part of the United States. Some are rare, some common, and many are showy and pretty.

Palms of tree size and smaller are numerous and at least eight are native, of which the royal palm is the most majestic. The best accessible known stand of royal palms in the county is in the Barron Collier Memorial State Park, on the south side of Tamiami Trail just east of the intersection of state highway 27 to Marco Island. Royal Palms were at one time more numerous in the hammocks and swamps of the Great Fakahatchee Swamp, from which the tall royal palms in Hialeah Park were taken. A third equally notable stand of royal palms is in Royal Palm Park, southwest of Homestead and now incorporated in the Everglades National Park.

Three species of mangroves grow in the county, the red, the black or honey, and the white, sometimes called white buttonwood. These are dissimilar in appearance and prefer somewhat different growing conditions. The red mangrove has an extensive prop root system that looks like braces growing from the trunk. Soldier Andrew P. Canova likened these to a lot of tent poles leaning together and a big tree growing on top. It is most common in shoal and shallow offshore waters and forms the outer zone of mangrove swamps.

Red Mangrove—note prop roots.

The black mangrove usually produces many erect roots called pneumatophores that stick up through the mud and water and resemble asparagus tips. It usually grows on inshore mud flats and forms a zone inland from the outer red mangrove zone.

The white mangrove is not so common as the other two. It seldom has pneumatophores and has thick oval shaped leaves that look alike on both surfaces. It may be found with the red mangroves but most frequently occurs further inland and forms thickets inland from the black mangrove zone.

The buttonwood tree usually occurs with the mangroves. It is so named because of its spherical group of flowers and fruits that look like round buttons. It is located inland from the flooded parts of the mangrove swamps, in near coastal hammocks, and low places in pine land. It is not so well adapted as mangrove to salt water and mud.

Of all the trees the pine and cypress alone have had great commercial importance. The mangrove is a potential source of tannin and charcoal and some wood utensils and some hope it may one day be used to make paper. Buttonwood was cut by pioneers for firewood and to make charcoal.

21

Photos by Taylor R. Alexander, Miami.

Black Mangrove—note pneumatophores.

Two of five main regions in southern Florida where wild life is most abundant today are wholly or partly in Collier County—the Ten Thousand Islands and the Big Cypress. Extending from Cape Romano to Cape Sable, the Ten Thousand Islands region includes the coastal rivers and coastal prairies and the great mangrove swamps and marshes near the coast. This area is still a wilderness and likely to remain one. The mangrove swamps and salt marshes are relatively inaccessible and provide ample food and cover for game. Great flocks of birds have roosts and rookeries there. The large water areas and the plentiful food and cover attract many ducks and other migratory fowl in season.

The Big Cypress provides almost as much food and shelter for its wild life as the Islands region, but is far more accessible to hunters. Most seriously hunted today are deer and turkey. Game here has been driven into small areas and into the less accessible Everglades and Ten Thousand Islands.

Of all the animals the alligator has perhaps been most important in the history of the county. Because three generation of hunters maintained themselves chiefly by selling alligator hides, the species is now nearly extinct and killing them is forbidden by law. Florida wildlife officers can testify that poachers still make raids on the rather easy-to-catch alligators and spirit the hides away to other counties where it is legal to sell them.

Florida deer once existed in great numbers but now survive only because the law protects them and nature affords such excellent cover for them. In the early 1940's they were almost lost to cattle raising when it was discovered that they carried the fever tick that preyed on the cattle. In Collier and Hendry counties hunters killed several thousand deer in two years to exterminate ticks near cattle ranges. But hunting is almost as important—to the sports minded people of the county and visitors—as cattle raising and the woods were restocked and the supply of deer somewhat replenished.

There were once Florida wolves but they were killed out by cattlemen and hunters nearly fifty years ago. The Florida panther or cougar is rarely found any more. The Florida black bear is also nearly gone but as late as 1956 an auto on Tamiami Trail struck a bear and they will get a new lease on life in the Everglades National Park. Numbers of otter still inhabit the waters of the county in spite of hunting and trapping them for their fur. The Florida bobcat, the gray fox, the raccoon, the opossum, and the "cologne kitty" or skunk, are still common, as are rabbits and squirrels.

The strangest and most unique mammal in southern Florida waters is the manatee or sea cow. It once ranged both the east and west coasts but the remaining few are probably outside Collier County waters. Manatees are slow and awkward and easily caught and they may be cut by a boat propeller. They are much sought after as food which is called sea pork and are in danger of extinction in spite of laws to protect them.

Many large and showy long legged wading birds have their rookeries, roosts and feeding grounds in southern Florida. In Pelican Rookery near Sand Fly Pass, pelicans, cormorants, Louisiana herons, Man o' War birds and snowy egrets nest. In the Corkscrew Cypress Rookery thousands of wood ibis nest high in the tops of huge cypress trees. This rookery is now preserved by the National Audubon Society and visitors may enter the swamp on a board walk and see one of the few stands of virgin cypress in the United States, as well as the nesting ibis, though in truth the best view of the nests is from the air.

The county shore waters have an abundance of fish in great variety. The mullet has been as basic to the economy of the fisherman as was the alligator to the hunter. In earlier days it was not uncommon for schools of mullet two or three miles long to be found coming in at the passes with the tide, and the splashing of so many fish is described as deafening. Pompano is another food fish not so numerous as formerly, but old-timers recall when they might be caught in Marco Pass with a throw net.

Mackerel, blue fish, and kingfish are commercially important in their seasons. Other food fish are weakfish or sea trout, grouper, snapper, jewfish, redfish or channel bass, sheepshead and robalo or snook. Snook and tarpon are the principal game fish. Every community catering to sportsmen is likely to have a tarpon tournament and report regularly on the catches. The snook is relatively unimportant as a commercial food fish and there has been a growing disposition to make it a game fish. Bass, bluegills, catfish, and blackfish or mudfish inhabit the fresh water, the first two being most sought after.

In a class by themselves are the shell fish in nearby waters. Huge mounds of shells, mostly oyster, clam and conch testify to the abundance and importance of these for nearly two thousand years. Piles of clam shells at Marco and Caxambas give evidence of the many clams collected by two canneries in a half century. Shell fish beds are no longer worked commercially.

All that has been said about resources in timber, fish and wild life should never obscure the fact that the soils of Collier County are its basic resource whether used for farming or cattle raising or tree growing. The United States Bureau of Plant Industry and the Florida Agricultural Experiment Station have made a joint survey of the soils of the county and soil type maps of the area are available at the county courthouse. There are many kinds of sand soils but the prevalence of a great variety of organic soils, especially in the Everglades, and the presence of many kinds of marl soils over large areas are considered the outstanding soil features of this part of the state. There are also peat, muck and marl soils in the coastal mangrove swamps which in some instances are over fourteen feet deep and in many places average seven to ten feet deep.

How these resources have attracted people to the region and how they have affected the lives of pioneers and newcomers makes up much of the content of succeeding chapters. It is upon these that the economy of the county is built.

2

Indian Antiquity:
The Calusa and Their Ancestors

I N THE LAST two thousand years four successive waves of population have made their way into the region that is now Collier County. The Calusa Indians were the first. The Spaniards, the Seminole Indians, and the forerunners of the present day inhabitants, White and Negro, all came more recently. Except the Seminoles, and the Negroes who may have been slaves, all came voluntarily, attracted by the climate and the abundance of natural food sources. And though the Seminoles had reluctantly moved southward under pressure from the white man, they soon found this area one of the best places where they could live their own lives. Because of this, they have steadfastly resisted any effort to move them away or deprive them of the use of its resources.

The ancestors of the Calusa Indians came into the region at least two thousand years ago, or before the beginning of the Christian era. Whence they came and by what routes is not entirely clear. But it seems most likely that they were part of the great Indian migration that moved southeastward across the continent and peopled the Atlantic seaboard of North America. That they may have come by way of Central America and the West Indies as is sometimes suggested seems improbable.

This writer is indebted to Dr. John Goggin for permission to use as source material an unpublished manuscript which summarizes the latest findings on the history of the Calusa and supplies much of the data that appears here.

By all accounts the Calusa in the sixteenth century was the most important Indian tribe in South Florida. Its leaders exercised a limited political dominance over other widely scattered small tribes and collected tribute from many of them. Its peoples occupied the southwest Gulf Coast below Charlotte Harbor, with their main village near the mouth of the Caloosahatchee River, probably on Mound Key in Estero Bay. Other writers have placed the principal village of the Calusa near present day Naples and around Pine Island. They extended inland to the Everglades and are said to have dominated the Mayaimi Indians around Lake Okeechobee politically if not culturally. The Florida Keys may also have been under their political control at times.

Best estimates place the population of the Calusa at the time of discovery at somewhere near two thousand people living in thirty villages ranging in size from ten to two hundred inhabitants. Archeological evidence available suggests that coastal towns were larger than those inland; that is, they lived mostly along the seacoast with some concentration at the mouths of creeks, rivers and inlets and on the nearby islands.

The Calusa were, according to most accounts, a non-agricultural people who lived by hunting and fishing and gathering wild plant foods. This would be especially practical in Collier County where there was a natural abundance of fish and wildlife. There is almost overwhelming evidence in the southern part of the county that they lived almost exclusively on seafoods which explorers found them roasting, broiling or eating raw.

The Calusa house was a round, thatched, wooden structure. The Cacique, or chief, had a very large house with windows and an interior platform on which the people sat. The Calusa men wore a belt around their loins and the literature describes the women as "naked except for a covering in front." Early travellers found the Cacique's wife wearing a pearl and stone necklace and a necklace of gold beads. Others report necklaces of beads four or six fingers in width. Beads might be worn on the wrist, upper arm, under the knees or above and on the ankles. Shell ornaments collected by archeologists and others in the Ten Thousand Islands show that they must have been in common use.

One of the more interesting of the early accounts of the Calusa was that of Hernando D'Escalante Fontaneda. Born of Spanish parents in Cartagena, he was being sent to Spain at the age of thirteen to receive his education when he was shipwrecked on the east coast of Florida and spent the next seventeen years mostly among the Ca- lusa. Of his captors he wrote: "These Indians have no gold, less silver, and less clothing. They go naked except only some breech- cloths woven of palm, with which the men cover themselves; the women do the like with certain grass that grows on trees. . . . The common food is fish, turtle and snails (all of which are alike fish), and tunny and whale: . . . . Some eat sea-wolves; not all of them, for there is a distinction between the higher and the lower classes, but the principal persons eat them. . . . "

Polygamy was being practiced by the Calusa chiefs when the Span- iards first began to visit them. It was probably a common practice by many people of that and other tribes, one of the women being consid- ered the principal wife. There was also considerable marrying out- side of the tribe, particularly by the chiefs. Cacique Carlos was re- lated to the Cacique of Tequesta, and planned marriage with the daughter of another chief.

Body painting or tattooing may have been a typical practice, for the Creek name of a group, possibly the Calusa, was "painted people." This according to William Bartram writing in the British period, 1764- 1783, was applied because of numerous designs of animals, plants and flowers on their bodies.

The Calusa traveled by canoe or by walking. The canoes were probably dugouts, although no description appears in the literature of the discoverers or explorers. For seagoing voyages that occasion- ally took them as far as Cuba, they sometimes lashed two canoes together, leaving them a little distance apart. There is ample evidence of their canoe trails in the Everglades as well as regularly traveled overland trails in such areas as the Big Cypress.

The Calusa had a relatively complex social organization that permitted considerable numbers of them to live together and rather effectively defend themselves. Some of their towns must have had several hundred people, as one of them, probably the largest, had thirty-six houses which may have been multifamily homes. Many of the small concentrations of people may have been temporary seasonal camps rather than permanent villages.

War making was a highly developed activity among the Calusa. Their principal weapon, which they used with great skill, was the bow and arrow; but they also used clubs and spear throwers. They took human heads rather than scalps as trophies, and carried them in victory dances.

They were good enough fighters to discourage the Spaniards who gave up the early effort to subdue them and plant missions among them. That the invaders could have conquered them is fairly obvious, but they appear to have thought it not worth the effort since it might be necessary literally to kill off the greater part of them. So it was nearly two centuries after discovery before any Spanish settlements were planted there.

Religion was also well developed among the Calusa who had special shamans or priests and a series of regular festivals throughout the year. The Cacique combined certain shamanistic powers with his temporal power, which may partly account for his exercise of absolute power. Dances and various ceremonies with priests and people participating were common. Priests sometimes wore masks, described by Spanish Jesuits in 1567 as "horrible," which were kept in a temple built on top of a special mound, probably the same place in which the idols of the tribe were stored. These idols were animal and other figures to whom captives were on occasion sacrificed.

In view of the fact that they lived there for about two thousand years, the Calusa left surprisingly little impress upon the development of the area. They left scarcely a place name, and most had disappeared before the Seminoles or modern white settlers moved into the area. In fact, they were probably almost all gone by 1800. Those who had not been killed by warfare or disease, or carried off by Europeans, seem to have left with the Spanish in 1784 and were settled in Guanadacoa, a suburb of Havana, where the baptismal records show them as Indians from St. Augustine.

The Calusa and their predecessors did, of course, leave enormous and impressive monuments to remind us of their occupation, namely, the many shell mounds on the mainland and on the coastal islands. In Collier County and in mainland Monroe County many of these mounds stand intact, though further north much of the shell has been used for roadbuilding and other mounds have been leveled for purposes of the white man.

The shell mounds consist principally of conch, oyster and clam shells, the proportion of each differing somewhat from place to place. The different ratios reflect the ecology of the region, oysters being more common near the mouths of rivers, and conchs in the calm waters of the brackish bays. All are to be found throughout the county but principally on the coastal inlets and on a hundred or more of the Ten Thousand Islands. There was a great concentration of shell on Mound Key northwest of the county, fewer of them down the coast to Marco Island where there were enormous collections at Marco, at Caxambas and at Goodland. Further south the great shell heaps are on Chokoloskee Island, whose nearly 150 acres are primarily shell, and about a half mile up Turner River on the east bank. The mounds of shell continue at intervals on down the coast as far as Lostman's River, below which there are very few.

Clarence B. Moore in 1906 described two shell deposits on Lostman's Key comprising ten acres. He and others have described extensive deposits on other islands, notably Panther Key, made famous as the home of John Gomez, Dismal Key, Fakahatchee Key, Russell's Key, Wiggins Key, on Sand Fly Pass, Addison Key, Crawford Place, Horr's Island, Little Marco, McIlvaine Key and Pavilion Key.

Because of their number and the extensive area and depth of the shell, these mounds have attracted a great deal of attention. They have been the subject of much conjecture and some scientific study as to their origin and uses. Conservative anthropologists suggest that the Calusa came into the low lying country when the sea level was not quite so high as now. The mounds, they say, started as refuse heaps and grew until they became obviously useful as a refuge in time of storm and high water. Then perhaps they became permanent habitations and continued to grow in size and depth, serving more and more effectively as living sites.

This supposition is enough to account for their origin, but more imaginative observers have projected the hypothesis that the shell islands in particular are a product of careful design, planning and execution. This is especially true of the view taken by Frank Hamilton Cushing whose findings were published in the *Proceedings of the American Philosophical Society,* Vol. 35, in 1896, under the title, "Explorations of Ancient Key Dwellers on the Gulf Coast of Florida." If it be true that his conjectures are somewhat fanciful, they are nonetheless intriguing. For a descriptive analysis of the 1400 by 1700 foot midden at Goodland see John M. Goggin "Cultural Occupation at Goodland Point, Florida" in *Florida Anthropologist,* Vol. II, Nos. 3-4, November 1949.

In 1895 Captain W. D. Collier at Marco was digging muck with which to fertilize some fruit trees when he found a number of objects, mostly made of wood, which he guessed might belong to Indian antiquity. By a fortunate coincidence he called them to the attention

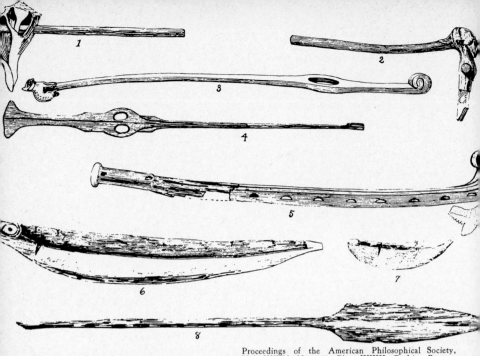

Proceedings of the American Philosophical Society, Vol. XXXV, No. 153, Plate XXXII. Cushing Report.

"Types of implements and weapons: toy canoes and paddle."

of Colonel C. D. Danford, a British gentleman visiting in the area. The Colonel suggested that some of the specimens be sent to University Museum in Philadelphia where Cushing was visiting. Dr. William Pepper, head of the Department of Anthropology, then arranged the Pepper-Hurst Archaeological Expedition under the joint auspices of his department at the University of Pennsylvania and the Bureau of American Ethnology in the Smithsonian Institution.

Collier's find proved to be one of the richest collections of carved and painted ceremonial and utilitarian objects unearthed anywhere in Florida. It was apparently their submergence in a muck deposit that had preserved them. For in the course of his explorations which began at Pine Island near the mouth of the Caloosahatchee, Cushing examined nearly a hundred of the shell islands, but nowhere did he find such remains of aboriginal Indian culture as at Marco. Nor have others, such as Clarence B. Moore, been able to duplicate the find. One must conclude that either Marco was a unique case or that nowhere else were conditions favorable to preserve the highly perishable items, mostly of wood or other vegetable fiber.

Included among the items Cushing discovered were wooden stools, cypress tubs two feet deep, wooden mortars, pestles and trays,

1   2   3   4

Proceedings of the American Philosophical Society,
Vol. XXXV No. 153, Plate XXXIII. Cushing Report.

"Animal Figureheads with correspondingly painted human masks."

pillows of rushes filled with moss or deer hair. There were tools with handles in place on some and remains of the thongs that bound them. There were wooden replicas of the sacred panther and a painting of the jay bird or kingfisher, and many human, deer and turtle masks. He found headdresses made of bark, and wooden ear and lip buttons worn for adornment. He concluded that some women wore a short deerskin skirt from waist to knees or a garment made of Spanish moss, and the men wore a scanty breech cloth of deerskin or braided cords.

For weapons, he asserted, they favored spear throwers and used a cleverly sharpened deer foreleg as a dirk or stiletto. They had also fashioned cutting and carving knives from shark's teeth and fitted them on wooden handles. Implements of shell are abundant in the islands, most of them conch shells perforated to receive a handle. Some have beaks ground down almost to a cutting edge while other shells, used as hammers, have blunt beaks. Among the shell remains are a fair percentage that were used as tools, some worn and broken and thrown aside, and a few still fairly perfect.

As to Marco and the other shell keys, Cushing concluded that they were artificial, that they had been carefully designed and built up as habitation sites. He reconstructs for us a picture of the inhabitants to stir the imagination and presents aboriginal Florida Indians in an entirely new light.

When built and occupied, the Marco site, like others of its kind, stood out in the open water, probably at a considerable distance from the mangrove-covered shoreline. Cushing noted that Marco was not yet joined to Caxambas Island save by a wide and low mangrove swamp that was still washed daily by high tide. At the time of abandonment by the Indians the extensive mangrove swamp area bordered open water to the southward. The main tidal currents between the key and Caxambas Island further to the south flowed past the easterly portion.

The northeastern edge of Marco Island, he reported, had been worn away by the sea. Originally it extended a little more than two hundred feet out in this direction. Marco was exceptional in this respect, being one of a half dozen keys to suffer such erosion. So carefully were the sites chosen, and so expertly were the foundations laid that storms and hurricanes which many times altered the contour of the region left these keys relatively untouched.

Sites far out on the flats and shoals seem to have been chosen both because of their nearness to food supply and their remoteness from the almost unbearable mosquitoes and other insects of the sub-tropic mainland. No waters in the world produced a greater quantity and variety of food, but for the few people dwelling inland this abundance was completely inaccessible because of the difficulty of shoreland navigation. These key dwellers therefore located their homes out in the midst of the navigable but not too deep shoreland seas. And before the intervening area toward the low and marshy shoreline filled in and grew up with mangrove, Cushing surmised that the inhabitants may have been free of insects and mosquitoes. If so, they were more fortunate than the present day inhabitants of the islands.

Other archaeologists support Cushing's observation that shell keys of the Marco type are not mere refuse heaps. They are skillfully designed and constructed to utilize the shell refuse as building material. On them the Indians erected special purpose mounds and provided canals to give easy access for their canoes. Fish ponds with outlets to the sea caught and held some of the fish which they used for food. Their homes were located on platforms or terraces.

Modern white settlers first made their homes on these shell mounds, finding them the highest and most fertile land. Such plantings as tomatoes, however, could not be put out without first sifting the coarser shells from the soil in which they were to be planted as the sharp edges would sometimes cut the stem of the plants deeply enough to kill them. After years of deterioration the shells were a positive detriment to cultivation and the large ones that had not decomposed had to be removed.

The Spaniards and the Spanish Indians

The Spaniards came to Florida early in the sixteenth century and long before the founding of St. Augustine they tried to establish themselves on the southwest coast. Their efforts were unsuccessful because of natural conditions and the hostility of the Indians mentioned earlier, but this coast was the first to become well known to the Spaniards.

This book is not the place to debate the landing place of this or that explorer. The stronger argument seems to favor Charlotte Harbor or Tampa Bay as the points at which the early Spanish explorers landed and made their futile attempts to subdue the hostile natives and the equally hostile terrain. But Mr. David O. True of Miami, a student of the early voyages, maintains that Ponce de Leon entered by way of Estero Bay on the northern extremity of the county which Freducci, the map maker, named Stababa in honor of the Calusa leader there. The late David Graham Copeland studied the records and early maps and argued with some reason that the Spaniards could not possibly have passed up such a likely inlet as Caxambas Pass, and that somewhere in that area, possibly on the south end of Marco Island, they had made a landing.

The Spaniards made little impression on southern Florida during the nearly three centuries that they held the region. When they surrendered the territory to the British in 1764 there were settlements only at St. Augustine and Pensacola and a military post at St. Marks on the gulf coast south of present Tallahassee. The presence of pottery and trade goods shows that the Spaniards traded extensively with the Calusa and that the Indians substituted Spanish ornaments and tools for many of their own. However, this was probably through itinerant fishermen from Cuba and not from other parts of Florida.

Little more is known about the region until it became a part of the United States in 1821. Then we begin to find reports of Spaniards and "Spanish Indians," presumably remnants still operating fishing ranches at Charlotte Harbor and points south where they salted and dried fish for the Cuban market.

In 1824 Commodore David Porter sent the U. S. Schooner *Terrier* to investigate these fisheries in connection with his campaign against Caribbean pirates. Lieutenant Commander James M. McIntosh reported from Fishermen's Key off the mouth of the Caloosahatchee that Spaniards were extensively engaged in fishing and cultivating the soil. A considerable part of the key was cleared and planted in corn, pumpkins and melons. They had nine neat, well-thatched houses, an extensive shed for drying fish, and a storehouse for salt and provisions. He reported two other similar places, one a mile up the Caloosahatchee River and the other near the entrance of Charlotte Harbor.

In 1831 William A. Whitehead, Collector of Customs for the Key West district, found four establishments at Charlotte Harbor employing 130 men, one-half of them Indians. He reported thirty Indian women and between fifty and one hundred children. Their vessels regularly entered and cleared at Key West, paid the tonnage duty there, and bought some of their supplies.

Some of these ranches existed as far south as Marco Island, if not further. John Lee Williams (*The Territory of Florida,* New York, Goodrich, 1837) visited Caxambas Pass in 1824 and among other things wrote: "To my great surprise I have found several well cultivated plantations long hid from the civilized world. There are several plantations near this sound. That of John Durant, a native of Savannah, lies on the south side about a mile from the western limit. Another by the eastern inlet is owned by a mulatto man. They all employ several native Indian families to assist in cultivating. The produce of the farm sells at a high price to the fishing companies, who, in turn, furnish them with clothing, powder, lead and C." Coasting vessels passing through Caxambas Sound could avoid the long trip around Cape Romano shoals by employing one of the native pilots.

There certainly were several different Indian groups in southwest Florida in the early nineteenth century. There were Seminole bands and individuals of mixed Indian and Spanish ancestry. There may have been a Choctaw group and a Calusa settlement. There was a band of Spanish Indians who may have been Choctaw, or a Calusa remnant, or even perhaps a more independent Seminole tribe. (For a thorough discussion of the identity of the Spanish Indian see W. C. Sturtevant, "Chakaika and the Spanish Indians," in *Tequesta,* XIII, 1953, pp. 35-73.)

Whether or not they were Calusa remnants, they had little association with other Indians, or with Florida white men until they became involved in the Seminole Wars. As Williams described the situation, "The inhabitants of several large plantations around Caximba Inlet, the heads of the Hujelo's (Yonge's River below Cape Romano), St. Mary's, and other southern streams, never appeared at the agency to draw annuities, but lived by cultivating their fields, hunting, trading at the Spanish ranchos, bartering skins, mocking birds and pet squirrels, for guns, ammunition and clothing, and sometimes assisting in the fisheries . . . Their knowledge of the passes of the country and their long connection with the Spanish traders and fishermen afforded perfect facilities for supplying the Seminoles with arms and munitions of war . . ." (Sturtevant, p. 41; Williams, p. 242.)

The Spanish Indians became directly involved in the Seminole War in 1839 when they participated in the raid on Lieutenant Colonel W. S. Harney's camp on the Caloosahatchee River. They next appeared on the east coast in the well-known raid on Indian Key in which Dr. Henry Perrine was killed on August 7, 1840. The final chapter was written when Harney left Fort Dallas on December 4, 1840 vowing to bring back the scalp of Chakaika, the chief of the Spanish Indians who had led them in the earlier raids. Harney's men did find Chakaika's hideout, and Private Hall of the 2nd Dragoons shot him through the head, after which Harney had the body hanged up on one of the lookout trees on Chakaika's island, presumably with the new rope he had purchased from a fisherman at New Smyrna for that express purpose.

This ended the life of the Spanish Indians and their appearance as a separate unit in the record of the war. In any case, the Calusa and the Spaniards had played out their roles and the stage was set for the third group to occupy the land.

3

The Wars of Indian Removal

THE WARS to remove the Seminole Indians from Florida had a double significance for the Collier County region. The Big Cypress County became the last refuge of the Indians and those who successfully resisted removal became the successors to the Calusa and the Spaniards as occupants of the land. Military expeditions seeking to round up the Seminole remnants made the first explorations of the interior and supplied the earliest maps and other data on what had hitherto been a no-man's land.

In 1821 when Florida became a part of the United States there were already several Seminole settlements near Tampa Bay, and the west coast had been for fifty years a favorite hunting ground for Seminoles from much farther north. The Seminoles had long been familiar with both the east and the west coasts of the lower peninsula where they came into contact with Spaniards from Cuba and Britishers from the Bahamas, but they apparently knew little of the interior of Florida. When white settlers were ready to move into northern Florida they found much of the best land there occupied by Seminoles numbering in all about five thousand. The frontiersmen made an immediate and vociferous demand for their removal, which at first meant further down into the peninsula.

The Seminoles were themselves comparative newcomers to Florida. They had begun to cross the line into Spanish Florida during the first half of the eighteenth century. Two circumstances combined to bring about this migration. Except for those gathered around St. Augustine under the protection of the Spaniards, the original inhabitants had all been killed, captured and carried away, or had died from European-introduced diseases, leaving a highly desirable land unoccupied. At about the same time the Indians of Georgia and Alabama were under increasing pressure from the English, and instead of moving fárther westward as many of their fellow tribesmen did, small groups of them began to move into Florida where they soon made the country their own.

The Seminoles were mostly settlers from the Creek Confederacy which included the Creek and several other linguistic and political groups. Hitchiti speaking Indians such as Oconee and Mikasuki were the major element in the eighteenth century migration. After the Creek War of 1812-1814, the defeated Red Stick faction provided numerous Muskogee immigrants to Florida who came to outnumber the Hitchiti speaking already there.

The first effort to solve the problem of Indian removal from Florida came in 1823 at a conference on Moultrie Creek near St. Augustine with a number of principal chiefs not in attendance. The Indians agreed to accept a reservation of five million acres south of the Withlacoochee River and north of Lake Okeechobee. On the west the reservation line ran to within fifteen miles, and on the east to within twenty miles of the coast. The lower peninsula seems at that time to have been completely disregarded.

At Moultrie Creek, Eneah Emathla expressed the apprehension of himself and his fellows at the prospect of moving southward when he said: "We rely on your justice and humanity; we hope that you will not send us south to a country where neither the hickorynut, the acorn, nor the persimmon grows; we depend much on these productions of the forest for food; in the south they are not to be found." This seems to suggest that the food resources of south Florida were unfamiliar to at least some of the Seminoles. The hickorynut might be missing, and the acorn and the persimmon less plentiful, but the wild foods, both plant and animal, would prove abundant.

The Indians did, however, make the first of a series of moves southward that would eventually bring them to present day Collier County. In 1832 John Lee Williams was told of an Indian settlement near the Caloosahatchee where they had large numbers of cattle and ponies and raised two crops of corn a year. In March of the following year he learned of several towns near the Peace River. Wiley Thompson reported in 1835 the existence of "several unauthorized settlements of Negro Indians and Spaniards" in the peninsula of Florida, and considered all of the Indians to be Seminoles subject to removal. Indians also were reported going a hundred miles south of the reservation on their annual hunting trips. Williams later recalled a deserted Seminole clearing seen in September 1832 up the St. Mary's River near Cape Sable. In the same month he had met an Indian in the bay of this river going to trade at Indian Key.

The Moultrie Creek Treaty was at best only a temporary solution for it left all of peninsular Florida to the Indians and pressure from white settlers to move them still farther would surely come. Nor were the Indians at all pleased with their new lands which proved to be inadequate for their needs, the area being too small and largely unproductive. Increasing the size of the reservation did not produce much greater satisfaction and soon both sides were violating the reservation limits.

In 1830 the Congress of the United States provided an answer that Floridians immediately adopted. All Indians would be moved to lands west of the Mississippi River far beyond the possibility of any contact with white men. The Federal Government recognized the ominous signs of an explosive situation in Florida and sent Colonel James Gadsden to negotiate with the Seminoles for the cession of their lands in Florida in return for lands in the West.

The Seminoles were reluctant to treat with the Whites but in the spring of 1832 Gadsden induced some of the chiefs to meet at Payne's Landing, seventeen miles from Fort King along the Oklawaha River. Seven chiefs and eight sub-chiefs signed the resulting treaty whereas thirty-two chiefs had signed the Treaty of Fort Moultrie nine years earlier. Removal was to be accomplished in three years, afterward extended to 1836. A delegation of chiefs was to examine the new country and if it proved satisfactory, the treaty would be binding on the nation.

The seven chiefs and an interpreter left with the Indian agent for the West to examine the country and signed a supplementary treaty at Fort Gibson, Arkansas, in March 1833. This agreement infuriated the remaining chiefs who asserted that the tribal nation should make the final decision, and they repudiated the treaty. John Hicks, a leading chief who favored emigration, died suddenly and Charley Emathla, the next most important supporter of the move, was assassinated. With their deaths, the leadership of the Seminoles passed to men determined to resist at all costs. Hostilities broke out in

38

December of 1835 as the deadline for being ready to move approached, and as the government showed signs of being about to enforce the terms of the treaties.

This is not the place to relate the story of the Indian wars except as they affected the area of our immediate interest. After seven years of effort by an army that often numbered more than all of the Seminoles, men, women and children, about one-tenth of the Indians were still in the Florida wilds. The redskins had powerful allies in the climate, which made military operations all but impossible in the summer because of rain and heat, and in the trackless wilderness so suited to the ways of the Indian and so baffling to the Whites. As the Indians retreated southward their numbers became smaller; some were captured and others voluntarily gave up the struggle and joined their fellows in Indian Territory. But the remnant found their shrinking numbers more than compensated for by the advantages of refuge in such areas as the Everglades and the Big Cypress where subsistence was easy, and safety from pursuit assured.

No real battle occurred after that at Lake Okeechobee on Christmas Day of 1837 in which two hundred Indians participated. Thereafter the redskins broke up into small bands to confuse the troops and conceal themselves more easily. Small war parties raided in widely scattered places and raced for safety to their refuge in the wilderness.

The campaigns of the later years of the war brought the center of activities closer and closer to the area of present-day Collier County. Two series of forts had been built to provide bases from which to launch attacks on the Seminoles on the southwest coast. One was on or near the coast, the other along the line of the Caloosahatchee River and southward toward the Big Cypress. In March of 1837 the army established "Old" Fort Foster on Rattlesnake Hammock, nine miles out of Naples toward Immokalee. This was an oval shaped stockade with a small creek flowing through one edge. It stood on an old Indian trail from the head of Henderson Creek northward to Bonita Springs and Fort Myers. Fort Dulany at Punta Rassa near the mouth of the Caloosahatchee, Fort Poinsett at Cape Sable and Fort Harrell at the head of New River followed soon after. Comparable bases on the east coast were at Fort Dallas on the Miami River and Fort Lauderdale on New River.

In January of 1838, units of the Seminole-hunting army first crossed the Caloosahatchee and established posts there, some of which later became settlements with the same name. General Persifor S. Smith gave the name T. B. Adams to a camp on the north bank and Fort Denaud on the south bank where he crossed. The same force marched to the mouth of the river and founded Fort Dulany, designed to be the principal base of operations in that area. Barracks, warehouses and a hospital were built there. A severe hurricane on October 19, 1841 completely destroyed the installation, however, and the base was moved up river nineteen miles to Fort Harvie, which eight years later was re-named Fort Myers.

On the return trip from Harvie, Smith's forces moved southward and established Fort Keais on the western edge of the Okaloacoochee Slough, then marched northeastward and established Fort Thompson at the head of the Caloosahatchee. A military map of 1840 shows the pattern of action down toward Collier County. A trail from Fort Denaud, twenty-seven miles up river from Fort Harvie, ran twenty-one miles south to the edge of the Big Cypress. From this last position other trails led twenty miles further south.

Interestingly enough, this map also shows a route for small boats from the north end of Key Biscayne across the Everglades to Fort Keais "as reported by the Indians." Actually the commonly accepted location of Fort Keais is thirty miles west of the edge of the Everglades on the eastern edge of a large cypress strand now known by the name Camp Keais Strand. It is unlikely that the water level ever was high enough for the last thirty miles to be navigable.

In 1839 it seemed as if the wars might be terminated by negotiation, but it provided only a brief truce. General Alexander Macomb reached a verbal agreement with the Indians under which they were to retire to the region below Peace River. To avoid any further clash with Whites a trading post was to be established in the reservation on the Caloosahatchee River. James Baxter Dalham received the permit to operate the store and four civilian employees accompanied him, a Mr. Morgan, a clerk, a carpenter, and the captain of the sloop. Lieutenant Colonel W. S. Harney, with a company of dragoons and two Negro interpreters, Sandy and Samson, established a military post nearby to secure the operation.

The Negro Samson, a slave, had been captured by the Indians at Micanopy in 1837, and lived with Osceola's band for a time. He escaped, became an interpreter and was present at Fort King in May 1839 when General Macomb made the agreement with the Indians. He accompanied Colonel Harney as guide and interpreter and later gave an eyewitness account of events at the new post. (Reprinted in *Tampa Tribune* January 2, 1955.) For his services in the war he received his freedom and developed a plantation on Simmons Hammock south of Lake Thonotosassa.

A large group of Indians had camped on the opposite bank of the river and commenced what appeared to be friendly trade, not waiting for the completion of the trading post. The soldiers had taken no precautions, not even putting out sentries. On the third night after their arrival at the new post young Indians warned the Whites not to cross the river to see Indian dance, saying that the old Indians were drunk, but this seemed no cause for alarm.

At four o'clock on the following morning, July 23, 1839 a force of about 160 Indians fell upon the unsuspecting Whites. Chakaika, chief of the Spanish Indians, led the attack on the camp while Hospetarke led those moving on the trading post. Present also were Holatter Micco, better known as Billy Bowlegs, and Cho-nock-Hadjo. Dalham and Morgan, sleeping outside the store, were killed. The two interpreters, the other three civilians and a Sergeant Simmons became captives. The carpenter and Sandy lived four days, the clerk accompanied a hunting party and disappeared, and the captain of the sloop escaped. Samson, befriended by Billy Bowlegs, was allowed to live but had to wait two years to escape. Thirteen soldiers died in the attack and fourteen, Harney among them, escaped by way of the river, perhaps because the Indians stopped briefly to plunder the quarters.

An explanation for the sudden resumption of hostilities is not difficult to find. The Indians had assumed that General Macomb's agreement was binding but nobody else did. When the newspapers of the territory attacked the War Department on the negotiation, the Secretary replied that this was only a move to pacify the Indians and make easier their removal. The suspicious Seminoles must have heard about this statement. Harney explained his negligence on the ground that he had not known about the published statement of the government's real purpose which so aroused them.

Another famous south Florida raid occurred early in the morning of August 7, 1840, when Chief Chakaika led seventeen canoeloads of Indians in the raid on Indian Key. Dr. Henry Perrine and six others were killed, stores were looted and buildings burned. Four kegs of powder in the loot were turned over to the chief in the Big Cypress.

As a direct consequence of this raid, Harney was ordered to seek out Chakaika and his band and eliminate them. Smarting under the defeat he had suffered a year earlier, Harney set out with firm purpose to find his man. Ninety men in sixteen canoes left Fort Dallas on the Miami River on December 4, 1840. They surprised Chakaika and some of his band, shot the chief and then hanged him.

Harney's raid demonstrated that white men in canoes could follow the Indians to their Everglades hiding places, a fact that induced the Indians more than ever to retreat to the Big Cypress. At the Green Corn Dance in the Spring of 1841, a council of the remaining chiefs decreed death to any of their number discovered in contact with Whites. They worked out plans for rapid communication with each other and adopted the strategy of ambushing any of the enemy who attempted to follow them, firing upon them, doing as much damage as possible and then running. The Indian chiefs carefully guarded the powder they secured in the raids on Harney's post and on Indian Key. They doled out a powder horn full to each Indian in a war party and for hunting allowed five charges in exchange for a hog. Indians began to kill bears and turkeys with bow and arrow, partly to save powder, partly to avoid announcing their presence by the sound of gun fire.

The most extensive military campaign in the Collier County area occurred in December of 1841 and January of 1842. This was an effort to get at the Indians by way of the many short water courses along the Gulf coast. Under command of Captain George Wright the expedition moved from Punta Rassa to Big Marco Pass where it split into two groups, one going northeast through Marco River and Henderson Creek and thence inland. A second group went eastward through present Marco Channel for some distance, then sharply southward around an "unusual island," possibly Goodland Point, to Gallivan's Bay. From there they ascended one of four possible streams, Royal Palm Hammock Creek, Blackwater River, Whitney River, or Pumpkin River; thence to "Wakika" which was probably either Fakahatchee or East River. (These are D. Graham Copeland's conclusions after studying the rather confused and confusing maps and accounts of the expedition.) They then moved inland on a reconnaisance and from there crossed an interior bay to Turner River where they again made an inland trip. Next they went to present-day Huston or Lopez River and upstream to Fort Harrell on present-day New River from which they progressed to an island called Talca Chafse, thence to and up another stream called on the map "Fahkahatchee," but clearly present-day Chatham River, and finally to Chitto-Hatchee or "Snake River."

This expedition located no Seminoles but made the first extensive exploration of the coastal waters of the southern part of the county. The Indians were now being crowded into the Big Cypress from three directions, on the east by canoe, from Ft. Lauderdale and Fort Dallas through the Everglades, on the north from Fort Harvie and its satellite bases, and on the west and south by way of the rivers.

What might have been the consequence of this pressure had it been continued one can only guess. For on August 14, 1842, Colonel William J. Worth, commanding the troops in Florida at the time, declared the hostilities had ceased. At that time Worth estimated the number of Seminoles remaining in Florida at 301 "supposed" to be in eight widely scattered bands of whom 112 were warriors able to bear arms and 189 were women and children. He agreed that this remnant might remain within the section south and west of Lake Istokpoga, and west of a line from the mouth of the Kissimmee River down through the Everglades to Shark River. This involved no treaty making. The Indians were already there and they were merely ordered to stay there. The order at least implied that they might have some claim to the use of the land.

But this was little more than a truce and in it were the seeds of trouble since Florida Whites would not permit such a settlement of the Indian problem. In fact there continued to be some fighting until April 14, 1843 when a small engagement took place at the Great Wahoo Swamp after which another band of 120 went west.

Yet the truce persisted and relations between the two peoples seemed to improve. The Indians stayed within the bounds of the "reservation" and assumed responsibility for the behavior of any individuals who committed acts against the Whites. They at times captured and turned over for punishment anyone accused of crime and gave assistance to distressed Whites whenever they found them.

The demand to remove the remaining Seminoles from Florida received new impetus in 1850 when Congress began to debate a proposal to turn over to the states the federally owned swamp and overflowed lands which the Seminoles occupied and had come to consider their own.

Two policies were urged as a means of getting the Indians off these lands. Indian Agent Captain John Casey proposed to organize systematic pressure upon them to force them to migrate or fight. He would forbid trade with them and cut off supplies, survey lands, build roads, and send military patrols into the region they regarded as theirs.

Before Casey was allowed to proceed Federal officials decided to try the alternate plan of persuasion again. Billy Bowlegs, who had become the recognized leader of the southernmost of the Seminoles refused in 1850 an offer of $215,000 on the grounds that he could not induce his people to go. The Government of Florida, a state since 1845, became impatient with Federal policy and in 1851 authorized the governor to raise a regiment of volunteers and spend two million dollars to speed the removal. But the Secretary of War was to have one more try at using peaceable means.

Luther Blake of Alabama became Indian agent, replacing Casey, to put the new plan into effect. With the help of western Seminoles brought back for the purpose, he induced Billy Bowlegs and three other chiefs to go to Washington and treat directly with the Great White Father. The Indians were sufficiently impressed to agree to use their influence in favor of migration. Blake then secured thirty-six Indians, two-thirds of them women and children, some allegedly captured or kidnaped, for transportation to Indian Territory at a total cost of $250,000. In 1853 this policy was given up as a failure and Captain Casey, restored as agent, initiated the pressure tactics he had earlier advocated.

Memory of all this payment-for-removal policy still lingers in Seminole memory and affects their relations with the government. One of the chief arguments of the present ultra-conservative faction is that the government is still trying to ship all the Seminoles west, and has secret plans to pay huge sums of money to Indians or Whites who aid in betraying the tribe.

By February of 1850, abandoned Fort Harvie had been reactivated and renamed Fort Myers. Similarly the Army reactivated Fort Denaud and Fort Thompson in 1854, and two new forts appeared down Collier County way. Fort Shackleford, a blockhouse on a pine island out on the edge of the Everglades one mile from Waxy Hadjo's Landing, was soon abandoned. But Fort Simon Drum near Immokalee became second only to Fort Myers in this phase of the war, expeditions going out east, south and west from it.

The Indians watched these movements with uneasiness and apprehension but showed no signs of changing their decision to remain in Florida. It was left to Billy Bowlegs to reveal what their answer

44

would be. In pursuance of Agent Casey's plans, Lieutenant George L. Hartsuff, a topographical engineer, set out with a patrol of ten men to explore the Big Cypress and report the location of Indian villages.

Under the circumstances their behavior seems foolhardy unless they meant to arouse the Indians to hostility, or unless they completely discounted the possibility of any Indian opposition. The patrol had visited Fort Simon Drum, found abandoned Fort Shackleford burned, and had stopped at Assinwah's town without incident. They then camped at Bonnet Pond, two miles from Bowlegs' town in the Big Cypress. Some of the men went to Bowlegs' garden, pulled some bananas and mutilated the plants, because they wanted to see "how old Billy would cut up." Nor did they deny responsibility when he charged them with it.

The response of Bowlegs was Indian-like and swift. The next morning, December 20, 1855, almost to a day twenty years after the first outbreak of Seminole hostility, at five-thirty in the morning, thirty-five Seminoles attacked the patrol, killing two and wounding four others, including Hartsuff. Thus was the final phase of the Seminole Wars, sometimes aptly called Bowlegs' War, set off.

There was not a single pitched battle in this war. What really broke the back of Indian opposition and induced Bowlegs and his people to leave was discovery and destruction of their homes, fields and crops hidden in the Big Cypress in the neighborhood of Deep Lake, Royal Palm Hammock and northward toward Lake Okeechobee.

In the winter of 1857 and 1858 the army struck its most telling blows. In November Captain John Parkhill's Company made one of the most effective raids. On Wednesday, November 18, 1857, under command of Colonel S. St. George Rogers, the Florida Mounted Volunteers left Fort Myers. One hundred and ten men were in the expedition. They reached "Chokoliska" Key on Sunday, the 22nd. On Tuesday Captain John Parkhill led seventy-five of the men on an expedition up Turner River from which he was never to return.

Nine miles up the river the party landed in the mangrove and marched three miles through swamps to higher ground. They moved on, scouting in a north and westerly direction for three days. Their guide was Captain Richard Turner, later to return to give his name to the river and make his home there.

On the fourth day out the scouting party discovered and destroyed

Billy Bowlegs, photographed in New Orleans in 1858 while being deported to Indian Territory.

a large Indian settlement in a palm grove in the neighborhood of Deep Lake or Royal Palm Hammock. On the following day they came upon two other large Indian fields and destroyed them. But here tragedy struck the expedition. Without waiting to send back for reinforcements Captain Parkhill set out to follow fresh tracks on an Indian trail. While the party was crossing a stream, Indians fired from ambush, killing Parkhill instantly and wounding five of his men.

This ended the progress of the expedition. The Indians fled as soon as the soldiers returned their fire and pursuit was out of the question. The men gathered the dead captain and their wounded companions and made their way back ten miles to where the tracks had been discovered and where a small detachment had been left. Next morning they started on the forty mile journey back to Chokoloskee. When they had brought Captain Parkhill's body back only fifteen miles they elected to bury it near a lake at the fork of the Fakahatchee River. A statue on the capitol grounds at Tallahassee commemorates this event.

The scouting party reached Chokoloskee on the night of the 30th, barely in time to avoid serious hunger for they had carried only seven days' subsistence. Meanwhile the base had been moved from Chokoloskee to Cape Romano. The supply of fresh water had given out at Chokoloskee and Cape Romano was described as the only place with a plentiful supply. Colonel Rogers made one scout from Cape Romano on December 19, 1857, another from Marco and continued raids into the Big Cypress in January of the following year. Though he found and destroyed several small villages, storehouses and fields, these were in a sense "mopping-up" expeditions. Captain Parkhill's expedition had revealed the hiding places of the Indians who were in no strength or position to defend them.

Early in 1858 the United States Government decided again to resort to persuasion to induce the remnant of the Seminoles to move to the west. Colonel Elias Rector, Indian Agent, brought forty Seminoles and six Creeks from the western reservation to convince their Florida brethren that migration was desirable. Final payments on a cash settlement with those who had already gone to the new land depended upon their inducing the Florida Indians to join them.

On March 4, 1858, Chief Billy Bowlegs again met with the negotiators. This time, he accepted five thousand dollars for himself and twenty-five hundred dollars for cattle he alleged had been stolen. Each warrior received one thousand dollars and each woman and child one hundred. The government agent also agreed to purchase all animals and property which the departing Indians could not take along to the new home.

Smithsonian Institution, B.A.E. from Harper's Weekly, June 12, 1858.
Billy Bowlegs' wife from a photograph made in New Orleans in 1858.

48

On May 8, Colonel Gustavus Loomis, commanding the Department of Florida, declared the Florida War closed. On the previous evening the U.S.S. *Grey Cloud* had departed for New Orleans. On board were Colonel Rector and his western Indian allies, Billy Bowlegs with thirty-eight of his warriors and eighty-five women and children. The steamer had stopped at Egmont Key to pick up forty-one other Indians who had been brought in by boat companies of Florida Volunteers for prize money, making 165 in all.

The *Grey Cloud* put in at St. Marks for wood. The old squaw Polly who had served as interpreter asked permission to go ashore and collect roots and herbs with which to treat some sick Indians. A dozen lightly guarded Indians went ashore and upon signal scattered and disappeared into the woods. Some were recaptured, but others, Polly among them, escaped to make their way back to south Florida. Albert DeVane of Lake Placid learned the story of Polly Parker from a daughter aged eighty-eight residing on the Brighton Reservation. Polly had lived until 1921 in the Florida she was so loath to leave. Rector returned to Florida and induced another seventy Seminoles to migrate the next year.

Andrew P. Canova, a private in the Florida Volunteers, went through the entire two and one-half years of the Bowlegs' War. He sent occasional dispatches to a Palatka, Florida, newspaper which were later published in book form. In one dispatch he wrote: "The Everglades and Big Cypress are great problems in themselves which can be solved only by time and ingenuity. It would seem as if the climate — the counterpart of which is found nowhere else on the globe—were not to enjoyed by the settlers here. But those who have had temerity to venture into these vast solitudes, have often returned with the consciousness of having had a very pleasant time; and the botanist and naturalist was never heard to complain of the scarcity of flora and fauna. . . .But I think somebody ought to turn his attention to the Big Cypress. There are islands there that, for fertility, are equal to the delta of the Nile."

Whereupon he related one of the tall tales for which he was well known, "One man, in walking over the soil (so says an old tradition) was so deeply impressed with its fertile appearance, that he took a tenpenny nail from his pocket and planted it near a tree which he marked for future reference. When six months had gone by he returned to the spot, and dug for the nail. To his surprise, he found that it had grown into a crowbar four feet long! . . ."

Collier County's Mikasuki Seminoles

THE LAST OF the Florida Indians to go west to Indian Territory departed in 1859. Just how many of their numbers remained in Florida nobody knows; probably it was somewhere near two hundred. This remnant remained in practically undisputed possession of a vast area south of the Caloosahatchee River, around and south of Lake Okeechobee until well into this century. Living in such complete isolation, the Indian culture remained amazingly resistant to change until in this generation.

The Seminoles had come to the Collier County region more than a century ago, fifty years ahead of any white settlers. Though their numbers have never been large, their role in the history of the county has been a colorful and significant one. Because of the undeveloped condition of much of the interior and its suitability to the Indian way of life, it is in many respects the last stand of their ancient culture, though even here it is rapidly giving way as those primitive conditions fall before what the white man calls progress. For everything that has spelled progress in the brief years of the county's existence has spelled doom to the ways of the Indian.

Their recent history in southern Florida paralleled their experience in northern Florida of gradually shrinking lands which they could use, and equally diminishing returns from the economy they inherited from their fathers. And as these changes have taken place, slowly but surely, their whole way of life has been modified. The Seminole has not yet received the white man's formal education and is nowhere near being assimilated, but he bears little resemblance in person or status to the proud people who once claimed most of Florida as their own.

By the time the effort to remove them to the west was dropped, they had already in the course of hostilities relocated themselves in southern Florida. So remote from any white settlements were they and so ill disposed toward any contacts with Whites, it was all of twenty years before any reliable data on them began to appear. The Commissioner of Indian Affairs confessed in 1879 that his office had no information on which to determine the number of Indians left in Florida, but he guessed there could not be more than 400. In that year R. H. Pratt, founder of the famous Carlisle Indian School, visited South Florida to report on the Seminoles and made the first useful account. ("R. H. Pratt's Report on the Seminoles in 1879," presented and edited by William C. Sturtevant, *Florida Anthropologist,* IX, No. 1, 1956.) Thereafter reports are fairly frequent. In the first three months of 1881 Clay MacCauley made a more extensive investigation and a fuller report which together with Pratt's gives a fairly adequate picture of the Seminoles as they had resettled themselves. (Clay MacCauley, "The Seminole Indians of Florida," *Fifth Annual Report of the Bureau of Ethnology,* pp. 469-531. Washington, 1887.) For purposes of comparison another report made fifty years later is very useful. (Roy Nash, "Survey of the Seminole Indians of Florida," Senate Document No. 314, 71st Congress, 3rd Session, Washington, Government Printing Office, 1931.) Nash made a careful comparison with the MacCauley report.

By the time of Pratt's visit, Florida citizens had apparently given up any purpose to remove the remaining Indians. They complained at times of Indian disregard of property rights, particularly in livestock on the open ranges, but the insistent demand for their removal seemed to have spent itself in the war period. In the Office of Indian Affairs, however, it still seemed the best solution and Pratt was instructed to discover how the Florida Seminoles felt about joining their brothers in the west. His report seems to have closed the subject.

Pratt concluded: "Their removal to the civilized portion of their tribes in the Indian Territory would do more for their advancement than any other policy, but, except by some unworthy trick, they could not be procured to go there. I very much doubt that they could be gathered into one community in Florida." He then reported a circumstance that was to plague all who sought to work with them. "To reach them in their present divided state and exercise any authority as agent would be extremely difficult even should the Indians be willing to accept such authority."

Pratt began his investigation at Fort Meade in Polk County. He learned, partly by observation, partly by inquiry, that there were four principal settlements of the Florida Indians. There were, as best he could determine, twenty-six in a small village near Fort Clinch, thirty-nine miles northeast of Fort Meade, called by MacCauley the Cat Fish Lake Settlement. At Fort Center or the Fisheating Creek settlement Pratt reported ninety Indians, but this was too high an estimate. Seventy-six others, led by old Chief Tigertail, resided in the vicinity of Old Fort Shackleford, somewhat scattered along the borders of the Big Cypress as far north as Devil's Garden. Finally there was a Miami group numbering eighty led by young Tigertail. To cover oversights or omissions he added twenty, for a total of 292.

The modern "Cow Creek" band, which includes the Cat Fish Lake and Fisheating Creek groups, lives on or near the Brighton Reservation and speaks Creek-Muscogee. The southern band, now ordinarily known as Mikasuki, speaks a different language, not mutually intelligible with Creek. It is ordinarily called Mikasuki in the literature, being a dialect of the language called Hitichiti in the North and in Oklahoma where it is now extinct. The Mikasuki and the Creeks are both members of the Muskogean language family. The Collier County Indians are all Mikasuki.

MacCauley in 1881 counted twenty-eight at Fort Clinch-Cat Fish Lake, only thirty-two at Fort Center-Fisheating Creek, twenty-three at Fort Shackleford-Big Cypress, sixty-three at Miami, and he added a small Creek-speaking settlement of twelve on Cow Creek for a total of 208. Since the Creek-speaking groups now constitute only a little more than a third of the total, MacCauley seems to be more nearly correct as to relative strength of the two language groups if not as to totals.

Two sources in 1898 provide additional data on the location of Seminoles, some of them in Collier County. Charles H. Coe, in *Red Patriots: The Story of the Seminoles*, reported their principal settlements on Cow Creek, on certain islands in the Everglades west of Ft. Lauderdale, and "in the neighborhood of Fort Shackleford, on the western edge of the Everglades, and of Chokoloskee Bay south of the Big Cypress, Lee County. The general location of the settlements is permanent but the camps are frequently changed."

In the same year A. J. Duncan, an Indian Inspector, reported to

52

the Secretary of the Interior a few near Chokoloskee and others in the region on the west side of the Everglades on land bordering on the Everglades, presumably in the eastern edge of the Big Cypress. Duncan further related that: "Within the Everglades, from 1 to 6 miles from the border, small hammocks are found quite numerous, and many of them are at present cultivated by the Indians. They vary in size from one quarter of an acre to 30 acres . . . The Indians themselves are very reticent and suspicious in regard to any inquiries appertaining to these islands. They are not of themselves desirable as residences, but only for cultivation. The following Indians have gardens on these hammocks and are cultivating them, but are all living on the mainland outside of the Everglades: Johnny Osceola, Jim Osceola, Charley Jumper, Charley Tommy, Charley Tiger, Robert Osceola, Jackson Charlie, Jimmie Tiger, and Old Mathlo. There are others but it is difficult to learn their names . . . These hammocks are more numerous in the southern part of the Everglades."

In 1923 J. K. Small wrote that the first Indians since Civil War times appeared at Everglades in 1882. Captain George W. Storter reported in an interview with D. Graham Copeland that Indians returned to the region about that time when they learned that there was a trading post at the small settlement there.

In 1930 Nash reported that the Atlantic Coast Line Railroad, a hard surfaced road and sugar plantations had crowded them off Fisheating Creek, and the Bok Tower looks down on the old Cat Fish Lake site from which Tallahassee and his band were driven in 1885. Both of these groups joined the Cow Creeks who alone "occupied swamps so little desirable that they have been suffered to remain there fifty years." Cattlemen from Fort Myers and hunters from LaBelle had crowded them out of Devil's Garden and compelled their retreat into the Big Cypress.

Nash prepared a map which showed a concentration of nearly a score of camps in Collier County in the Big Cypress near the Everglades, all east of the Everglades-Immokalee road and one each at Immokalee, Everglades and Turner River. There were a few camps in Hendry County, all south of Devil's Garden. There were three camps of the southwestern group in Monroe County and two in Dade. By 1930 Nash declared the Big Cypress and Cow Creek settlements comprised the only really Indian County, all the others being largely white man's creations.

Pratt himself had visited only the Cat Fish Lake Settlement

headed by old Chipco who reportedly had managed to remain neutral during the renewal of hostilities in 1855 and whose white neighbors had defended him from the Indian hunters. Pratt made an attempt to get the three west coast groups together at Fort Myers for a council which he had hopefully planned for July 7, 1879. Chipco was expected to be there and Captain F. A. Hendry of Fort Myers, a well-known cattleman and friend of the Indians, undertook to bring in the other two chiefs for the meeting.

When Pratt proposed that the United States provide help in making a livelihood and in educating his children, Chipco rejected summarily any "Washington talk," and insisted he needed no education or other help. The old Chief refused with equal firmness to attend the proposed Fort Myers conference, saying he was old and his pony lame, nor would he send a delegate. (MacCauley also later found them everywhere opposed to any talk of schools provided by the government.)

Captain Hendry was apparently having better luck with his invitations to the council. Tuscanugga and Chief Tigertail agreed to attend. On the appointed day four Indians arrived, and four days later nine more, all from the Big Cypress. Pratt decided to try talks with this one group but those present had nothing to say and did not wish to hear any Washington talk, nor was Hendry able to induce them to act otherwise. Pratt, meanwhile, had learned that Tuscanugga had been bitten by a rattlesnake and could not make the trip to Fort Myers. The agent concluded that any effort to have talks with the Indians would be futile.

Pratt found Chipco presiding over what seemed to him a rather progressive and prosperous community. He saw a good many hogs and was told there were more off in the pine woods feeding on pine mast. He reported, as have many others since him, that they made pets of the hogs and allowed them sleep about their homes. It is difficult to see how they could otherwise have any control over their swine and move them from place to place. They had plenty of chickens and eggs and a few ponies and cattle. The land and crops looked as good to him as any in the state. Each family had a separate patch of corn, rice, sweet potatoes, sugar cane and melons and the chief had a few stalks of tobacco. The total was only fifteen acres set in the midst of a dense hammock. Good farmer that he was, Chipco excused himself when a rain came up and went with his squaw to put out sweet potato plants.

Pratt in 1879 found one unusual feature in Chipco's camp that

Charley Tigertail's store in the Everglades, 1910, photo by Alanson Skinner. Built on a canoe run from the head of Rock Creek that joins Lostman's River and Broad River, toward forty mile bend. Both the house and the business were probably unique. He also operated a motor launch built for him by Captain George Storter of Everglade. He traded his furs, skins and feathers principally at Everglade and Chokoloskee. He finally acquired an automobile and drove it into the Tamiami Trail Canal and drowned.

he assumed was characteristic of all of them. There were ten substantial frame buildings with clapboard walls and clapboard or shingle roofs whereas "Four or five years back these Indians all lived in frail houses constructed of palmetto leaves . . ." MacCauley, on the other hand, in 1881 describes as typical the open type house or chickee with thatched roof. Fifty years later Nash reported the construction of these houses identical with that described by MacCauley with the single exception that nails were used in fastening the thatch. Formerly the framework was lashed together and the thatch tied on with any of half a dozen easily procurable fibers. He called the Seminole house arrangements "one of those perfect adaptations of means to an end which characterize a competent people."

Sturtevant, writing in 1956, points out that though frame houses of all sorts have been built from time to time, the open-sided Seminole house has proved better adapted to the South Florida climate and the readily available building material. In 1950-1953 when he made a survey of Seminole camps, he found only two Seminole-built board walled houses. All other occupied houses, except a few small cottages built by the Indian Service, were the open-sided chickee.

Sturtevant also points out that though the general form of the chickee remained the same, there were some changes noticeable in Mikasuki houses. MacCauley had shown open gable ends, like modern cook houses, whereas Nash mentioned thatched gable ends which all present Mikasuki dwelling houses have. Also by Nash's time nearly all houses, as today, had platforms of sawed planks rather than split logs shown and described by MacCauley. Furthermore, the use of nails to hold the house frame together made it possible to eliminate the center posts supporting the ridge.

Sturtevant has called my attention to a letter of W. H. "Bill" Brown who had lived among the Seminoles eighteen years and knew most of them. In a letter to the *Fort Myers Press* of June 24, 1897, Brown stated that "Cypress Indians" had twelve yoke of oxen, six or seven wagons, and not less than 800 hogs. The Seminoles, he said, were honest and independent, not asking nor looking for any assistance from the government, and unwilling to accept any. The present Indian agent had not been into any of the camps for eighteen months and the Indians could not be induced to visit the Indian station at the Allen Place (Immokalee).

Describing their economy, he said they grew corn and other crops on a piece of land for two years and then abandoned it, moving to a piece of virgin soil. When one Indian cleared a small patch of land, another Indian would join him, leaving only a narrow strip of bushes to divide the farms. Then others joined in and cleared their little patches until there was a vast farm cut up into small independent farms, making theirs the largest cooperative farm in Lee County. Brown said.

As to clothing, Pratt, on his visit in 1879, found women wearing short jackets and skirts made of calico and no covering for the feet. They adorned themselves with cheap beads, large and small, and in all colors "piled up in enormous fagging quantities about their necks." Three years later, MacCauley was equally impressed by what seemed

Mikasuki Seminole girls near Boat Landing, 1910. Photo by Alanson Skinner.

to him the burdensome quantities of beads they wore. In the Big Cypress settlement he tried to count those worn by young Tigertail's wife number one, who had come through the Everglades to visit her relatives. "She was the proud wearer of not fewer than two-hundred strings of good sized beads. She had six quarts (probably a peck of the beads) gathered about her neck, hanging down her back, down upon her breasts, filling the space under her chin, and covering her neck up to the ears. It was an effort for her to move her head . . .

Seminole Indians near the entrance to Kennedy, now Burdine Ranch.

Others were about equally burdened . . . Even girl babies are provided with a varying quantity."

By 1930 beads were worn in lesser quantities and since Nash's trip have decreased still more. Yet he commented on the beads worn by Sally Cypress: "String after string after string until a solid pyramid extends from shoulder blades to chin. Twenty-five pounds and a few ounces one set was found to weigh." Nash described her costume as consisting of "a skirt, a chemise with sleeves and a cape. Neither shoes nor stockings nor hats are worn. The chemise slips over the head and hangs down just enough to cover the breasts. The cape covers the elbows and meets the waistband of the skirt."

In 1881 the cape was merely a ruffle sewn around the shoulders. By 1930 it had become a separate garment, much longer and usually of filmy cloth. Worn over a bodice or blouse, it was usually briefer, but often with longer waist, than the blouse of MacCauley's day. The most striking change in women's dress has been the elaboration of patchwork design strips, probably connected with the use of the sewing machines. In 1881 the few bands of design were appliqued, not patchwork. Women's costumes and to some extent men's also,

58

developed independently of changes in white fashions. They started with adoption and adaptation of Euro-American styles but subsequently underwent considerable changes in style without further borrowing except in materials and sewing machines.

All early reports note that the Indian women are virtuous, modest and retiring, often refusing to speak to Whites. MacCauley pointed out that no white halfbreeds existed but there were three Negroes and seven persons of mixed Indian and Negro blood. In the nineteen twenties the reports of the Indian agents and doctors agreed that this feature of Indian morals was breaking down. Beginning in 1923 the reports of a social disease increase in frequency, as do references to Indian maidens bearing half-breed children with white fathers out of wedlock. All observers blame contact with Whites, particularly in amusement camps in Miami and St. Petersburg. Certainly the Indian taboo that once reportedly condemned violators to death broke down in these cases.

In 1879 Pratt found men wearing "the usual breech clout" and a calico shirt ornamented with strips of bright ribbons and a turban made of bands of bright colors folded and wrapped around the head. On special occasions they wore moccasins and leggings of buckskin and sometimes a light hunting coat of bright colors adorned with strips of ribbon or cloth. Men have more readily adopted the dress of the white men though they still favor a more highly colored shirt. In 1930 Nash reported the great turban was gone, buckskin leggings never seen, moccasins rare, and the white man's breeches common.

The bright colored patchwork shirt worn with store bought pants by most Collier County Seminole men today is a development out of their older skirted man's "dress" worn by some older men today. The Trail Mikasuki men are more conservative in dress than the reservation Indians. Turbans and leggings reappeared about 1953, but apparently are worn only on occasions calling for newspaper publicity or public exhibition.

In 1881 women "wrought their hair into an elongated cone with bangs in front." Fifty years later they were piling it on their heads, combing the front into a pompadour instead of bangs, slicking it down with grease, and confining it under a net. In the curious corona style of headdress which became almost a Seminole trademark, the hair is drawn up over a crescent of cardboard covered with black cloth, and held in place by a hairnet. This style developed during the 1930's, but was almost obsolete by 1950. Young women today wear their hair in white women's styles, although hair hanging loose was until a few years ago a symbol of a widow in mourning. Today most men cut their hair white man's style, but fifty years ago they cut it close to the head, "except a strip about an inch wide running over the front of the scalp from temple to temple and another strip about the same width perpendicular to the former, crossing the head to the nape of the neck. At each temple a heavy tuft is allowed to hang to the bottom of the lobe of the ear. The long hair of the strip coming to the neck is generally gathered and braided into two ornamental queues."

Pratt saw dozens of deerskins, buckskins and a few otter pelts in the camps of 1879 but Indians complained that game was getting scarce. He observed that their only weapons were old Kentucky rifles and bows and arrows. He was told that there were a few breech loaders and revolvers in other camps. MacCauley counted sixty-three Kentucky rifles, eight breech loading rifles, one shotgun and two revolvers, and said they were beginning to use traps to catch game. Pratt described the bow as being near six feet and the arrow near four feet without feathers, but with a conical metal tip of iron as an arrowhead. Bows and arrows sold as souvenirs by modern Seminoles are modeled on those still used as toys (and occasionally hunting weapons) by Seminole boys. An Indian demonstrated the effectiveness of the weapon for Pratt by shooting an arrow into a designated tree which proved to be 190 yards away. By 1930 rifle and double barreled shotgun had replaced muzzle loaders and bow and arrow. A recent newspaper feature showed Seminole braves practicing with bow and arrow to be ready to oppose exclusion from the Everglades National Park hunting grounds, but this was obviously a stunt to provide a feature.

Indian Council meetings have become more frequent in recent years, but are still fraught with difficulty. The Seminoles recognize no one who speaks for all of them and differ among themselves violently in matters of policy in dealing with the Indian Service. The Indian agent at Dania seeks to overcome this by developing a council on which each group has representation, but so far it is a rather nebulous institution.

One notable conference was staged in Collier County in 1947 in a hammock about a mile west of the Monroe Filling Station east of Ochopee. Present were Governor David W. Sholtz and his cabinet, David Graham Copeland, representing the Collier County Commissioners, and 273 Indians mostly from Collier County camps. To the question how best the county and state could help them, the Seminoles gave the old and simple answer: "Just let us alone." A monument fifty feet north of the Trail commemorates this event.

All agents agree on one observation. The greatest enemy of the Indians was whiskey. When they went to Tampa, Fort Meade, Bartow, Fort Myers, Fort Ogden in the early days or to Marco, Everglades and Chokoloskee later, they invariably got drunk—all but one who remained sober to look after them. Except for making noise, they were not ugly when drunk. Though Roy Nash was fullsome in his praise of Whitney and Sally Cypress, he lamented that they came in from Immokalee reeling drunk, but added, "What else could an Indian do at Immokalee?" C. G. McKinney, operator of a store on Chokoloskee Island until his death in 1926, wrote a weekly column of news in which he commented regularly on their drinking habits. He held it but justice in one instance when Indians were reported selling liquor to Whites. Thelma Smallwood at Chokoloskee also recalls how the Indians deposited their weapons and chattels at the store and went on a spree. At night they rattled the doorknobs on her home begging her father to come out and help them find their lost liquor. And one night some squaws tied an inebriated brave in a blanket and left him all night to the tender mercies of the shell beach and the mosquitoes.

From local informants Pratt learned back in 1879 that the Seminoles stole and killed a good many cattle, sometimes killing an animal for a small cut of meat. Owners estimated the loss at 150 to 200 cattle annually, or $1500 to $2000, since open range cattle were valued at ten dollars a head. They admitted that Whites also stole from the Indians. One had recently stolen sixteen hogs. An Indian had once bought fifty head of cattle from a white man and then had to give them up when they proved to be stolen. Nash declared in 1930 that Indians had given up efforts to run cattle on the range because of White disregard of Indian property on it. Earlier, when white cattlemen were fewer and less aggressive they had been friendly with the Indians since their own cattle sometimes strayed into the Seminole Country.

Indian agents were all sure that cattle raising was a logical activity for the Indians, but felt that it must be done on reservations under fence. In no other way would the cattle be safe from rustlers. Of course the day of the open range cattle industry was nearly gone anyhow. Today Indians under guidance run cattle on ranches at both the Hendry County and the Brighton reservations.

Until the last thirty or forty years farming provided a major portion of the Seminole support. At one time they depended on fields in the hammocks for most of their vegetable foods, corn, sweet potatoes, squash, melons, cow peas, and sugar cane. Thelma Smallwood recalls that when they first came to Chokoloskee to trade they made their own cornmeal for the sofkee, using mortar and pestle to prepare it, but more and more they bought grits at the store. Possibly two or three Mikasuki families on the Trail still do farming, but such fields are not common. Most of the families except at Dania still have a small garden patch near the camp in which they grow bananas, taro, elephant ear, and sometimes citrus, tobacco, potatoes and a little corn. Almost every camp has chickens, but hogs are less common. The growing reliance upon store food seems to be due primarily to the decrease in farming. Cash hunting is gone, but subsistence hunting and some fishing continue to supply food.

The Indian had relied on hunting as a source of income as long as possible, but this possibility has declined rapidly in recent years. Three things have now made hunting only a very limited activity. The area in which he can hunt has been drastically reduced as more and more land is put under fence for cattle raising, and hunting in the Everglades National Park area is forbidden. Secondly, laws forbid the killing of egrets and other birds for their plumage though arrests for violation occurred as late as 1920. The alligator may no longer be killed, and for other animals and birds there is a closed season and a bag limit. Finally, the white man has become a strong competitor for what hunting there is. Nash concluded in 1930 that the Indian was already a minority factor in the fur and skin business. A Fort Myers trader told him that Whites brought in sixty-five per cent of his trade. Only in the Big Cypress country was the Indian producing more than half of the skins. Indians were also regularly beaten at their own art. White men used better traps and exercised more care in handling the skins. It was the contrast between the dugout canoe and the gasoline launch.

Clearly the old Indian economy was doomed. He would find it necessary to go into a reservation where he would in a sense become a ward of the government and find his freedom of action restricted, or go into the white man's world and compete for employment. He has done both.

62

Wilson Cypress and ox team, Immokalee prairie early in the century.

The Indians were in a sense only squatters on public or private lands until reservations began to be provided for them upon which a fraction of them consented to live. As early as 1875 Indian agents began to urge that lands be set aside for them, admitting that they might not be ready to move onto them, but foreseeing the day when that would be their only refuge. In 1884 the Indian Service initiated a series of unsuccessful efforts to find suitable public lands. Ten years later when it became clear that all the south Florida land belonged to the state or to land companies the Commissioner began to purchase lands, and by 1930 Federal holdings amounted to more than 25,000 acres. And in 1917 the State of Florida had set aside nearly 100,000 acres in Monroe County north of Shark River where the Everglades breaks up into the Ten Thousand Islands.

When the Everglades National Park was created the state reservation lands became a part of it and the Seminoles received instead a tract of 104,800 acres in the heart of the Everglades next to the Big Cypress settlement. Few Indians had ever lived permanently in either of these areas. There are also Federal Reservations at Brighton, Dania, and in Hendry County down on the Collier County line.

But there was a serious difficulty. The Indian Service could not acquire the land which the Seminoles were using, and the Seminoles would not move onto the lands which the Service did acquire. The Indians did, however, recognize that reservation lands were good insurance for the inevitable day when they could no longer reside on privately owned lands.

Reservation policy developed slowly and haltingly. Before the end of 1920, 12,800 acres in Hendry County were enclosed by a twenty-mile fence, and another 1280 acres were fenced for a hog range. There was a complete set of ranch buildings but not a cow or a steer. The government had bought a few hogs but panthers killed forty in two nights. In 1926 the project was abandoned and nearly twenty years elapsed before it was revived and successfully developed.

There are still many Indians residing off the reservations but force of circumstances has pushed them more and more toward the reservation lands. In 1930 Nash reported 125-150 in Okeechobee camps, 40 at Dania, nearly 400 in the Everglades and Big Cypress. Collier County is still the home of the greatest number of off-reservation Seminoles. The 1945 state census showed 232 in Collier County, 187 in Glades, 132 in Hendry, 27 in St. Lucie, 22 in Broward and nine in Palm Beach.

Kenneth Marmon, Indian Agent at Dania, reported 918 on tribal rolls on February 1, 1954. Of these about sixty per cent were on reservations, 180 at Dania, 218 at Brighton and 140 at the Big Cypress. Another 75 to 80 lived in Miami and 305 along the Trail, mostly in Collier County. Other interesting statistics report 257 children of school age and 155 actually in school. Ninety-seven are in nine different public schools and 57 in Federal day and boarding schools. Most of the 102 not in school live in isolated places too remote to get to schools. This is in sharp contrast to the three in school in 1937 or even the 13 enrolled in 1939. In 1954 there were only five Seminole high school graduates and no college graduates. In spite of the gains in enrollment, there are conservative Mikasuki Seminole, centered in Collier County, who oppose schooling for their children. The same report counts 218 families, of which 825 members are full bloods and 68 mixed bloods with some white. Of these about one-third are dependent upon reservation resources, principally cattle raising, and the others work for wages off the reservations.

Today the Collier County Seminole is a familiar figure in many occupations. He works in the woods at the sawmills for the lumber companies; he works for cattlemen; he works at the vegetable harvest and at common labor. The largest single camp of workers is at Cope-

Gufney Tiger, John Malthers and, in stern, George Osceola.

land where the Lee Cypress Company maintains its logging camp and where there is a considerable amount of winter vegetable farming. He may have occasional employment as a guide to hunters, but the day of the Indian and his oxcart going out with hunters is largely gone. Such guiding as there is has become largely a white man's occupation. He may fish for food but he has never been a commercial fisherman, and the rewards of commercial hunting are limited and hazardous, being in most instances illegal. As mentioned earlier, hunting is largely a sportsman's preserve. The single exception, and it is a vastly important one, is frog hunting for their legs, which is now a major source of cash income. Seminoles hunt them with head lamps and spears at night from airboats. They are sold to fish wholesale houses by Indian and white middlemen.

As the Reverend James A. Glenn pointed out in 1928 on the occasion of the Tamiami Trail opening: "Their own private folkways have a cash value that must be bewildering to the Seminole." Already he had discovered that he could exhibit himself and his wares for a price in amusement parks at Miami and St. Petersburg for the information and entertainment of tourists. These parks regularly feature alligator wrestling and other such spectacles. The Indians, not to be

65

outdone by the Whites, have gone into business for themselves, setting up souvenir stands in "typical" Indian villages along the Tamiami Trail. These may keep alive traditional dress longer than any other force, particularly for women and children as men even there stick largely to white man's costume. Soon he may remain an Indian only in those respects which he finds economically profitable.

The souvenir business is the basis of some craftwork which is in the nature of a new industry for them. In recent years it has become a major source of income, especially for the Trail Mikasuki. They make and sell women's skirts, a modification of the Seminole costume, men's shirts, aprons, handbags—all decorated with patchwork designs —grass baskets, dolls of palmetto fiber, dressed Seminole style, pincushions, woven beadwork. All of these are made by women. Men also make souvenirs, but to a lesser extent, providing model canoes, wooden Seminole spoons, small bows and arrows, wooden tomahawks, miniature totem poles, model birds, tomtoms and the like. These are made for sale only, and are not based on types used by Seminoles themselves, except in the case of the canoe. The predominance of women's productions in the sales is notable and may serve to support the traditional independence of Seminole women.

The Green Corn Dance, the best known ceremony of the Seminoles, is held every year by the Collier County group. On the reservations, and in and near the city the festival may have lost its importance, but for the Trail conservatives this is the high point of the year, both religiously and socially. There are more white intruders and guests than formerly, but few if any outsiders have been present during the "court session" or have seen the medicine bundles. The Mikasuki also hold an annual Hunting Dance, sometimes called the Snake Dance, about three months after the Green Corn Dance. This is again an example of the survival of Indian practice in Collier County that has largely disappeared elsewhere.

The Mikasuki social organization is a conservative area of Seminole culture perhaps also better preserved in Collier County than elsewhere. Important aspects of this are the sibs, or clans, and the residence pattern. Mikasuki have about ten sibs, mostly named after animals. There are matrilineal descent groups in which an individual inherits sib membership from his mother. Their major function, still in force, is the control of marriage; two members of the same sib cannot marry.

A Seminole camp typically consists of a man, his wife, to whom the

Photo by Deaconess Bedell from Smithsonian Institution, Bureau of American Ethnology.

Ingraham Billy, Mikasuki medicine man, with his family in front of his camp and souvenir store on the Tamiami Trail, 1938.

camp belongs, their unmarried children, and their married daughters with their husbands and children. On marriage a Seminole man goes to live with his wife's family. Variations on this pattern are caused by individual circumstances. Widowers may be living with a sister or some other female relative of their sib, and some couples set up their own camp after living with the wife's family for a few years. The size of the household varies from a few, consisting of only a man and his wife, to those with twelve or fifteen occupants.

Important in modifying the Indian way of life and bringing him into closer contact with a money economy was the automobile. As Nash put it in 1930, the secondhand Ford was "a modern curse of which MacCauley never dreamed. . ." The dugout canoe still serves a useful purpose, but the wide water over which it once carried its owners are now drained away or closed to his use. The lowly oxen and cart which White and Indian alike found essential to travel in the wet woods are too slow for modern taste.

◄

Isolated Mikasuki camp in the Everglades north of the Tamiami Trail near the eastern edge of Collier County, 1948.

5

The Glade Cross Mission

THE GLADE CROSS MISSION headquarters in Everglades, presided over by Deaconess Harriet M. Bedell of the Episcopal Church, is a familiar sight to citizens who visit the county seat and an object of interest to a great many visitors from far and wide who have heard of this famous Collier County institution. It might be said that the deaconess herself is an institution. Certainly she has been the heart and soul of the mission since 1933. Most people probably do not realize that its origin dates back almost to the beginning of white settlement in the county.

The mission began as part of the national movement in the final quarter of the last century to do something about the Indian problem. It was a product of an awakened social conscience that sought to undo some of the wrongs that had been done to these first Americans. It came at a time when frontiersmen had dispossessed the Indian all the way to the Pacific coast. At the legislative level it found expression in the Dawes Act of 1887, which assumed that the Indian could learn and live the ways of the white man. It looked to the day when he would become property-owning, self-supporting, self-respecting, fully participating citizen.

In 1888 the Missionary Committee of the Women's National Indian Association began investigating conditions among the Florida Seminoles. In March of 1891, Mrs. Amelia Quinton, its president, and two other ladies, accompanied by Captain Francis A. Hendry of Fort Myers, visited the camps on the western edge of the Everglades. Mrs. Quinton bought for the association four hundred acres of land west of Immokalee and Dr. and Mrs. J. E. Brecht came to establish a mission in June of that year.

Almost immediately the Indian Association induced the Federal government to assume responsibility for the project. Dr. Brecht became Indian agent and remained in charge until 1899. On eighty acres of land acquired from the ladies, a program of far reaching importance was planned. The Indians were to receive employment and at the same time be inducted into the ways of the white man. To those ends a saw mill and a farm were to be provided.

The project directors moved quickly, for the *Fort Myers Press* on October 22, 1891 reported that the boiler, engine and saw mill were brought around from Punta Gorda by the schooner *George Jurgens* the previous week, and added, "It will be quite an undertaking to move it out to the Allen place some thirty miles east of Fort Myers." How they moved the heavy machinery over the wet and muddy trail is not recorded but by early 1892 the saw mill was set up and ready for use. Among other equipment supplied were ten mules and a wagon, ten oxen and a cart, two logging carts and farm implements.

A year later when the mill house, the planing mill and a large quantity of shingles burned, the Indian service was still sufficiently interested to make good the loss. In addition to the mill there was a store to sell at cost to the Indians and pay fair prices for hides and furs. Also in 1891 Lee County provided a teacher for what was intended to be an industrial school that Whites as well as Indians might attend. Apparently the Indian Association was to pay for teaching the Indians and the County for the Whites. A visiting inspector discovered that since no Indians attended the school, the teacher gave all of the white children Indian names and reported them to the Association.

But the hoped for results did not follow. The Indians were indifferent if not hostile and refused even to visit the community being provided at such great cost and effort to benefit them. Seminole mistrust of the motives of the Whites and their preference for their own way of living are perhaps enough to account for this attitude. Supporters of the school blamed local Whites for the failure, charging that traffickers in whiskey had told the Indians the mission was part of a plan to trap them, that the steam whistle at the saw mill would be used to signal soldiers to seize them.

The government gave up the effort, but the mission was not to die. The saw mill proved a blessing to the white settlers when W. H. Tolles bought and operated it. The Indian Association offered the property and the project to the Episcopal Church. After his consecration on January 1, 1893, the Right Reverend William Crane Gray had become the first Bishop of the Missionary Jurisdiction of Southern Florida. He already had some interest in the Indians and went to inspect the proffered land and buildings, travelling to Punta Gorda by train, and from there to Fort Myers by boat, where he found a man who was willing, if paid enough, "to drive me by pony cart through sand and water and clouds of mosquitoes, forty miles into the interior through an almost *terra incognita.*" On the 320 acres he found a dwelling, a school house, and stables, with the government agency nearby.

Bishop Gray accepted the property and called the place Immokalee after the Seminole word commonly assumed to mean "my home." The name, however, is more like the word immokli meaning his home. This is a mistake easy to make in dealing with interpreters for the Mikasuki word for my home is ammokli. In any case, by this means the Allen Place became known as Immokalee. The bishop also built Christ Church there and the first service was held on July 5, 1896 with three other ministers present.

The effort of the church to attract the Indians to Immokalee was no more successful than that under other auspices had been. Bill Brown reported in 1897 that the Seminoles visited neither the church nor the school. But Bishop Gray did not give up so easily. If the Indians would not come to the mission, he would take the mission to the Indians. Accordingly he purchased for the church a section of land within three miles of Boat Landing where Bill Brown had a thriving trading post that many Indians visited regularly. Brown had given the Bishop the idea for he had moved from Immokalee to the landing to be nearer the source of the Indian trade. Boat Landing was at the head of canoe navigation on the western edge of the Everglades, an important way station and resting place for the Indians, in what is now the Federal Indian Reservation in Hendry County.

There in 1898 Glade Cross Mission was born. As Bishop Gray described it, "using a fine palmetto tree, prominently located, for the standard, I had placed across it for the arms of the cross a large cypress beam." Everglades Lodge was built as a home for the missionaries who spent part of the year there and the remainder at Immokalee. This was also a rather extensive project. Besides the lodge there was a store, a small hospital and outhouses and sheds. Workmen dug drainage ditches and fenced some fields where they grew corn, cane, potatoes, bananas and citrus on some island hammocks.

But the church still did not succeed too well in reaching the Indians who came only to the Brown Landing store three miles away. In the belief that the offer of medical services might have some appeal, early in 1905 an English missionary and pharmacist, Dr. W. J. Godden, joined the staff at Glade Cross.

One more move was to come before Bishop Gray and his associates could reach the Indians. Bill Brown was ready to retire from the Landing and return to Immokalee. In February, 1908, he sold his store to the bishop and the functions of the mission and the trading post were combined. Dr. Godden became manager of the store and hospital, and lived there until his death in October, 1914.

From Parkhill, H. R., The Mission to the Seminoles in the Everglades of Florida, 1909.

The Glade Cross and the Medical Missionary, Dr. Godden.

In July of 1909 Dr. Godden erected a new building as a store and dwelling and fitted up the old store as a chapel and rest room. A heavy duck curtain veiled the chancel, altar and organ at one end when not in use, and served as a screen when the missionary wished to show stereopticon pictures. The hospital too was moved to the Landing.

There is not much record of the success of this dual venture. The Fort Myers newspaper frequently reported Dr. Godden's visits to town and annual visits of the bishop to the mission. Dr. Godden came in a great covered wagon drawn by three yoke of oxen as Bill Brown before him had, to bring in the feathers, furs and hides he had accumulated and take back the goods for the Indian trade and supplies. One may reasonably conclude that the project was not too successful in bringing Christianity to the Indians for when the good doctor died in October of 1914 the mission became inactive. Bishop Gray had resigned in October 1913 and his successor did not continue the efforts among the Indians. Meanwhile, in 1913 the Reverend Lucien A. Spencer, an Episcopal minister, was appointed Indian agent and held the position until his death in 1930, but attempted no missionary activity. The Seminoles were not ready to receive the white man's religion on any terms.

The Glade Cross Mission was inactive for eighteen years after which it was revived when Deaconess Bedell came to Florida. How she came to Florida and her story before that time explain much about the work she has done in this frontier mission.

Born in Buffalo, New York, in 1875, educated in the public schools and teacher's college there, she worked for ten years in Doyle School in the Polish district of her home. She taught English and history and there was little sign that she was to find her life work in another field of service.

Harriet Bedell was always active in the social and philanthropic work of the Episcopal Church in Buffalo. When in 1905 a call came for a missionary to teach in China, she offered her services and received an appointment to go to Hankow after a year of training. She entered St. Faith's New York training school for deaconesses where she received instruction in theology, nursing, the rudiments of medicine, notably first aid, and practical experience in social work.

But the new deaconess was not to go to China. Her family so opposed her going that she asked to be allowed to remain for a time in the home field until her family should become more accustomed to her being away from home. She received an assignment as a teacher at the Whirlwind Mission to the Cheyenne Indians, forty miles west of Watonga in western Oklahoma. The new teacher was the only white person at the mission where Indian families had gathered to build their tepees, in order that their children might attend the school. To assist her and serve as interpreter she had an Indian deacon, David Oakerhater.

The deaconess taught the forty children, cared for the sick and provided social and religious activities. At the mission she rode on horseback or in a democrat wagon. Once a month she journeyed by train across the territory to Chilocco government Indian school just across the state line from Arkansas City, where 900 Indians from forty tribes came together. About one hundred of them were of her denomination and she gave them instruction in the morning and spoke to the entire body in the afternoon.

74

Deaconess Bedell lives in supreme confidence that her work will always be provided for. It has always been so. One morning the boy who cared for the horses came in to report, "Billy, he die." One of the horses was dead, a major calamity on the frontier. But in the mail that day was a letter from a Mrs. Buckingham writing from Washington, D.C., to express interest in the work and ask the deaconess to relate her day's experiences. The good lady, when she read the sad tale of Billy, sent a check for five hundred dollars to buy a new team.

Years later when she came to Florida and needed an automobile for her work, the deaconess wrote to Mrs. Buckingham describing her need. It was a depression year and the check was for only three hundred dollars, but it went for a second hand model T Ford, the first car she ever drove and almost the first one in which she had ridden.

The Cheyennes adopted her into the tribe and gave her the name Vicsehia. In the ceremony the chief said, "You must have a name. Vicsehia is the best name in our nation. It means bird woman. Birds are always happy. They never get sick. They sing too." Florida Seminoles have not adopted her into any family or clan, but they know her as Ing-koe-shop-pee, one who prays, the word used generally to mean Christian.

In 1916 the United States Bureau of Indian Affairs made a change of policy that was to send the deaconess to another field of activity. The Indians must move away from the mission and live on their own allotments of land, reside in little four room houses built for them, and their children could attend the grade schools. The deaconess doubted that the new plan would work, but had little to say in the matter.

Asked if she would go to Alaska to teach in a boarding school maintained by her church at Nenana, she said yes, and in three weeks she was on her way. Here she would be one of five white workers. Perhaps this was too civilized for the deaconess who was by now accustomed to being the only white person at the post she served. At any rate, after a year of teaching there she found an opportunity to go further out on the frontier. The missionary at Stephens Village became ill and had to come out of the far north. The bishop objected to her going, saying that she was needed to teach at Nenana, but a teacher would be easier to replace.

Stephens Village was 185 miles up the Yukon from Nenana and 160 miles down river from Fort Yukon. In the village were 42 children of school age whose parents lived chiefly by hunting and trapping.

75

It lies just outside the Arctic Circle where the sun shines less than two hours in the shortest days of winter, and where in summer it is light all the time. The moon gives some light but children usually came to school by lantern light in winter. It is on winter, moonlit nights that the Indians have picnics on the lake at forty degrees below zero, with five feet of snow on the ground.

Deaconess Bedell recalls two memorable trips on snowshoes and dog sled. Such travel is possible until the temperature falls below fifty degrees below zero. Boats cease operation in early October and until next June the only travel is by snowshoe and sled. So Stephens Village learned about the Armistice of November 11, 1918 in June of 1919 when the first boat came through. One April she took a sick child to Fort Yukon over a route that meant breaking trail all the way and sleeping out of doors. There were two dog teams of seven and eight dogs. The child recovered.

On another occasion the deaconess played cupid. A girl in the village wished to be married and accompany her man on the trap line but the bishop would not come until after the ice broke up in the river. So the deaconess was one of a party that made its way 500 miles to Nenana where the couple could be married.

A change in the Indian economy altered the life of Deaconess Bedell again. The supply of furs became too limited and the price of furs too low in the early nineteen thirties to enable the Indians to keep their children at the school. But the resourceful missionary worked out a plan to save the mission. When the bishop came on his annual visit she asked permission to set up a boarding school at Tanana for a part of the year. An old hospital building there might be used and the Stephens Village buildings could be dismantled and moved.

The bishop approved and with no help but that of the Indian children the new project was launched. They took the logs down, numbering each one carefully and lashed them together in a raft on which the deaconess rode down river two days and a night. The new project could not be supported on the slender resources of the Indians and the small post. Her own diocese in New York paid off the $2200 deficit.

In that year, 1932, the deaconess came home on furlough, never guessing that she was not to see Alaska again. While she was at home in Buffalo the Florida Chain of Missions asked the Board of Missions of the Episcopal Church for a representative. Deaconess Bedell accepted the opportunity to lecture on Alaska to Florida audiences in communities down the east coast and up the Gulf side.

On her first visit to Miami she observed something she did not like and proceeded in her forthright manner to say so, as indeed she has ever since. She objected to Indians being exhibited to curious tourists. Show Indian crafts, she said, but never Indians. At their invitation she took her case to the Miami Woman's Club and aroused their interest in her cause, but did not succeed in stopping the practice.

She guards with equal care the authenticity of the Indian crafts which she encourages. She scarcely acknowledges that even Indian ways of doing things do change. To the Indian who argues that the white man does not know the difference, she retorts, "No, but you do."

The deaconess returned from her Florida tour to New York expecting to return to Alaska when her year of leave expired. But in Florida she had heard the story of the Glade Cross Mission and it had intrigued her. It was not feasible to reopen the abandoned Boat Landing site, but the Seminoles needed a mission.

When she asked for an appointment, she was reminded of the depression and told there was no money for it. She replied that her furlough pay would be sufficient for the time being. The temporary assignment has grown into nearly twenty-five years of service. As she now had to learn yet another mode of travel, she learned to drive a car. She also proudly exhibits one picture of a journey upriver in an Indian canoe. But roads and trails together provide access to the places she wishes to visit.

She made the new headquarters of the Glade Cross Mission at Everglades, in the small cottage she still occupies. She has received increasing support for her work from the Collier interests as well as from the growing number of people who come to know about her efforts. At first she rented the home, then she used it rent free until finally it was deeded to the Church. For a nominal sum she rents the land on which her mission buildings stand, and the Collier Development Company still provides the meat for her annual Christmas festival at the mission for the Indians.

Her start with the Seminoles was slow indeed. They had never been friendly to very many Whites and possibly less so to a woman. As steadily as they rejected her overtures, she persisted in patient and friendly readiness to help them. Sometimes she won them by having them help her. One of her first successes was to induce some of the younger Indians to drive her car.

Mikasuki Seminoles visiting the Glade Cross Mission in Everglades, 1940.

Gradually winning their confidence, she went from camp to camp and sometimes spent several days. On these visits she was learner and helper rather than exhorter. After all, dealing with Indians was no new experience to her.

Nor has she sought to make the Indian over in the image of the white man religiously, socially or economically. She has always thought that he should be all Indian or white man and recognizes his present status as one of transition from a way of life he has not entirely lost to one for which he is not yet ready even if indifferent Whites would admit him to it. She hopes to build on the best of the Indian traits in him some of the qualities that will enable him more easily to be assimilated.

She conceives her mission to be one of social and economic helpfulness and spiritual guidance and nothing must be allowed to interfere with the spiritual function. But even there she has not tried to work a revolution, limiting her teachings to what the Indians can understand in terms of their little experience with systems of belief other than their own. She will take no sides in any of their differences among themselves or with the Indian Service. Thus she hopes to keep her work above the level of any sort of factionalism.

Deaconess Bedell visiting a Seminole family on the Tamiami Trail, 1940.

After about seven years of working with them, the deaconess made her first effort to get them together for a religious meeting. She rented the use of an abandoned Indian village site and provided materials with which she induced the Indians to build a mission complete with chickees, a bath house and improved outdoor toilets. Here again her approach was for more than the purely religious. Here she invited the Indians on such religious occasions as Easter and Christmas and taught them something of what they mean to Christians. On occasional house parties she would spend one or more nights at the mission with Indian girls showing them something of the adaptability of the white man's way in their own environment.

She has aided the Indians economically by teaching them to help themselves. If they want money they must bring some craft work to exchange for it. This was a much neglected side of the Seminole culture which has come to be of increasing importance. Now they sell more and more of their works in their own camps along the Tamiami Trail, but the deaconess is still an important middleman in the business.

In off seasons, meaning out of the tourist season, she accumulates quite a large inventory in the Indian room of her cottage. If her slender resources are exhausted she gives orders on local stores instead of money and redeems them in season when the craft work is sold. Some of the Indians who operate the souvenir shops buy from her a portion of what they sell, knowing that she seeks no profit in her role in the exchange.

79

This work brings more and more Indians to the cottage in Everglades and the deaconess finds less time and need to go to the camps. And every contact is an opportunity to spread the Christian teachings as well as to exhibit such an example of helpfulness. They also bring her letters to read and ask her to write letters for them. In case of illness, or birth, or death, she may be called to a camp.

Examples of her willingness to compromise with her own convictions and teachings are common. At Indian funerals she might only say a prayer for the deceased who is already buried in some secret place according to the Seminole ritual, or she may share the service with the medicine man, or perhaps read the Episcopal burial service. Once when an Indian couple brought a sick child they consulted the physician and administered treatment at the cottage through the night. When the child's progress did not please the couple and they wished to resort to the medicine man, the deaconess obligingly took them in the car. The child did soon recover which was, after all, the object of all the ministrations.

Actually, nobody who has observed Deaconess Bedell over a short time would suggest that she ever compromises on principle or loses sight of her main objective to win the souls of all with whom she comes in contact, be they Indian, White, or Negro. It is so much a part of her that it comes out in all forms of social intercourse as well as formal religious service.

Measured in the terms of the number of formal conversions and confirmations the success of her mission might be called slight. There is no satisfactory statistical measurement for her achievement. She is more a social worker than a crusading evangelist. Measured in terms of the number of lives she has touched and brightened, the achievements of the Deaconess Bedell assume monumental proportions.

This missionary to the Indians ministers to all with whom she comes in contact. At Caxambas Miss Elizabeth Wood, a white visitor, had been conducting an Episcopal Sunday School class during the winter. The deaconess took it through the summer and when Miss Wood died she took over her work. Each Sunday afternoon she goes to Goodland where the mission now stands, conducts Sunday school and Evening Prayer and spends the night at the mission, returning on Monday morning to the cottage in Everglades. She appears at the assembly programs in the public schools, is called upon to read the invocation at many meetings, and visits the county jail to do what she can for the welfare of the prisoners. In 1947, appropriately

Photo courtesy of Deaconess Bedell.

The Caxambas mission and Miss Elizabeth Wood (extreme right) who conducted it from 1924 to 1939.

enough, she sat on the platform with other dignitaries who came to dedicate the Everglades National Park and said the invocation.

Christmas is her busiest day and her greatest opportunity. She begins with a Christmas feast and a Christmas tree for the Indians. The meat for each family is provided and cooked separately, and gifts for the children and women are on the tree. Episcopal churches in southern Florida and friends of the mission provide the food and the gifts. In the afternoon she has a service at the county jail, and in the evening a Christmas service and a tree from the children at Goodland winds up a busy day.

In 1943 at the age of 68 Deaconess Bedell was forced to retire, but retirement was a matter of form that altered her life only in that she receives a monthly retirement pension check instead of a salary. She still presides over the Glade Cross Mission. At eighty-two years of age she confesses to never having been bored or lonely. She has not had time for such luxuries. She is brisk of manner and step and forthright and direct in her speech and opinion.

Deaconess Harriet Bedell is the Glade Cross Mission; and whatever usefulness and character it has is the stamp of her own personality upon it. She probably fits into no simple category of missionaries that her church knows. She has always been a pioneer; and she has been at home in Collier County which proudly calls her its own.

81

Deaconess Bedell with Doctor Tiger and small boy, 1936.

This humble woman of God and servant of all who come to her, whose indomitable spirit has carried her from the east to the west and then to the far north and to the deep south in Collier County, gives one the impression she might go on forever, as indeed her spirit will.

Barron G. Collier: *Twice A Pioneer*

SELDOM has one man been so singlehandedly responsible for the creation of a county and for the course of its early development as was Barron G. Collier for the county that bears his name. Not only did he own nearly ninety per cent of the land in the county and pay a proportionate share of the taxes: but whether he willed it or not he was inseparable from the county and its affairs and it bore the indelible stamp of his influence from end to end. No man could hold such a position and not make enemies, but even they conceded his vision, energy, and resources in opening up the area.

Barron Collier was as much a pioneer as the other builders of the new county whose exploits will be related here. He had from his youth pioneered in the business world and had already achieved success enough to satisfy most men before he turned his attention to South Florida and another new venture.

He was born in Memphis, Tennessee, on March 23, 1873. His education was limited by his own choice to what the public schools of the city offered. Eager to make his way in the business world, he began working at the age of sixteen. In less than ten years he was ready to migrate to New York where he built up the nationwide business in street car advertising that provided the means for the Florida venture.

His rise to financial fortune started with the Illinois Central Railway in Memphis, for which he solicited business. Always alert to new opportunities, he saw that lighting of the streets in his home city could be improved and secured a contract to do the job with a new-fangled gasoline lantern manufactured in Cleveland. He was also associated with an uncle in the office of the Memphis *Appeal-Ava-*

lanche where he had a brief experience in advertising and selling.

More prophetic of the future was his acquisition of a half interest in the small G. S. Standish print shop where he began to publish the *Daily Hotel World*. This listed the names of all hotel arrivals in the city and included train schedules and other information of interest to travellers, as well as advertising. The shop also printed advertising placards for horsedrawn street cars, a business which grew rapidly under young Collier's energy and resourcefulness. Electric street railways were then rapidly replacing the horsedrawn variety and he observed that their advertising possibilities were unrealized and undeveloped. He began to contract for street railway advertising franchises, beginning with Memphis and expanding to Little Rock, Chattanooga, Birmingham and New Orleans.

Far from putting Collier out of business, the panic of 1893 and the depression of the mid-nineties sent him to New York City where while still in his twenties he set up the Consolidated Street Railway Advertising Company. In time he became the owner of the street railway advertising franchise in practically every city in the United States. The story of his business career is of interest to us here only in that it produced the experience and capital he eventually brought to South Florida for its development.

Such towns as there were along the lower Gulf Coast at the turn of the century had long been the winter vacation resorts of a number of wealthy families who usually came in yachts, some to live in their own winter homes, others in the small hotels maintained largely for them.

Barron Collier came to Florida first in 1911 upon the invitation of his friend and business associate, John M. Roach, president of the Chicago Street Railway Company. Roach had acquired Useppa Island just off the coast of Fort Myers and had built there a home and a small hotel, the Useppa Inn. Collier bought this property in that year and it became his Florida home and, after 1926, his legal residence. One of Collier's sons thought that this purchase might have been part of the cost of the Chicago street railway advertising franchise.

Be that as it may, Collier became increasingly interested in the region and learned more about it each winter he visited there. He knew that development was reaching down that way but he could have been under no illusions about the nature and extent of the problem associated with opening up the land to settlement and the development of its economic potential.

He made his first purchase in what was to be Collier County in 1921 when he acquired Deep Lake Hammock and the grove that Roach and Langford had planted there early in the century. This included the fourteen-mile Deep Lake Railroad down to the river at Everglades. In the next two years he quietly bought up land in large tracts from land and timber companies, from the State and from local residents who had homesteaded, pre-empted or purchased it. His holdings reached over nine hundred thousand acres in what became Collier County. Land acquired in south-

Courtesy of the Collier Development Company.
Barron G. Collier.

ern Lee and Hendry Counties pushed the total to just over a million acres.

Practically all this land was "swamp and overflowed" and patented to the State of Florida under an Act of Congress of 1850. The State, through its Board of Internal Improvements, had pledged the lands to underwrite railroad building, guaranteeing the principal and interest on the bonds. The Board subsequently granted lands outright to subsidize drainage and railroad projects.

Recipients of subsidy lands sold them in turn to land and timber companies to raise money for their construction endeavors, receiving, according to one spokesman, from twelve to thirty cents an acre. In consequence, three land companies in 1921 owned 1,379,811 acres in Lee County and ten others together owned 423,935 acres, leaving 776,234 acres for homestead, school and private lands of which the state owned 52,700 acres.

Though they have long since been much sub-divided and sold off, large holdings were common in the new county. The tax rolls in

85

1926 showed, besides the Collier holdings, Lee Tidewater Cypress Company with 126,682 acres, Empire Land Company with 76,898 acres and the Atlantic Coast Line Railroad with 40,976 acres.

Resident citizens in the county, most of them holders of small properties, resented control by absentees of so much of the area of Lee County. They demanded that higher assessments be made for tax purposes, that the lands be opened up to settlers, that the owners cease their opposition to bond issues for public improvements. Spokesmen for the holders of large tracts, on the other hand, maintained that talk of development was premature. They could not sell grazing rights for enough to pay taxes, and timber, the only marketable asset, was located in inaccessible swamps and could not be brought out.

The *American Eagle* at Estero carried on a veritable crusade against the owners of corporation lands. Taxes were increased and by 1921 some of the owners were refusing to pay and the county was advertising the lands to be sold for taxes. Perhaps it was this experience that made so many people skeptical about Barron Collier's announced plans to provide drainage and transportation, open the land to settlement and get it on the tax rolls.

Both his activities and the new county were in a sense products of the Florida boom in the early twenties. This was but one of thirteen counties that appeared on the map between 1921 and 1925. In other respects Collier and his county were victims of the depression. He had maintained all along that this was no fly-by-night real estate venture, that no land would be sold until the public improvements were actually made. But it was two depressions and a world war later that development really began.

On many occasions Collier had to defend and reiterate his faith in Florida. He had reportedly made his original investments in property against the advice of New York bankers, but later argued the Florida properties were the only tangible assets he had. Possibly his interest in land grew out of the fact that his principal wealth came from such a fragile and intangible commodity as street railway advertising franchises.

In November of 1927 after the September 1926 hurricane and collapse of the Florida boom, the *Tampa Tribune* quoted him as saying, "We are going right ahead with our program as it was originally planned. We have not been affected by the boom, so we are not suffering from its collapse . . ." And he confirmed his faith in Florida by continuing to invest in banks, hotels and a newspaper. In November of 1932 he said, "Florida is all right. I find everything here that first sold me on the state and I know of no reason to change the opinion that I have always held."

But as the depression lengthened and deepened, his resources, if not his faith in Florida, gave out. In 1933 he could claim assets in excess of liabilities but he could not meet financial commitments he had made. His creditors and the Federal courts allowed him a moratorium on his obligations and, like so many others, he gradually worked his way back toward solvency. He died on March 13, 1939 before he was able to realize many of his dreams for Florida development. Nevertheless during his twenty-eight years of devoted interest in Florida, much was accomplished that in retrospect seems little short of miraculous.

While Collier himself was never the active director of his Florida affairs, he brought into his organization many local people and others from outside the state who remained to play key roles in the "company" and in the county. Among the latter the name of David Graham Copeland leads all the rest. He was a well trained engineer, a product of the South Carolina Military Academy, where he was graduated first in a class of 342 in 1903, and of Rensselaer Polytechnic Institute. In the United States Navy between 1906 and 1920 he rose from midshipman to Lieutenant Commander, serving in Europe in World War I. He came to Collier County in 1924 as chief engineer of the Alexander, Ramsay and Kerr Construction Company and directed the building operations of the Collier enterprises.

In 1929 he resigned as chief engineer but remained as resident manager of the Collier properties in the county until he retired in 1947. In 1929 he became a member of the Board of County Commissioners, a post he also held throughout his residence there. In 1945 he became state representative from the district and worked effectively for the interests of the small county block in that body.

Copeland became deeply interested in the history of the county he had helped to build and meant to write its story. Before his death he had collected much data from printed sources and from pioneers, and had personally visited every historic spot in the county. He died October 18, 1949 before he had completed his writing, and the story of his personal experiences was lost with his death. During the quarter century of his Collier association, he had guarded carefully the inseparable interests of the Collier family and Collier County.

Barron Collier left three sons to carry on his activities. After time out to participate in the second World War, they took over the active direction of the Florida enterprises. The second son, Samuel Carnes, worked for a year with Copeland before the latter's retirement. Sam met his death in 1950 in an auto racing accident at Watkins Glen, New York. Barron, Jr., the eldest son, who had been active in the management of the non-Florida interests, succeeded to the leadership of the Florida activities. Miles, the third of the sons, who perhaps had more of his father's imagination, love of the land, and sentimental feeling of the county and its people, died suddenly of a virus infection on April 4, 1955 at the age of thirty-nine, leaving Barron the task of directing the family enterprises. The resident manager, Norman A. Herren, who works with him today "learned his trade" under Copeland who built the Florida organization.

Many things in Collier County might be called memorials to Barron G. Collier, for they stand as symbols of his vision and his willingness to back it with the means to realization. He and his sons after him have given support to all public causes and have generally supported all conservation measures in the county and in such adjacent areas as the Everglades National Park. They have recognized that southern Florida has unique scenery and wildlife that are among its principal assets to attract tourists and hold permanent residents. They would probably be among the first to admit that this policy has been a combination of altruism and good business.

When roads were being constructed in the early years of the county's history they were, of course, nearly always laid out through Collier lands. Barron Collier told officials to decide where the roads should be located and go ahead and build them. No formal dedication of right-of-way was executed. But the county commissioners now find themselves buying right-of-way on lands that no longer belong to the Colliers that would have been cheerfully given when the roads were built twenty-five years ago. Because of the canals that border all of the roads the entire extension to make the required 150 feet must be on one side and sometimes it lies through real estate developments that make costs high. Collier was the principal taxpayer, but he was also the principal beneficiary of the road building, as it made lands accessible and valuable; and his heirs still follow the same policy.

The only formal memorial to Collier in the county is in Collier

Courtesy of the Collier Development Company.

The sons of Barron G. Collier with their resident manager, D. Graham Copeland. Left to right, Samuel C., Miles, Copeland and Barron, Jr.

Seminole State Park. This park site was planned when Collier bought his Florida lands. The Southern States Land and Timber Company reserved 150 acres at Royal Palm Hammock for what it hoped would be a national park to be designated "Lincoln-Lee National Park." The principal feature of the landscape was a magnificent stand of native royal palms. In 1924 Collier offered to add enough land to make the park and proposed it to the national government, but the offer was rejected.

The county began the development of the park before it became one of the state parks in 1947. In the 6,423 acres that constitute the park area are almost all types of land that are typical of the county. There are 1,152 acres of pine, 44 acres of prairie, 272 acres of hammock, 198 acres of scrub cypress, 36 acres of fresh water marsh, 1,558 acres of tide water marsh, 2,832 acres of mangroves and 366 acres of inland bays. This is scarcely a miniature Everglades National Park as has sometimes been suggested, but it has great potential as a park.

In the center of a cleared spot just south of the Tamiami Trail is the memorial to Barron Collier placed there by the county. On both sides of the monument bronze tablets mounted on native rock name the heroes of the Seminole War in that area, one of them listing the State and Federal Troops who gave their lives and the other naming the Seminole warriors who died there in a vain effort to hold onto lands which they had come to look upon as their own. In the background is a stand of the stately royal palms.

Just west of the road into the park stands the metal remains, (the wood having rotted away) of the old walking dredge that did such yeoman service in road building west of there on the Tamiami Trail. On the western side of the cleared area is the replica of a blockhouse of the sort constructed by the troops in the Seminole wars. This will, in time, become something of a county museum where visitors may see exhibits that tell the history of the county. Mrs. Ed Scott has led the movement to make a collection for the museum.

Among the trees to the west of the blockhouse are picnic tables, rest rooms, and limited accommodations for parking trailers. The local park board has proposed to the State Park Service that a raised walkway and bridge and a parking area be constructed just north of the Tamiami Trail to provide access to a cypress stand. They also proposed a canal from a point near the park entrance to Blackwater River one-half mile away with facilities for launching boats for trips down that river. They also suggest that footpaths be laid out, and that the trees and shrubs unique to the area be identified and marked.

Since the Everglades National Park first began to be talked about it has been a matter of great concern to the Colliers as to all other residents of the county. They have not all approved the park and there is a wide difference of opinion among its supporters as to what should be included in the park. People who have looked upon the Ten Thousand Islands as a hunting and fishing ground have their doubts about what might happen to those privileges. Others believe that the area has more value for farming or real estate development and that the park should lie somewhere to the south and east. And those who have dreamed of wealth from oil have been equally outspoken in their opposition to the inclusion of their lands in a National Park. The national park for sub-tropical southern Florida became a reality in 1947, but the fight over boundaries is not yet settled. Coming at a time of steadily rising real estate values, land acquisition has been expensive as well as difficult.

The Barron G. Collier Memorial in Collier Seminole State Park.

Collier family interests have increasingly supported an extension of park boundaries that would make Everglades the western water gateway to the big park. Whether this is to be a land or a water gateway is still a matter of debate. Many of the County's citizens and others on up the west coast favor a road down the coast to Flamingo to join the road coming in from the east coast. Two serious obstacles stand in the way of such a road. To build it close enough to the coast to enable visitors to see the most attractive parts of the area would be too costly. It would be trestle or bridge for much of the distance. Secondly, the road would violate National Park Service policy as it would interfere too much with the state of nature which they wish to preserve. Yet the islands and mangrove coast are unique with spectacular features and should be made accessible.

Miles Collier became the spokesman of the Collier family in the matter of the park. It was he who was instrumental in having the dedication by President Truman in 1947 held at Everglades rather than somewhere on the lower east coast. More recently the family has given in trust to the state of Florida some 32,000 acres of land east and west of Everglades in Collier County to be included in the national park. This will make possible the inclusion in the park area of almost all of the Ten Thousand Islands and make it easily accessible by water from Chokoloskee, Everglades, Marco, Goodland and Naples by inside or outside passage. The master plan of the Everglades National Park includes a detached site at Everglades to further administration and use of the park, and a museum at the county seat also.

But the interests of hunters, fishermen, farmers and developers are also involved and must be measured against those of the conservationists and those who hope to attract tourists. Conservationists are strongly of the opinion that the Turner River shell mounds should be preserved in the park, but the owners, logically enough, consider the commercial value of the shell for road building which is too high to make its purchase for the park likely. But here is one of the few large and undisturbed shell deposits that could be preserved and made accessible to visitors.

Other areas in the county have from time to time been proposed for preservation in their natural state. North of the Tamiami Trail along the edges of the Fakahatchee Cypress Strand is what Superintendent Dan Beard has called a royal palm forest in which he counted at least 5,000 fully mature specimens of that beautiful tree. There

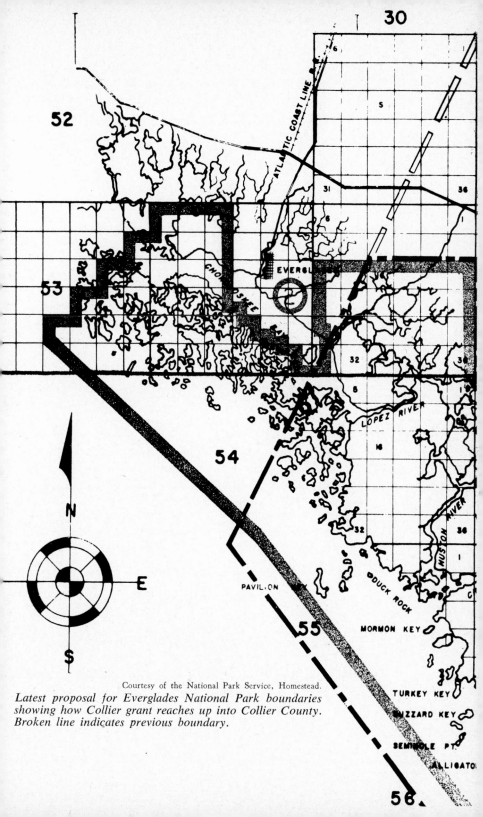

Courtesy of the National Park Service, Homestead.

Latest proposal for Everglades National Park boundaries showing how Collier grant reaches up into Collier County. Broken line indicates previous boundary.

is no likelihood of these being included in the national park, but in the early thirties there was a concerted move by conservationists to save them. This was inspired by the sale and removal of some of the trees, notably those that went to add so much to the beauty of the grounds at Hialeah Race Track.

David Graham Copeland, general manager of the Collier properties in Florida, and, incidentally, a member of the Everglades Park Commission from the time of its creation, assured T. Ralph Robinson in 1932 that the company was in favor of a park and in favor of saving the royal palms. The president of the Lee Tidewater Cypress Company gave assurances that his company was also interested. He gave an account of his company's origin and early experiences that is interesting in itself. Four men who comprised the company had purchased the lands in 1913 for $1,400,000. In 1922 they gave an option to an agent of Henry Ford who was to buy the Big Cypress Swamp for $2,250,000. Ford intended to give it to the state of Florida for a park, but the state was in no position in depression years to build the necessary roads and the matter was dropped. The price had risen to seven and a half or eight million dollars in the booming twenties, but at the time of the writing there were no bidders at the offering price of $3,000,000 and the president wrote that the taxes were eating them up.

Not until almost all of the cypress had been cut, and indeed, the last of it about to be marked for cutting, was anything done to save the last of the remaining original growth cypress and the ibis-egret bird rookery in them. Then a combination of local and national groups organized the Corkscrew Cypress Rookery Association to raise money and save the remnant as a museum stand. The Lee Cypress Company and the Collier families cooperated, each giving 640 acres in the area of the rookery and making it possible for the surrounding area to be added as a buffer zone at modest cost. A board walk now makes it possible to walk into the interior of the last area of its kind in Florida. An access road which will soon be built will provide easy access to the entrance of the swamp. If civilization has not come too close to the wary birds, visitors under the guidance of the National Audubon Society may see them there in season. They nest in the tops of the tall trees mostly in February and March.

The Collier family has been linked inseparably with the fortunes of the county that bears their name. What is good for the county is good for them and they have supported the development of the county in every respect. They increasingly share the ownership and control of the county with others, but they are still the largest property holders and still have the largest stake in the county's future.

When the senior Barron Collier came to southern Lee county, he found a half dozen small communities whose pioneer settlers had discovered the lure of the region fifty years earlier. These served as the nucleus for the Collier County we know today, and their story must be related before that of the county established in 1923.

7

Chokoloskee: *Bay, Island, Settlement*

SETTLEMENT in the pioneer communities of Collier County at Chokoloskee, Everglade, Marco, Caxambas, Goodland, Naples and Immokalee, all began at about the same time. Yet each of them had, and indeed, still has, distinctive features in its history and growth.

Seminole Indians gave Chokoloskee its name, meaning "old house," but no legend survives to relate the reason for the name. Long time residents pronounce it "Chuckaluskee" which is closer to the Indian sound than the spelling might suggest.

Chokoloskee now denotes only the island in lower Chokoloskee Bay and the settlement on the island, but until about 1900 it embraced the entire region touching on the bay. This bay is a shallow inland sea almost ten miles in length and less than two miles wide lying roughly southeast to northwest along the shore of the mainland, nowhere more than five feet deep. A protecting fringe of the Ten Thousand Islands screens it from the Gulf of Mexico.

The island is located in the lower end of the bay just off the mainland, and is less than 150 acres in extent. It owes much of its importance to its elevation. In a region where most of the land is barely above sea level, Chokoloskee at its highest point rises to more than twenty feet. The only higher point on the lower southwest coast of the peninsula is at Caxambas on the southern end of Marco Island.

Chokoloskee also proved unusual in another respect. Reliance upon cisterns for a supply of fresh water is characteristic of such islands, but Ted Smallwood, exploring for water in 1918, tapped an underground source that provided him with a flowing well. This with two other artesian wells on the island gives a plentiful supply of water. In the twenties Barron Collier also found fresh water in a well on nearby Sand Fly Island.

The name of the first modern day settler on Chokoloskee is difficult if not impossible to determine. That he came in the early 1870's is fairly certain. George Dwight Allen, whose father lived at nearby Everglades from 1873 to 1889, wrote that Captain Dick Turner settled on Turner River and gave it its name about 1874. The island at the mouth of the river "then called Big Island," he continued, showed signs of having been inhabited many years before, for there were large lime trees growing there. This may easily be accounted for by the presence of occasional visitors or even temporary residents, possibly Indian or White. No other evidence of occupation is mentioned.

John Weeks, with his wife, one son and two stepdaughters, was the first settler of record on the island. This may have been before or after the time he lived near the mouth of Barron River. Weeks was something of a wanderer who seems to have lived at one time or another at most settlements between Cape Sable and Naples. His son, Alfred, now living at East Naples, recalls an amazing number of places his parents pointed out as having once been sites of their homes. But by no means are all of the numerous Weeks clan in Collier County descended from John.

Weeks established the first claim to the island but his family did not like living in such isolation and he induced Adolphus Santini to join them there by granting him half of the island. Where and how Weeks met Santini is not known. The Santinis came to Florida from Corsica by way of Charleston, South Carolina. A fragment of Santini's diary shows him living on Sanibel Island in 1869 and 1870 where he and other members of his family engaged in fishing, sponge fishing and turtling. They also made frequent trips to Key West and Cedar Keys and points in between. One entry mentions an Allen and it may well have been the William Smith Allen who founded the Everglades settlement, and who also may have been the means of Santini discovering the area.

John Weeks shortly sold his half of the island to Captain William H. Von Pfister who had been a member of a Union volunteer corps at Key West during the War Between the States. The new owner was never a permanent resident on the island but he built a house there, kept an overseer and manager there who carried on farming operations, and he was himself a frequent visitor. He later sold his claim to the Santinis.

Throughout the last twenty years of the century the Santini family owned most of the island and was the most influential. Other members of the family who joined Adolphus and stayed for at least a time were his parents and his brother Nicholas Santino with his family. The Santinis engaged in farming, fishing, turtling and operating boat services to and from Key West. When the Santinis left the island in 1899 the Smallwoods succeeded to their property and leading position.

About 1875 a Mr. Jenkins and family settled on the island. Mrs. Jenkins had two small children and two boys and a daughter by a former husband named Daniels. The daughter was married to Nicholas Santini.

C. G. McKinney came to the island in 1886. He recalled that there were two Catholic families on the island at the time, obviously the Santini brothers. An account four years earlier indicates that five families lived there or had property there.

Population grew slowly. Settlers came, remained for a short time, and moved on. In 1897 when Ted Smallwood settled there, he found only five other families. They were the McKinneys, two Santinis, the John Browns and one Murphy. A son-in-law of Adolphus Santini, Joseph Santana, came and lived on the island for a time. In 1903, the widow Maria Rojas, a sister of Santana, came from Cuba with her children. Nine of the children were girls and Chokoloskee offered the family little opportunity to earn a livelihood. Fortunately for them, the Burnham Clam Cannery was opening at Caxambas on nearby Marco Island. After a one year stay at Chokoloskee the Rojas family moved to Caxambas and found employment there.

C. G. McKinney, who became known as the "Sage of Chokoloskee," was as important in the early history of the island as was Ted Smallwood in its later development. McKinney was a man of many interests and resources. Born in Sumter County, Georgia, in 1847, he moved to Columbia County, Florida, in 1854. His father was a blacksmith, wheelwright and carpenter. The younger McKinney tanned leather and made shoes in the early years of the War between the States. At 17 he joined the army and participated in one raid near Ft. Myers and later got into an artillery company at Brooksville. He reported in his reminiscences that he "moonshined" for John Grimes in Alachua County after the war for a brief time, but returned home in 1867-1869 to farm cotton. In 1869 he went to Texas where he was a carpenter at thirty dollars in gold a month. Returning to Florida, he homesteaded 160 acres on the Santa Fe River. He put up a water mill on the Santa Fe where he ground corn, ginned cotton and sawed lumber. Meanwhile he was operating a cotton farm and running a grocery and dry goods store. He later moved to High Springs to be located on a railroad. For a time he took over a "booze" shop at Fort White from his brother's widow.

Because he had chills and fever every fall in Alachua and Columbia counties and had pneumonia twice, McKinney sold out and went to Chokoloskee in 1886 for his health. There his health was completely restored and he attributed his long life and vigorous well-being to the simplicity of life on the frontier. On August 8, 1925 in his whimsical and philosophical manner, he wrote: "Well, we are 78 today and feel as good as new in some respects, but our ears refuse to function as formerly. One of them hears just a little bit and the other a little bit more, but they are very handy to have to hang our glasses on anyway . . ."

He was the nearest approach to a doctor the region ever had except for a few years when a Doctor S. L. Greene lived there, residing with Will Wiggins on Sand Fly Island and later on Half-Way Creek. Quite possibly "Doctor" was a title to which McKinney was as much entitled. At any rate he practiced midwifery for fifty years, for which he was registered with the State Board of Health and the birth certificates of many children born on the island bear his signature. He extracted teeth for White, Black and Indian, but he also welcomed the occasional visits of itinerant dentists.

Thanks to McKinney's efforts, Chokoloskee early had a post office. He had been accustomed to receive mail twice a day before he came to the frontier village. There he was lucky to get it twice a month. In 1890 he secured a dozen signatures on a petition for a post office. As if to see if it could be done, he was told to work at getting the mail off to Key West for a year.

Marked on the post office at Chokoloskee is the date November 27, 1891 on which it was established. He had proved by sending mail by every passing boat that reasonably regular mail service might be established. For a few months the new post office bore the name

POSTOFFICE
CHOKOLOSKEE
FLA

TED
SMALLWOOD
TEN
THOUSAND
ISLANDS

C. S. "Ted" Smallwood standing in post office door, Chokoloskee.

"Comfort," after which it was changed on June 30, 1892 to Choko-loskee. In 1906 Ted Smallwood became postmaster and held the position for thirty-five years. In earlier days when the schedule was somewhat uncertain, the arrival of the mail boat was announced to people around the bay by the blowing of a conch shell horn. Mail for Chokoloskee was coming by water from Everglades only six miles away in 1955 when the road was completed to the island.

Charles Sherod "Ted" Smallwood, who succeeded the Santinis to become the owner of most of the island and its principal citizen, was born in Columbia County, Florida, in 1873. Some of his childhood was spent in south Georgia with his grandparents and some years with an uncle near Fort Ogden in Florida. He first came to Choko-loskee Bay in 1891 and stayed for a short time at Half-Way Creek.

Before he finally made his home at Chokoloskee he had visited around the lower peninsula from Tampa Bay to Biscayne Bay. He stayed briefly at Madeira Hammock, and had a longer season of employment at various places on Biscayne Bay. From this last place he took time out for a trip to Nassau and Bimini. He also homesteaded briefly on Anna Maria Key in Tampa Bay.

In 1896 he returned to Chokoloskee Bay and farmed for a time with D. D. House on Turner River. Living on the same farm was Miss Mamie House whom he married in the following year. The future Mrs. Smallwood had come to Florida from Spartanburg, South Carolina, at two and one-half years of age. The family had lived briefly near Ocala and at Arcadia before making their way to Turner River.

The Smallwood couple established themselves in a small two-room house on the east side of Chokoloskee Island. In 1903 they moved to the south side, where the family home now stands and lived out their lives there. Ted lived until January 15, 1951. (For Ted Smallwood's reminiscences and a more detailed story of the Chokoloskee Bay Country see the author's *The Story of the Choko-loskee Bay Country with the Reminiscences of Pioneer C. S. "Ted" Smallwood*. Coral Gables, University of Miami Press, 1955.)

It was about 1900 that Ted Smallwood and his father bought out the Santinis who had built several houses on Chokoloskee Island in the twenty-five years of their stay. He bought from Adolphus Santini the home which he first occupied on the island. The Small-wood home now stands on the site of one of the two larger Santini homes. The new owner tore down the old houses in which the timbers were pinned together with wooden pegs and used a part of the lumber in building the house which the family has occupied for half a century.

Adolphus Santini had pre-emption papers to "160 acres more or less on Chokoloskee Island among the Ten Thousand Islands of Florida" dated 1877. It was his claim that the Smallwoods acquired in 1900. Captain Dick Turner had a similar claim to 80 acres on Turner River dated July 1878. Other settlers in the Chokoloskee Country probably had only squatters' rights, but the state of Florida in granting lands reserved the right of such occupants to retain their claims by paying the state price for the land. This was the legal status of the property until the Shands Survey in 1902. Up to that time what was bought and sold was principally squatters' rights.

But all such rights required validation before the title could be cleared. As long as squatters made up most of the population they resisted the suggestion of surveyors and titles which to them meant paying for the land and paying taxes or eviction.

By 1900 the principal landowners in the region were Captain George W. Storter, Jr., at Everglade, and Ted Smallwood on Chokoloskee Island. They became interested in establishing clear land title to the lands. When they sought to acquire the land from the United States government, they discovered that it had been granted to the state, which had granted it to railroad companies to subsidize railroad building in other parts of the state.

They also found that the railroad companies had in turn sold to timber and land companies. These lands had never been surveyed and located as the owners were not yet ready to open them up to lumbering and settlement. The timber company acknowledged the rights of the Chokoloskee Country claimants but refused to do anything about the surveys. In 1902 the company and the claimants entered into an agreement providing that Joseph F. Shands of Fort Myers, Surveyor for Lee County, do the surveying, the claimants to pay the cost. Since the timber company refused to deed the land in small lots to individuals, it was necessary for the claims to be lumped together and subdivided later. So Ted Smallwood got the deed for the eastern half of Chokoloskee Island, and his father, R. B. Smallwood, for the west side. George W. Storter, Jr., played the same role at Half-Way Creek and Everglade.

In 1906 Ted Smallwood started a trading post in his home which was set back on higher ground about one hundred yards from the

Photo by George C. Trabant, St. Petersburg Times, 1957.

Interior of Smallwood Store. Thelma Smallwood standing behind counter; her sister Mrs. Marguerite Williams and her nephew and niece, Chris and Lynn Hancock.

water's edge. In that same year he succeeded C. G. McKinney as postmaster and moved the post office there also. He held this position until 1941 when he retired. Since that date his daughter, Thelma Smallwood, has been in charge of the post office. After 1906 the Smallwood place became increasingly the trading headquarters for the region, being rivaled only by that of Captain George W. Storter, Jr., at Everglades.

This business success was not due to chance. Ted Smallwood was an enterprising and resourceful man. In 1917 he built the store that now stands on the water's edge. At first it was built only slightly above the water level, but a 1924 storm sounded a warning. The door blew in, four feet of water stood in the store and the building was moved six inches on the foundation. The next year he raised it on pilings in the manner it now stands—and barely in time, for it would otherwise have been destroyed in the severe 1926 hurricane.

One other major problem remained to be solved before the possibilities of the trading site could be fully realized. The deep water channel was offshore some hundreds of yards. Only small boats such as skiffs and canoes could come all the way into the dock at the store front. Two fish houses stood out on the edge of the channel and at this writing a few of the posts that supported one of them still stand to mark the point to which boats of heavier draft came. In 1918 Smallwood dredged a channel extending several hundred yards along the shore from deep water to his dock at the store front. The fish houses were then moved onto the land, one on either side of the store. This channel gave a considerable commercial advantage to that side of the island and rewarded the enterprise of Ted Small-wood.

Priests from Key West came to administer the sacraments to Catholic families and the Santinis had attached to their home a small chapel. Adolphus Santini's journal records frequent visits of priests to Chokoloskee, Marco and sometimes up the coast. In between such visits Catholic families often visited Key West where they had the advantage of all the services of the church. Itinerant ministers or missionaries sent by Protestant organizations from upper Florida provided for some of the religious needs of the Protestants.

In its early history the Chokoloskee Country faced north and south. Its mail at first came by sailing vessel from Key West. But soon it was coming from the railroad at Punta Gorda and later Fort Myers. Its people looked first to Key West and then to Fort Myers for local government until it was brought closer to home by the creation of Collier County in 1923. Its markets followed the same pattern. Key West with its contact with Mallory Line steamers to New York was the center at first. But as the railroads reached deeper into Florida around the turn of the century, residents looked northward to use that means of access to new markets.

Life went on with relatively little change. Sometimes a citizen revealed sensitiveness to the isolation and obscurity in which he lived. In 1912 McKinney complained that the importance of the island and its people was being overlooked. Two letters had lately been addressed to him at Everglade. "Now I wish folks could learn that there is another part of this neck of the woods besides Everglade. Everglade is a small place beside Chokoloskee. We have two business houses . . . we have ten families living here."

A survey of property holdings on the island in 1935 showed its 144 1/6 acres divided up into 27 parcels. Eleven owners held an acre or less. Seven of them had between one and three acres each. Five owned between ten and sixteen acres each. Ted Smallwood, owner of the largest tract, had 35½ acres. The Coast Realty Company held 27 acres. Three-fifths of an acre belonged to a church, and 1¼ acres to the school. Clearly land ownership was widely distributed on the island. When Barron Collier was buying up the greater part of what is now Collier County he did not acquire any of Chokoloskee Island. His brother C. M. Collier, however, was the principal owner of the Coast Realty Company.

John Henry Thompson, the oldest inhabitant on Chokoloskee Island in 1957, was born in Key West seventy-eight years ago. He came up to Chatham River in 1892 and worked on the farm of notorious bad man Ed Watson for five years after which he operated Watson's boats for a time. He next moved down to Lostman's River where he married and spent several years at farming. The 1910 storm wiped him out completely, destroying his palmetto shack and wrecking an eight ton schooner in the swamp. He recalls placing his six weeks old daughter on the net board of a skiff and turning a wash tub over her, placing the remainder of the family in the skiff and pushing it inland to a heavy stand of timber where they rode out the storm.

Like many other pioneers, the Thompsons maintained a home in one place and took up temporary residence in a palmetto shack while they farmed or fished for a season. Their first home was on Dismal

Photo by Dr. John K. Small, in Chas. T. Simpson, In Lower Florida Wilds, p. 67.
This is described as a typical palmetto thatch on Chokoloskee Island at the turn of the century. But many of the so-called shacks had as many as four rooms.

Key, and it was only a temporary dwelling that was destroyed in 1910. They next took up temporary quarters on Pavilion Key and dug clams in the nearby waters. They then returned to Lostman's River for another period of farming, after which they moved their home base to Caxambas and built a house there, but soon sold it to J. M. Barfield and returned to Dismal Key. They next spent some time on Fakahatchee Island and at Lane's Place on the mainland on upper Chokoloskee Bay. After two years they returned to Fakahatchee and built a house there. They came to Chokoloskee in 1917 and soon thereafter built the house in which the head of the family still lives, his wife having died four years ago. The father of eleven children, he has been a trustee of the Chokoloskee school for twenty-two years.

From time to time McKinney reported the ups and downs of school life in the remote fishing village and trading post, revealing a rough and tumble frontier community where the weak and fearful did not long survive. Mr. Lions, an elderly Irishman, taught the first school in an old outhouse. There were only about seven or eight pupils. McKinney and George Howell then built a palmetto shack for a school house and Miss Annie Metcalf taught there. In 1898 Lee County provided the lumber, citizens did the labor, and Chokoloskee had its first public schoolhouse.

But in November, 1924, McKinney wrote, "We have no preaching at all and no school. We heard of a he-teacher who started down here and got as far as Marco and found out he did not have his fighting spirit along; so he went back up the coast." He added that the islanders had recently bidden a lady teacher good-bye. Of the recently departed lady he had written: "Our school teacher, we understand, is going to give up her school today; it is too much for her nerves. She seems to be a nice refined body and we are sorry for her. She had a trying time here, but we can give her praise for her endurance . . ."

But the school was not abandoned. At the end of May 1925, McKinney reported: "Our school is moving slowly being somewhat crippled up, the swamp angels (mosquitoes) being so fearful just now. It is hard to run anything here successfully now except a spray gun."

McKinney would have been proud to know that in 1940, long after his passing, the first Chokoloskee graduate was to receive a high school diploma. There had been a good elementary school on the island but no one had gone beyond the eighth grade until that date. Belle Thompson, whose father was a guide and fisherman, completed high school in the same year at Everglades and Leola McKinney was within one year of graduation at Naples High.

Like all frontier communities, Chokoloskee had its itinerant preachers, an occasional resident minister, and sometimes a revival meeting. The island was for a time very active as a center for the Pentecostal sect. Writing in the *American Eagle* in January of 1913, McKinney reported: "We have not heard from our preacher but we are getting on fine with the Pentecost now. It is the best that we have had in this neck of the woods. It has captured some of the worst sinners we have, and I am told that it makes them want to pay their debts, but if it doesn't make them have the energy to get around and make the wherewith to pay, it is of no benefit at all."

McKinney's reference to "our church" was the one he helped to build. He claimed to have given the lot, bought the bell and the lumber for it. There may have been other churches in the region, but the Reverend James L. Glenn reported in 1926 that a small mission church at Chokoloskee with no pastor was the only one in the county in 1923. This is still the only church on the island. It is now designated as the Church of God and the congregation is engaged in replacing the small wooden building with a concrete block

Photo by Taylor R. Alexander, Miami.
Church of God, Chokoloskee, June 1957.

structure more in keeping with the island's new importance.

If one may judge from McKinney's comments, what he called "low bush lightning" was the worst enemy of the islanders. In 1923, for example: "Moonshining is still on the boom; good demand for pure cane syrup, bottles, jugs and cork stoppers. The Karo syrup will not give the desired results in the moonshine business, they say."

Chokoloskee Islanders felt their isolation and listened hopefully to all the proposals to extend highways or railroad down their way. In the early twenties the realization of their dreams came tantalizingly near when Barron G. Collier came to southern Lee County, became its principal land-owner and showed promise of lifting the region out of its obscurity.

In 1923 when Collier County was created, the town of Everglade, six miles away on Barron River, became the county seat. The channel out to deep water was improved. The county seat town grew rapidly. The Tamiami Trail showed signs of eventually being completed and only four miles of road would be needed to connect Everglade to that highway. Another six miles would extend the highway to the island, but four of those miles would be across the bay and difficult to construct.

In February, 1919, Captain J. F. Jaudon, perhaps the foremost promoter of the Tamiami Trail, had picked up a party of thirteen notables at Marco to inspect the proposed route of the Tamiami Trail. The party went to Chokoloskee on the Jaudon yacht *Macushla*. Two local guides took them up Turner River to visit the Trail site and they returned to supper at the Smallwood residence. For the islanders, this was their first real promise of escape from isolation.

Chokoloskee's outlook was completely changed by the opening of the Tamiami Trail. The islanders had previously looked entirely to the waters of the Gulf of Mexico for contact with the outside. They now turned inland to the growing town of Everglades which soon had highway connections and, in time, a railroad.

Contact by land seemed within reach, but hopes of an early highway to the mainland were doomed repeatedly to disappointment. Anticipation ran high in 1935 when it appeared that such a road might be made a W.P.A. project. Chokoloskee news had largely disappeared from the local newspaper after McKinney's death in 1926, but several items regarding the possible road now appeared. The correspondent to the *American Eagle* reported that they had appealed to everyone from President Roosevelt to Governor Sholtz without result and added: "but guess will have to turn to Mr. Copeland, our last resort in time of trouble." Mrs. Ted Smallwood wrote in support of a road and bridge to the mainland. She thought the more than twenty families deserved a road.

The county commissioners of Collier County did take the first steps to build the road. They constructed a grade about one and one-half miles long a short distance inland and parallel to the shore line. This extended to Half-Way Creek. They planned to continue this grade to the point at which the island is nearest to the mainland. From that point the plans called for a causeway out to the island. World War II intervened and road making stopped.

In 1948 the County Commissioners revived the project. They released for the Chokoloskee road a quarter of a million dollars held by the State Road Department for new construction in Collier County. But the road was not yet to be built. Engineers of the State Road Department considered unsatisfactory the original plans for the road along the shore to a point opposite the island. They concluded the most feasible and least expensive route lay directly across the bay.

The engineers maintained that the road along the shore would be adequate only if the muck were removed down to hardpan and the

Air photo by Captain Frederick Forte, U.S.A.F.
Chokoloskee Island six months after the road was completed.

roadbed built up from that. Road building experience elsewhere indicated that roads built upon muck were unsatisfactory. They recommended instead a road directly to the bay from the courthouse circle in Everglades built up from a solid foundation. From that point a hydraulic fill out to the island would provide a better and cheaper road. Plans included a bridge at Half-Way Creek. But nothing was done immediately as funds were inadequate.

Funds finally became available in 1954 and construction was started late in the year. The muck was removed from the roadbed from Everglades down to the bay. In the beginning it looked more like a drainage canal but soon it was filled to make a sound roadbed. The pumping up of the sand fill required about six months. By the end of the summer in 1955 autos and trucks began to make their somewhat uncertain way over the new causeway to the island. By early summer of 1956 the roadbed had settled sufficiently to apply the hardsurfacing, and Chokoloskee at last had access to the mainland.

· Bulldozers began to transform the appearance of the island as soon as equipment could be moved across the new road. They cleared the land of most of the trees and undergrowth and leveled the mounds and ridges on three-fourths of it, revealing how completely the island is built up of shell. A fishing camp, a small boat dock, and a motel appeared at the point where the road reaches the island. A little further on the east side of the road Ted Smallwood, son of the first of that name on the island, dredged a channel into his property and used the shell fill to raise and level the surrounding area.

Near the old Smallwood home and store, another member of the family has built a motel, dredged a channel and a small turning basin and operates a fishing camp. A little further around to the west two fish houses have again appeared on the island to handle the catch of its many commercial fishermen. The school boat is no more, having been replaced with a bus. The elementary school for the first four grades will remain for another term but its life appears limited. The youngsters will join their older brothers and sisters for the daily trip to Everglades.

Chokoloskee has taken on some of the aspects of a modern real estate development, but as long as the store remains, with its hoop skirt counter and relics from the days of Old Ted Smallwood, there will be an authentic touch of the good old days.

Since Chokoloskee was the southernmost settlement in the Ten Thousand Islands it was the headquarters for people from a wide area. Captain Dick Turner, Seminole War scout, came back in the early seventies to the river that bears his name. He occupied the shell mound site about a quarter of a mile upriver until near 1890 when he sold it to a Doctor Harris of Key West. The doctor apparently planned extensive farming operations for he built a packing shed 50 x 100 feet, a stable and an office building. To catch an adequate supply of fresh water he constructed the large cistern that alone now marks the site. Back from these buildings was a two story frame dwelling house.

The House family moved to Turner River in 1895 and purchased the Turner - Harris property for two thousand dollars. Dan R. House, now living in Naples, remembers that they kept their hogs in the stable at night to protect them from panthers. They also moved the office building up to the house to make an additional room. In 1900 the Houses moved to Chokoloskee. High water had salted much of the farming land on the river and it could not be cultivated successfully until after rain had washed the salt out of the soil. The gigantic 1910 storm destroyed the packing house and the property was occupied only occasionally after that time.

A huge cistern on the bank of Lopez River some miles down the coast from Chokoloskee marks the place where the Lopez family settled and lived for two generations, giving their name to the river. Further down the coast on Chatham River was the homesite of the well known Ed Watson who carried on extensive cane growing and syrup making and operated his boats between Key West and Fort Myers. Banana trees, a huge royal poinciana tree, remains of the machinery used in syrup making and part of the dwelling house complete with the ever present cistern mark the famous Chatham Bend place. On nearby Sand Fly Pass Charles T. Boggess and others farmed the rich shell mound soil planting mostly tomatoes.

Everglade: *On Allen's River*

I N 1893 when the Post Office Department rejected the name Chokoloskee first submitted for the new post office on Allen's River,
Bembery Storter proposed that it be called "Everglade." And this
was its designation until 1923 when the letter "s" was added to
make the present day "Everglades." The history of that community
before and after adding the letter is so strikingly different that it
may well be treated as the history of two settlements that happened to
occupy the same site.

Barron River bears little resemblance to the narrow, somewhat
crooked stream that was known before 1923 as Allen's River, so
named after the first permanent settler. Before his time it seems to
have been known as Potato Creek. Legend has it that soldiers planted
the potatoes there in the Seminole War and that they had continued
to grow wild, or, as crackers put it, "volunteer." There is no reason
to believe that the stream was ever that important in the Indian wars
and if early settlers found potatoes growing there, some itinerant
Indian or White occupant of the site must have been the planter.

Certainly there were temporary settlers on the banks of the river
before William Smith Allen became its first permanent occupant
shortly after 1870. Among these was John Weeks, who later moved
to Chokoloskee Island. The War between the States brought Weeks
and Allen to Key West and from there to Collier County in completely unrelated ways.

The conflict between the North and the South left the Collier
County region almost completely untouched. Official records note a

few blockade runners being taken in the Marco Channel-Cape Romano area, but most such activity was further up the coast. Undoubtedly the many channels and passes of the Ten Thousand Islands provided hiding places for deserters from both armies and hiding places of a temporary sort for small boats.

Key West remained in Union hands throughout the war and Unionists made their way to the island in such numbers as to create problems of housing, food and employment. Key West authorities sought to meet all these problems in one move. They supplied seeds and tools for farming at Cape Sable and points north, possibly including some of the islands. Obie Hall, a well known pioneer resident who sailed on his father's schooner and kept in touch with these outlying farmers, reported that they did very well for a time.

The success of these early farmers probably first called attention to the farming possibilities in the region. John Weeks was among those who chose to return there after the conflict. He reached the mouth of the river some time in the late sixties and settled on the west bank. Two plume hunters, William Clay and his partner, Lowell, also reportedly sold Allen squatters' rights to the land where he wished to locate. It was not unusual for such "claim jockies" to pre-empt sites and sell their claims to newcomers.

William Smith Allen, who remained to be the first permanent settler and to give his name to the river until 1923, was born in Enfield, Connecticut. He moved to Ithaca, New York, where he met and married Jane Sprague. The couple moved to Georgia where he taught school for a time. The next move was to Jacksonville, Florida, where he kept books for the Fairbanks sawmilling firm. At the outbreak of the Civil War, Allen went to Key West along with other Union sympathizers.

George D. Allen, a brother, was collector of Customs at Key West and secured the appointment of William as deputy collector. The Allen brothers owned a drug store in Key West. A scarcity of castor oil induced them to attempt the growth of castor beans on Sanibel Island in 1868. Since the castor bean grew in a wild state in Florida they reasoned, why not cultivate it? The venture died a-borning when a storm destroyed the crop, and Allen loaded his tools and equipment and headed back to Key West.

Because of unfavorable winds little headway could be made. Off Chokoloskee Bay water was running short, so the retreating Allen put in to look for water. There he found John Weeks living at the mouth of the river. He secured his supply of fresh water. He also observed how richly bananas, sugar cane, pumpkins and cow peas grew in the small Weeks clearing and noted that there was similar soil on either bank of the river. He thereupon decided that he would one day return to the area. Some accounts suggest logically enough that he left his tools with John Weeks and took on board some of the sugar cane and bananas to market for Weeks in Key West. And by that set of circumstances a Connecticut Yankee found his way to what was one day to be the county seat of Collier County.

Allen put up a small house on the present Rod and Gun Club site and anchored it on two-foot blocks. As the site had not been filled to its present height above water level, a hurricane in 1873 flooded the place to a depth of six feet, putting several feet of water inside the home. The owner thereupon jacked up the building another four feet and placed three foot square posts under it, mixing beach shell, homemade lime and cement to make the concrete.

Allen owned and occupied all of the Everglade townsite along the river from 1873 to 1889 when he returned to Key West where he soon died. He had planted his crops along the river front on the east side from the mouth of the river to Port DuPont, the north end of the present settlement. Allen was also a Justice of the Peace, and in that capacity he held court and performed marriage ceremonies. In the absence of a minister, he also conducted funerals.

The real founder of Everglades, however, and its first citizen for over a quarter of a century, was George W. Storter, Jr., who became William Allen's successor. He was born at Eutaw, Alabama, July 1, 1862. In 1877 he came with his father and a brother, R. B., to Fort Winder (now called Platt), Florida, three miles west of Fort Ogden.

The younger George recalled that the family had made the trip from Alabama in true pioneer style in a covered wagon. In September of 1881, the senior Storter made the first trip to Everglade. He traded an ox-cart for a sloop and John Cash sailed her from Charlotte Harbor to Allen's River.

Storter first farmed with William S. Allen. In the first year they produced for the Key West-New York market a crop of cucumbers, eggplant and tomatoes. The sons, George W., Jr., and R. B., came down in February, 1882 to help harvest the crop, and remained until May.

John Cash, having used the sloop for his own purpose during the winter months, returned to Everglade where he picked up the Storter

Courtesy of Claude M. Storter, Naples.
Captain George Storter at controls of Deep Lake Railroad "engine" with Mrs. Storter and Harry Magill.

men for the return to Fort Winder. R. B. related to D. Graham Copeland in 1946 that the only inhabited places along the way were at Punta Rassa where there was a telegraph station, Wiggins Pass where Joe Wiggins operated an apiary and a small trading post, and at Marco where W. T. Collier had established himself.

August Swycover and his wife settled at the Port DuPont site in 1882. They planted sugar cane along the west bank of the river below where the bridge now crosses. Swycover shipped his sugar cane to Key West in a boat which carried 1200 to 1500 cane at a trip.

In 1883 the father of the Storters established himself at the north end of the present townsite. In the fall of 1887 George W., Jr., came with his wife and one small daughter. He purchased the property of the Swycovers and made his first home there. On January 1, 1889, the first white child born in Everglade, Frances Eva Storter, was born there.

When William Allen returned to Key West in 1889, George W. Storter, Jr., purchased all the Allen property, comprising the entire Everglade townsite, for eight hundred dollars. Storter bought the land unsurveyed, but Allen had a certificate giving him prior right to purchase the land. The new owner set himself up at the Allen homestead. From that vantage point he directed the destinies of Everglade until 1922 and continued his farming operations, particularly the growing of sugar cane.

The senior Storter was a tinner by trade and in the early years made cans for the syrup. George, Jr., better known as Judge Storter in later years, and, like many others, also called "Captain" Storter, was famous for his sugar cane growing and syrup making. In 1912 the *Fort Myers Press* reported thirty acres of cane that would produce 9,000 gallons of syrup. He was then using a gasoline driven cane grinding mill that would crush two tons of cane a day. Seven years later the *American Eagle* reported that he had grown cane on the same land for twenty years without replanting, without fertilizing and without cultivating after the first year. At that time he reputedly owned 700 acres of land of which sixty were in cultivation. Twenty-five acres of it planted in cane would yield 500 to 800 gallons of syrup per acre.

In 1892, George, Jr., established a trading post just down river from his home which became a gathering place for Indian and White alike. The original building had a dirt floor, home made shelves and counters, and an open screen front with a canvas curtain to keep out the rain and cold.

He gradually enlarged his home to accommodate the increasing number of hunters, fishermen and yachting parties that came for the winter season and set a lavish table with all the products of that country. This was the foundation of the modern Rod and Gun Club built around the Storter House, and always famous for its cuisine. In 1898 he planted the great madeira mahogany tree now growing in front of the club.

The second Storter son, R. B., better known as Bembery, was equally active in the growing of cane and the making of syrup. Whereas his brother used large iron kettles of eighty and one hundred gallons capacity in which he cooked the cane juice, Bembery used the evaporator type of pan in which the juice started in one section and moved through nine sections to emerge on the other end as syrup. Both Storters grew cane on Half-Way Creek and brought it around to Everglade to be processed. The huge cane barge provided a refuge on which to ride out the 1910 hurricane. Bembery also operated a passenger and freight service on his schooner, the *Bertie Lee,* one of the most famous sailing vessels on the coast.

The Storter store and warehouse made up the business section of Everglade.

The *Bertie Lee* grew with the community's expanding trade and travel, being rebuilt and enlarged twice. Originally the sloop *Falcon*, it caught fire at the dock in Key West where the fire department sank her to extinguish the flames. Storter raised the vessel and brought it to Everglade where he rebuilt and enlarged it and renamed it the *Bertie Lee*. In 1898 it was redesigned and a two cylinder Globe engine installed for auxiliary power, the first gasoline engine in the area. On the first Sunday after the installation, every person in the village had a ride.

Other settlers came to the Allen River community, some to remain permanently, others to tarry only briefly. In 1879, Mr. and Mrs. Madison Weeks with their three sons and two daughters came from Fort Winder to stay briefly on Half-Way Creek before they settled at the mouth of the river on the west bank. They raised cabbages and turnips for market. For his home Weeks built two twelve-foot rooms with a passageway between. It was made of palmetto logs and the roof was thatched with palm fronds. In 1883, John J. Brown bought the Weeks property, moved his family there from Half-Way

Creek, and lived there until he died. About 1914 one of his sons, C. M. Brown, sold half of the property to George Bruner of Kokomo, Indiana, and later sold the other half to Barron Collier.

Opposite the Rod and Gun Club site, Mrs. Willie Gandees, a widow, lived from 1887 to 1897, when she sold the property to George W. Storter. The next year Storter sold it to H. K. Stevens who occupied it until the 1910 hurricane when he abandoned it and it reverted to Storter. In 1911 Storter sold it again, this time to George Kingston who retained it until he sold out to Barron Collier. Kingston planted the royal palms and madeira trees now standing on the property occupied by "Uncle" Charles Boggess.

In 1882, the Storters, on their way back to Fort Winder, found Joe Wiggins operating an apiary and a small trading post at Wiggins Pass on Surveyor Creek or Imperial River. He announced at the time that he was about to sell out to Joe Williams. The next year Wiggins settled on a shell mound near the head of Allen's River where he raised cabbages for shipment to Key West and also operated a small trading post.

About 1886 after Wiggins moved again, this time to Sand Fly Pass, a Mr. Lennart of Tampa bought the trading post site from Wiggins, but abandoned it after a month to return to Tampa. After several other changes in ownership, George W. Storter acquired the property and traded it to Thomas Myles of Bartow for five acres of land at Bartow. Myles never cultivated the land and finally abandoned it.

Andrew Wiggins, himself an old settler, related that his uncle sold the Sand Fly Pass place to a Mr. Porter from Michigan. Joe Wiggins later had yet another store at Broad River for a time. When asked for an article he didn't have, he invariably replied that it was ordered and coming on the next boat. He would then crane his neck to see if the boat was coming up the pass.

Charles T. "Uncle Charley" Boggess, the oldest pioneer in the southern part of the county, now lives at Everglades, but has lived part of his life at Sand Fly Pass, Chokoloskee, Half-Way Creek and Fakahatchee. He came from Fort Ogden at the age of three, seventy-five years ago. His wife of sixty years also came to Florida at three years of age from Rockville, Illinois, with her father who sought the warmer climate and salt water as a cure for arthritis. The two attended school together at the Everglade School and were married in February of 1897.

Uncle Charley combines in his experience most of the principal occupations of pioneers. For years he grew tomatoes at Sand Fly Pass, built his own packing shed and boated his crop to the Key West market. He later turned guide to winter visitors who came to fish and is recognized as dean of the guides though he now rarely goes out. He has also been a boat builder, designing and building many of the cabin cruisers that make up the Everglades fleet of charter boats. He was the first person to make the trip to Chokoloskee by land when the new road was under construction, wading fifty yards of the distance. He is one of the best story tellers—yarn spinners—in the county. He now lives in semi-retirement but exercises all of the rights and privileges of the area's oldest pioneer.

Half-Way Creek, appropriately enough half way between Allen River and Turner River, had an early development that rivaled Chokoloskee and Everglade. Farmers settled on both banks of the creek where they specialized in bananas and sugar cane and vegetables. In the early 1890's Ted Smallwood reported those living there. On the north side were George Howell, Ben Brown, Will Gardner, Jimmie Lockhart, and Charles Gardner, and on the south side, Charley Boggess, Dave Black, George Christian, and Bill Brown. And at that time there was an Adventist church there.

About ten years later the Shands Survey of 1902 showed the names of only four property owners on the creek. George Storter appears as the owner of two tracts and he apparently had begun to buy up the properties of those who abandoned the Creek as a place to live. The others at that time were Byrd, Johnson, Lockhart, and Chas. Bogus (Boggess).

Ted Smallwood also recalled that the first election held in the Ten Thousand Islands was at Half-Way Creek in 1892. Will Gardner brought the ballot box from Key West and "All the poll tax receipts, a jug of licker, a box of cigars. All we had to do was vote." Today the banks of the creek are completely overgrown and only the remains of an occasional cistern mark the old homesites.

The church soon made its appearance alongside the other institutions of civilized living. The Florida Conference of the Methodist Church sent the Reverend George W. Gatewood to survey the field in 1888. In a later account of that experience the pioneer minister wrote that he had made his way to Fort Myers where he engaged passage on the sailboat *Ploughboy* under the command of Captain Joe Williams. There were two other passengers but before they reached their destination Williams engaged in a fight with one of

Sunday School at Everglade about 1906.

them, killed him, and hid out for years. The first act of the new minister was to bury the murdered man. Very soon thereafter the minister and his flock built two chapels, one at Half-Way Creek and the other at Marco.

Having surveyed the field and its potentialities, the Reverend Gatewood made his report to the Conference which thereupon dispatched the Reverend H. S. Miller to the field for a year. He seems to have preached at Half-Way Creek, Marco and Naples, traveling by boat.

But the Reverend Gatewood returned as resident pastor, living with Captain G. W. Storter until he married in 1892 at Everglade. When the Seventh Day Adventists began to take over the field at Half-Way Creek, Methodist services were held at the schoolhouse in Everglade. When this was destroyed, a small church was built on the adjoining lot.

Pastor Gatewood remained on the circuit four years, making friends with the Indians who came to Everglade to trade. They sometimes came and sat crosslegged on the floor throughout the services although he doubted they got much good from the sermons since they knew no English.

The Gatewoods received little money for their services, but said they never wanted anything. There was always an abundance of seafood, wild game, native fruits and vegetables. The first church officials were the Storter brothers, George and R. B., James Lockhart and George Christian.

The Conference apparently did not continue to maintain a minister at Everglade. The news items supplied by local correspondents indicate that itinerant preachers of various denominations preached occasionally, usually in a home. A Baptist minister, G. F. Giles, in May, 1913 undertook to reorganize the Sunday School which had died down "since the arrival of Pentecost folks." He would also preach on Sunday afternoon. The correspondent exhibited his preference in the matter of churches when he added "glad to hear somebody besides Pentecost."

So slowly did the community grow that not until the fall of 1893 were there enough children to induce the county officials to establish a school. In that year J. W. Todd, a native of Tennessee, taught the first school. The teacher and his dozen pupils met in a room provided by G. W. Storter in what was then his home and is now the Rod and Gun Club. In the winter of 1895-1896 Allen B. Clare, later Mayor of Key West and County Attorney for Monroe County, taught in the new schoolhouse down near the mouth of the river on the east bank.

A cyclone destroyed the schoolhouse and the county built another on the same site. In the 1910 hurricane that one floated up river and broke up in the swamp. The third building on the site was being used in 1923 when Collier County was founded.

Mrs. Bertie Storter Ison of Bonita Springs, eldest daughter of G. W. Storter, Jr., recalls teaching at Everglade when there were more than thirty pupils, thirteen of them Storters. Swimming was the main feature of the physical education program. A couple of boys watched for alligators while the others dived into the river. Alligators never attacked any of the youngsters but when a dog attempted to swim across the river, it was likely to be caught, and this made the swimmers more alert.

The Shands Survey listed the properties and their owners in 1902, beginning on the right bank of the river down near the mouth. First came the public school, then in order, the parsonage, the church, R. B. Storter, the Post Office and three parcels marked Storter, presumably George W., and on the left bank C. M. Brown, near the mouth of the river, and further up, Storter, Russell, Nobles and James Demere.

Fourteen miles north of Everglade was Deep Lake Hammock which derives its name from the lake of the same name. Deep Lake is important in its own right, but its history has from the beginning been inseparably linked with that of Everglade and Everglades.

Shortly after 1900 Walter Langford of Fort Myers and John M. Roach of the Chicago Street Railway Company acquired the Deep Lake Hammock. It is nearly three hundred acres of relatively high land, and what is more important, the tropical vegetation there appeared to have survived the freeze that had wrought such havoc in groves further north. Maybe this was the frost-free land they were seeking.

The partners cleared two hundred acres of the hammock and planted it in Marsh seedless grapefruit trees. This was done at considerable cost as everything had to be brought from Fort Myers without benefit of even an Indian trail for much of the way. They planted the grove with the reasonable assumption that canal, highway or railroad would soon provide access to market for the fruit. Until that time it would be hauled overland to the head of navigation on Allen's River fourteen miles away, from which it would be shipped by barge to Fort Myers where it would be packed and sent to market.

In 1913 the owners of the grove apparently despaired of getting any public means of transportation and decided to provide their own. They shipped to Everglade by water the rails and rolling stock to build a railroad from the river to Deep Lake, Collier County's first. Power came from a Ford automobile engine mounted on a four wheeled carriage, the wheels being flanged to run on the rails. The flat cars were also small four wheeled affairs.

On May 21, George Storter, Sr., drove the first spike in the laying of the rails, and his son George, Jr., the second. The road ran across the swamp by a somewhat circuitous route without benefit of grade, and in wet weather large sections of it were under water. The *American Eagle* reported in 1917 that 17,000 field boxes of grapefruit went to market over the road that season.

This was hardly yet the railroad age come to the wilderness, but it was enough to excite newspaper comment on the possibilities it opened up. The *American Eagle,* July 3, 1915, quoted the *Key West Journal* as it took notice of this railroad activity. The island newspaper saw the railroad eventually reaching Key West and opening the entire region to her commerce. It was only 50 miles from Key West to Cape Sable, "the most beautiful spot in all Florida, and there

Courtesy of Mrs. Bertie Storter Ison, Bonita Springs.
Storter House which was expanded into the Rod and Gun Club, Everglades.

is no doubt the road will be pushed in that direction as soon as possible, opening up to tourists and agriculture alike, the dream of the ages—a perfect climate and nice and easily worked soil with no malaria or other scourge of the tropics.

"From Cape Sable there is not more than three fathoms of water across to the inside keys with only shallow water between there and Key West. This route presents less difficulties than the one chosen by the Florida East Coast and there is no doubt that with the advantageous position enjoyed by Key West as the gateway to the Panama Canal and Central America another railroad will soon be built to Key West."

In 1922 Barron G. Collier began buying land in Lee County from land and timber companies and from individuals. Among his important purchases were the Deep Lake property and the considerable holdings of George Storter who held most of the land in the Everglade-Half-Way Creek region. When he chose the town of Everglade for the center of his activities, he ushered in the second phase of its history. Everglade was about to become Everglades.

When Collier came to this remote trading post and farming community less than a dozen families were living there. The only habitable land was a narrow strip on both banks of the river, nowhere more than two hundred feet wide. Back of that strip lay tide washed mangrove swamp. But it was already known as a paradise for fishermen and hunters. Two sportsmen from Kokomo, Indiana, George

Kingston and George Bruner, had built winter homes there and yachting parties anchored in the lower end of nearby Chokoloskee Bay. The Storter House was already more than a local institution. The stage was set for a new era.

Everglades: *County Seat in The Mangroves*

I N 1923 Everglade added an "s" and became Everglades and the county seat of newly created Collier County. Over-night, it had become the capital city of Barron Collier's Florida holdings and as such was a beehive of activity. It was now a transportation and communications center and the site of two giant engineering projects: building a town and directing the construction work both on the Tamiami Trail and on a north-south highway from Everglades to the Trail, on up to Deep Lake and Immokalee.

To a casual observer it might have appeared doubtful that a town of any consequence could ever develop there. Back from the low ridge of slightly higher ground that bordered on the river there was only salt marsh and mangrove swamp for four or more miles. This half land-half water tangle of roots, subject to overflow at high tide seemed an impossible barrier to the building of a town. The only way out of town northward was by way of the flimsy Deep Lake Railroad which came to a dead end fourteen miles away. The river was narrow, not very deep, and crooked, and Chokoloskee Bay into which it flowed was nowhere more than five feet deep, but must be crossed to reach the deep water of the Gulf of Mexico.

What prompted Barron Collier to choose this rather than some higher and more accessible point only he knew and he never said. As he was thoroughly familiar with the entire region, one must conclude that he chose the area because it was located nearest the center of his holdings and it was all his to develop as he pleased. What nature had failed to supply, his imagination, vision, managerial skill, and, above all, his capital, would soon provide. The new Everglades first took form in the mind of this man who had set out to develop the county to which he gave his name, and most of which he owned.

Everglades next appeared bit by bit on blueprints in the offices of Collier's associates and engineers. For the building of this town was first of all an engineering feat. The level of the land must be raised above the mangrove swamp and beyond the reach of high tide, for less than ten per cent of the 660, later 760, acres was high land. This was accomplished by building seawall or bulkheads along the river banks and pumping the fill from the river bottom into the townsite. As the level of the land rose, the channel of the river became wider and deeper and more nearly straight. When the river no longer supplied enough fill the dredge was moved to a point east of town where it dredged out the large lake now there.

The big dredge "Barcarmil," named for the three sons of Barron Collier, Barron, Jr., Carnes (better known as Sam) and Miles, was a familiar sight and sound in Everglades from late 1926 to 1929. Earlier a six inch machine had been used to make the fill for the basic buildings near the river. The big twelve inch machine was designed and built in a machine shop at Port DuPont and usually operated twenty hours a day. It could deliver its load a distance of 4500 feet which made it possible to extend the channel well out into the bay while filling the townsite. The two machines together pumped nearly two million cubic feet of fill into the townsite. Other dredging as late as 1950 has filled other areas and extended the usable land.

Everglades was from the beginning laid out in two parts. At the north end of town was the industrial section called Port DuPont. Collier felt that this isolated community must be made as nearly self-sufficient as possible. The operations at Port DuPont went a long way to achieve that end. Here were machine shops to maintain the equipment being used to transform the town of Everglades. And the same shops did an even more important job of maintaining equipment on the Tamiami Trail construction. When broken or worn parts could not be mended, they were often made outright for to wait for parts and service from distant Fort Myers or Tampa would be far too costly in time and money.

Dredge "Barcarmil" pumping in fill for townsite.

The first shop was built in 1922. By 1927 the machine shop alone was keeping in repair 11 dredges, 30 cars and trucks and several tractors. Closely allied to the machine shop were a blacksmith shop and a garage. A sawmill with a daily capacity of 10,000 feet provided lumber for the numerous building projects. There was also a planing and finishing mill. A boat yard kept in operation floating craft of all sizes and description and new boats were constructed when need for them arose.

The offices of the engineers charged with planning and carrying out Barron Collier's major projects were also at Port DuPont. The engineering and construction firm of Alexander, Ramsay and Kerr was organized to execute the major projects such as roadbuilding. Barrack-like buildings with central mess halls provided living quarters for workmen, White and Negro, until houses could be built for men and their families.

The Deep Lake Railroad which John Roach and Walter Langford had built years before to get the annual grapefruit crop to market now began to assume much wider importance. In addition to the passenger and freight service to Deep Lake, logging trains brought in the pine and cypress logs to feed the sawmill. And until the road north to the Tamiami Trail was opened the little railroad functioned effectively as a supply line to haul supplies and men for the Trail building operations. The railroad in 1927 owned two small loco-

The street car "System" in Everglades in the middle twenties.

motives and operated at least one train a day. Three tractor trains ran daily to and from the logging camps.

The river provided the new town with its only street for many months. Mary Hayes Davis writing in the *American Eagle* in January 1924 thought it the "most unique" main street. Amid all the bustle of activity she saw not one automobile or wagon. The river, on the other hand, was crowded with the going and coming of floating craft of all types.

Before the town had an exit by highway or railroad, it achieved the unique distinction of operating the only street car south of Tampa. This was a single, battery powered car, but complete in every detail including advertising cards. Aside from any utility it represented, the street car was a novel advertising stunt. Perhaps also Barron Collier wanted this symbol of the Street Railway advertising business enterprise that provided the means for his Florida enterprises.

It had arrived on a seagoing barge. On another barge was 400 tons of 90 pound rails. The track was laid down parallel to the road to DuPont and Carnestown. It operated only to and from Port DuPont and no fares were collected.

The life of the street car "system" in this case was relatively brief, but not without incident. On the night of June 27th, 1928 fire damaged the car. A short circuit when the batteries were being charged caused a fire that did slight injury to eight batteries and two of the seats. When a hurricane in 1929 did considerable damage to the track the car was retired. By that time there was less need for the car's services and certainly less money for such luxuries. But the Everglades Railway Light and Power Company that had operated the one-car street railway system continued to operate the town's power plant and water works until they were sold to the city in 1954.

Step by step the town's isolation began to be overcome. A Collier subsidiary bought out the Fort Myers Steamship and Navigation Company with its wharves, warehouses and offices in Fort Myers. It became the Collier line, and the terminal facilities bore the Collier name also. This was done primarily to serve Everglades but it grew into a service for the entire southwest coast of Florida. The line started out with the *City of Everglades*. Later additions included the *City of Tampa, City of Fort Myers, City of Punta Gorda* and *City of Punta Blanca*. This was a flourishing enterprise for a few years, but the Tamiami Trail was officially opened in 1928 and the railroad was already pushing southward. The Collier line had done its work and had its day.

From the earliest days of the new Everglades development, it had telephone connections with the outside world. Collier workmen had immediately set to work stringing line north to Immokalee which connected with Fort Myers and provided a long distance connection to New York and elsewhere. This line, established primarily to serve Everglades, grew into a Collier owned subsidiary that served nineteen counties in that area of Florida. And when the new county assumed responsibility for construction work on the Tamiami Trail, telephone lines kept the Everglades offices of Alexander, Ramsay and Kerr in direct contact with "front line" operations.

As soon as the road was open to Naples and points north toward Tampa, Collier buses and trucks provided a passenger and freight service to the new town appearing in the mangrove swamp of southern Collier County. This grew into a bus system that served the entire southwest coastal area.

The final step in opening up Everglades to the outside world came in 1928 when the Atlantic Coast Line extension from Immokalee, 41 miles away, reached the town. The first passenger train puffed into Everglades in June of 1928, one month after the first work train.

This was destined to be the southern terminus of that railroad. Rumor said at the time that it was only part of a plan to extend the line on to Key West to rival Flagler's East Coast system. The 1929 economic collapse put an end to the possibility of any further extension of the railroad at the time.

The Collier interests rebuilt the Deep Lake-to-Everglades portion of the new railroad. The right of way was straightened and the new road built to Atlantic Coast Line specifications. And in a single operation the Alexander, Ramsay and Kerr dredges, in addition to building a railroad bed, prepared a roadbed for a new highway and dug out a sizeable drainage canal. When the Deep Lake Railroad was thus rebuilt it was taken over by the ACL.

House building proceeded more slowly. But as rapidly as the townsite was built up new streets were laid out and building operations were begun. Planning included ample space for tree planting and other landscaping to add to the natural beauty of the setting. Everglades today scarcely represents fulfillment of the founder's dream, but when its growth is more complete there will be gratitude for the foresight of the planners.

Architects and builders sought to design each house to fit the building site and thereby give individuality to the homes. Perhaps because they knew it was a "company" town, perhaps because in spite of the planners the buildings exhibited too much similarity, observers commented on the company town features. Mary Hayes Davis, who was quick to observe the unique features of the place, also noted that the houses were almost uniformly painted a deep cream with green or dull red roofs. W. E. Dahlgren, representing the Field Museum, wrote in "South Florida Wonders, II" "Instead of the primitive fishing village I had expected there was a trim and clean-cut, thoroughly modern, spotless looking town. At first glance it reminded us of nothing so much as of an up-to-date quarantine station in the tropics, but the uniform color scheme, yellow buildings with white trim and green stained roofs, gives it a character of its own."

No part of what should make a model town and county seat was overlooked. The Bank of Everglades opened its doors at 9 o'clock Monday July 9, 1923 and weathered both the Florida and the national depressions. The first bank building was down near the river on the north side of Broad Street. Before the present building was occupied in 1926 the bank operated from a small building across the street where there is now a barbershop. The first issue of the *Collier County News* appeared that same summer and served the county as an official organ. It was printed on the presses of the *Fort Myers Press* until 1954 when it acquired its own office in Naples. The Manhattan Mercantile Company which has recently moved its grocery department into new quarters up near Court House Circle, maintained a well stocked general merchandise establishment.

What had been a one-room school quickly grew into a two-room school with two teachers and forty-five pupils in the fall of 1923. A launch brought the pupils from the Port DuPont end of town. The present high school building was constructed in 1926, two rooms were added in 1936, a steel fire escape in 1945 and the one-story elementary school in 1939.

In the summer of 1927 attention was called to twelve Negro children who needed a school. In June of the same year the Negroes opened their own church built for them by Barron Collier. The small Negro congregation had formerly met in the Negro mess hall. Barron Collier, F. Irwin Holmes and D. Graham Copeland attended the dedication services at which it was announced that the pastor, the Reverend Hamilton, would open a school for Negroes in the fall. The Port DuPont Church has had a pastor intermittently, and it has been Methodist or Baptist as the minister happened to belong to one or the other of the denominations.

The County has since maintained DuPont School for Negro Children in the Everglades area through the eighth grade. High school pupils are transported to Immokalee where they attend Bethune High School. Carver School at Naples is also limited to the eighth grade. High school pupils are transported to Fort Myers in Lee County where they attend Dunbar High School. When the highway from Naples to Immokalee is completed it is assumed that Negro high school students from Naples will also be transported by bus to Bethune in Immokalee.

Since late 1925 Everglades has had a community church. It was established and nurtured by the Presbyterian Church until 1940 when the congregation became self-supporting and independent. The National Mission Board also helped to maintain the new church and the pastor was assigned to work among the Seminole Indians. This he did until 1933 when the Glade Cross Mission was reactivated. The congregation met in the theatre building until May 5, 1940 when they dedicated the church now standing on Broad Street. The Sunday

School-social room addition was added in 1957. Until the present pastor arrived in 1956 the pastor was always a Presbyterian but the Community Church is now served by the Rev. J. C. Simms, a Baptist. The interdenominational type of organization has proved successful here, the officers of the Women's auxiliary being Methodist, Baptist and Episcopalian.

In 1956 Baptists in Everglades organized a congregation and acquired a lot east of the school house. When C. J. Jones closed his sawmill at Jerome he donated to them the church he had built for the small sawmill village. They have moved it to Everglades, made additions to it, and the Reverend E. P. Strickland is the pastor of this first congregation apart from the Community Church.

In 1929 the Juliet C. Collier Hospital was completed and opened. In the same year Collier built and gave to the community a library, located on Broadway across from the Bank of Everglades. After an initial gift of money and books the library was to be maintained by gifts and fees paid by users. This is one project yet to be fully realized.

In July of 1927 the new town installed its first fraternal order when the Tamiami Trail Lodge of the Masons was founded. The previous affiliation of the officers of the new lodge gave some indication of the places of origin of some of the town's people. D. W. McLeod, worshipful master, was a past master of Peace River Lodge #66 of Arcadia. Dr. W. A. Brewer, senior warden, came from Summer Avenue Lodge #729 of Memphis. Junior Warden, Thomas B. Monson, came from Tropical Lodge #56 of Fort Myers. The nearest other lodges at the time were at Fort Myers, Key West and Miami.

The possibility that Everglades might grow as a winter tourist resort was never lost sight of. In this respect the new regime could build upon the long established reputation of the Storter House and the doings of Barron Collier both of which were widely reported. People heard about Everglades and the wonders being wrought there. As the Storter House had grown by several additions to what was once a family residence, the Storter House by additions became the Rod and Gun Club. The older building remained the nucleus of the hostelry that has attracted sportsmen year after year. Today some thirty charter boats operate regularly from the Rod and Gun Club docks from about January 15 to April 15, the height of the season.

A new 45-room hotel, the Everglades Inn, was under construction by early 1924. To the Inn as maitre d'hotel came a man destined to become one of the most famous of the many employees and associates Collier brought to his town a-building in the wilderness. Travelling in Bavaria, Collier liked the dishes served at an inn where the maitre d'hotel was Claus Senghaas. He induced the young German to come to Everglades. Collier must have described Everglades as it was to be. "Snooky," as Senghaas came to be known, liked to relate how he came by way of Cuba and Key West and by small boat to Everglades just before Christmas in 1923. Instead of a brilliant city, he found what was little more than a construction camp in the wilderness. He was dismayed by what he saw—or did not see, but he learned to love the place. He was once reported to have requested burial in Royal Palm Hammock.

Snooky contributed much to the fame that Everglades acquired in the winter sports world. He soon became manager of the Everglades Inn, and when the Rod and Gun Club was opened in 1925 he became manager and maitre d'hotel there also. He made the Club famous for its hospitality and food, including the lunches packed for all-day fishing trips. Snooky's real province was the kitchen. While he played host to the great and near great he kept a watchful eye on the culinary domain.

After World War II, Snooky retired to a small house of his own. His home had rooms for three or four guests, and he remained associated with the Rod and Gun Club in the capacity of consultant. Snooky died on February 22, 1954. His death marked the passing of yet another of the small number of Barron Collier associates still in Everglades.

The Everglades Inn was not designed to be a hotel. Its ground floor had three stores and the second was to house personnel of the Collier organization until houses could be built for them. Mrs. Mattie Lybass Thompson (Mrs. Sam) supervised the furnishing of the rooms and was its first manager. So great was the demand for hotel accommodations that in 1928 the building was remodeled and a third floor added, the lobby was enlarged and it received the stucco finish one sees today.

During World War II, the Coast Guard took over the Inn for a time but later moved to the Rod and Gun Club. The Inn never reopened as a hotel and is now given over to offices and apartments. A drug store occupies what was once the lobby. The Rod and Gun Club continued to attract many people in season. Those who come to fish or hunt during other months stay at one of the nearby motor courts. For a time guest facilities at Everglades included the Seminole

"Snooky" Senghaas with General and Mrs. Eisenhower, the guests of the Rod and Gun Club of whom he was probably most proud.

Lodge which had been the home of R. B. Storter. In recent years this has been used as a community hall.

The same Florida State legislature that created Collier County provided for the incorporation of the town of Everglades. The charter provided for a three-man council. These were always duly elected, but it can scarcely be said that the town government functioned as provided in its charter. The principal function of the Council was to pass ordinances in order to give necessary legal sanction to what was being done. Otherwise it functioned largely as a company town for thirty years. The Collier Company was almost the only taxpayer, the principal exceptions being the commercial fish houses, the railroad and the telephone company.

So the town's principal owner and taxpayer simply provided what the town needed. These included water works, electric power plant, ice plant, street maintenance equipment, fire fighting facilities, and mosquito control machinery. Barron Collier certainly did not mean to keep up such a paternalistic system, but adopted it as the readiest, if not the only way to get things going. He owned all of the houses and practically all of the residents were his employees. Furthermore, he was not ready to sell any property until it was fully developed. Clearly Barron Collier had no intention to maintain Everglades as a company town, but the Great Depression dried up the sources of revenue for any further development of Everglades. His death in 1939 found him still in the business of owning and maintaining a town.

By 1953 the Collier enterprises were showing signs of renewed vitality. Property was being leased and sold throughout the county, One major decision was to get Everglades out of the company town category which had been conceived originally as only a temporary status. The Company began to sell the homes to people who had been renting them. In the fall of 1953 when a freeholder's election was held, 63 persons had become home owners and 18 more were under contract to buy.

The 1953 legislature authorized a new charter and the citizens approved it. Everglades now became a city. Its citizens elected a mayor, council, clerk and an attorney. Under the old charter one of the three councilmen acted as mayor and another as clerk. The new mayor was Daniel W. McLeod who had also been mayor for 30 years under the original charter. The new municipal government set out to assume all the responsibilities of the city government, which

Photo by Captain Frederick Forte, U.S.A.F.
Everglades in 1956 looking south into the Ten Thousand Islands.

included collecting taxes and paying its own bills. It meant providing services for which the company had been paying around forty thousand dollars a year. Everglades is in a state of transition, but it will be less and less a company town. In fact, it was never intended to be a true company town where everything else is subordinated to the interests of the owner, for this type of community could in the long run serve no purpose of the Collier family.

In February of 1954 the city council agreed to buy from the company a garbage truck, a Willys Jeep with mosquito fogging attachment, a road grader, and a fire truck with some 1050 feet of hose. The price tag on the combination was four thousand dollars. Sam Bonard, fire chief, would also operate the mosquito control equipment and be responsible for garbage disposal. R.E.A. electric service replaced the Collier owned light plant in 1955 and the old machinery is maintained on a standby basis. Electric lines from Fort Myers have been extended to Immokalee, Ochopee and Marco Island.

Everglades is still intimately associated with the Collier enterprises. But as new property owners come in, as enterprises independent of the company become important, as Collier properties decrease in importance as the only potential tax source, Everglades will become more and more an independent and self-sufficient community as its founder undoubtedly intended it should.

Considerable money and effort went into the building of Everglades, and considerable attention must still be given to the same problems that faced the founder. The channel across Chokoloskee Bay must be maintained if fishing and shrimp boats are to continue to come to the town's industrial section. The pressure of a growing population and the attractiveness of the region will increasingly draw people to Everglades as to the entire county.

Possibly the greatest asset of Everglades is its relation to nearby Everglades National Park to which it is the western water gateway. At the moment it is a sort of "back door" entrance but it will ultimately become an important entrance if not another front door. Everglades and Chokoloskee afford the most accessible and protected way into the coastal and island portions of the park.

Early in 1956 a boat tour under the auspices of the Park Service began to operate from a base in Everglades. The tour goes up Half-Way Creek, over to Turner Lake and into Turner River, and down that stream past the historic shell mounds and into the bay at Chokoloskee, returning by a channel against the mainland and parallel to the new causeway.

The Duck Rock and Corkscrew Cypress Rookery tours of the National Audubon Society also originate at Everglades. The people of Everglades and the Collier interests are fully aware of the importance of these activities and afford them every possible encouragement and assistance.

10

Marco: *To Rise Again*

CONFUSION about Marco has been so widespread among writers that many have understandably fallen into error about it. There is Marco Island, largest of the Ten Thousand group, about 6800 acres in extent. Then there is Marco townsite on the north end of the island. There were two other settlements, Caxambas on the south end, once as important as Marco, and Goodland, just south of the point where the highway bridge reaches the island. So there are two post offices on Marco, but only one at Marco. Members of one Collier family were the first settlers and another unrelated Collier family became the owner of ninety per cent of the island, but not of Marco townsite, the stronghold of the first Colliers. In 1926 as part of a real estate promotion the state legislature was induced to incorporate the entire island as Collier City, named for the pioneer Collier, not the newcomer as is commonly supposed.

In Marco Island's slightly less than seven thousand acres there is a remarkable variety of landscape ranging from salt marsh and mangrove swamp to sandhills. There are nearly 700 acres of sandhills that rise to sixty-seven feet at the highest point, 2000 acres of high pine land, nearly 700 acres of sand prairie, 149 acres of beach front and slightly more than 3000 acres of mangrove swamp. Besides the relatively high elevation, it has six miles of sand beach on which the waves of the Gulf of Mexico wash up millions of multicolored sea shells, and it has deep channels at the north and south ends.

The island's ancient history, as indicated in Chapter Two, is relatively more important than its recent. The three important sites occupied by the Calusa Indians have been taken over by modern man as townsites. Marco is, as yet, little involved in the contemporary development of the lower west coast, but not because it is not highly desirable land. Across the channel on the north, between Johnson and Tarpon Bays and lying across the old Marco road, there is a giant reclamation project providing water front real estate, known as the Isles of Capri. A ferry service from Marco to the project brings back memories of the time when the only access to Marco was by that means. A road under construction partly following the route of the old Marco road will soon provide highway access from the Tamiami Trail. South of Marco Island, with beautiful sand beaches and high land, but lacking a bridge to the mainland is Cape Romano, already marked for subdivision and probably one day to be reached by bridge or causeway.

Much of the history of early modern Marco Island may be told in the lives of three families who have played leading roles in the three centers of population. They are the W. T. Collier family at Marco, especially one son, W. D., "Captain Bill," the James Madison Barfields at Caxambas, the Pettits at Goodland Point. Since 1922 when Barron G. Collier became the principal landowner on the island, he and his sons have largely guided the destiny of the island and its people.

W. T. Collier, by common consent the founder of the modern Marco townsite, came to the island in 1870 from Tennessee. He had married Barbara Hedick from North Carolina at Gainesville, Florida, in 1848. The couple had lived at Clearwater for some years where eight of their children were born. Another was born at New Smyrna just prior to the move to Marco and three others at Marco.

This Collier family came down the Atlantic coast of the peninsula from New Smyrna in the two masted schooner, *Robert E. Lee.* They ran into a storm at Indian Key which damaged the sailing vessel but a shipload of lumber wrecked in the same storm provided material to repair the ship. The foresighted Colliers took on board some 15,000 feet of lumber with which to build a house when they reached their destination.

On the west coast the cruising family went as far north as Buckingham and unloaded their lumber. Before a decision to build a home was made, however, they reloaded the lumber and sailed back down to Marco. At that time they found no white person living between Punta Rassa and Marco. Probably John Weeks down in Chokoloskee

Bay was the only settler between Marco and Key West. They did find four Negro squatters farming on Marco Island. Collier bought their claims and paid their transportation back to Fort Myers.

The foresight and effort that went into bringing the lumber for a house went to naught. Three months after it was built, it caught fire from a palm frond thatch around the chimney and burned. Then the Colliers started out as did most other pioneers by building a palmetto shack in which to live for several years until lumber could be purchased and brought in. Their first place of residence was out on the Gulf front south of the channel, but a storm induced them to abandon that site and move to a high shell mound in the present townsite.

The first money crop of the Colliers was a patch of cabbage grown for the Key West market where it brought a good price because of a large contingent of naval vessels stationed there. Fern Riggs, who fished for pompano in Big Marco Pass from 1898 to 1903 and camped with a crew on the beach, recalls going to the Collier store one day to seek some vegetables to add to their limited diet. Collier replied that all he had was one head of cabbage if that would help. When he brought it out it was found to weigh fourteen and one half pounds. Riggs also had a vivid memory of the mosquitoes that had pestered the fishermen, remarking "all we could do was burn Bee Brand insect powder to drive them away."

Other families came to Marco in time and the Collier enterprises grew with the small community. In the 1880's a sailing vessel began to make regular trips from Key West to pick up fish along the coast. This attracted other settlers to the island community, and fishing became a basic feature in the economy of its people.

Sport fishing has been since 1890 an all important part of the life of Marco Islanders. Winter visitors fished principally for tarpon or hunted on the islands or the nearby mainland. Today the principal occupations of Marco's inhabitants are commercial fishing, catering to winter visitors who come for the sport fishing, or serving the growing number of fishermen who come year-around to fish in the nearby Ten Thousand Islands waters. Since 1938 when the bridge to the mainland gave easy access, charter boats and guides and boat liveries supplying skiffs, motors and bait have become increasingly important to the island economy.

A weekly column of Marco news appeared more or less regularly in the *Fort Myers Press,* founded in 1884. In the pages of that weekly newspaper one follows the hopes, aspirations and achievements of the growing island community. In December of 1884 the Marco correspondent wrote that they wanted a mail route to Key West, buoys and beacons in the pass, and a light on Cape Romano. The people needed a church too. A building site had been given, so he called for contributions to put up a house of worship.

In the next month the office of the U.S. Lighthouse inspector at Pensacola announced that the Lighthouse Board had approved the placing of buoys in Marco Channel.

On October 20, 1888, William D. "Captain Bill" Collier received a commission as postmaster, making Marco the second post office in the county. It had been called Malco for some time because of the mistaken assumption that there was another Marco in Florida.

In December, 1888, the *Press* reported Marco's first school, with fifteen pupils, was flourishing. A Miss Murdock was the first teacher. Apparently the school had been opened in an unfinished building as temporary quarters while a schoolhouse was being put up. By March of the following year the schoolhouse was reported finished.

On December 19, 1899, fifteen years after the need for a house of worship had been noted, the local correspondent announced that the first sermon at Marco would be preached that night by the Reverend Gatewood. He concluded: "We feel proud to be honored by a church and a school."

Today a Church of God, founded in 1941, is the only organized religious group at Marco. In the early days when there was a considerable number of Roman Catholics among the population they had occasional visits of priests or went to Key West for the services of the Church.

"Captain Bill" Collier was to be the guiding genius of Marco until the early twenties of this century. During that period it had a larger population and considerably more varied and active economy than it now has. The *Press* reported in 1896 that he had completed his hotel. It had twenty sleeping rooms, a parlor, a dining room and a bathroom. Somewhat enlarged and with a cluster of cottages added, it still caters to a select winter season clientele.

The captain also had a boat yard which had more than a local reputation, since boats were constructed there for Key West shrimpers, for the Naples Company and for Miamians. He established and built the store which still stands at the water front. To it came Indians bringing hides, furs and feathers to trade. Hiram Newell,

Captain W. D. "Bill" Collier inspecting road work.

an 1889 arrival on the island, recalls when thirty or forty canoes sometimes gathered there. The Indian trade later went more to Everglade and Chokoloskee but the store had a growing clientele of local citizens.

Like so many others on the coast, "Captain Bill" operated a boat service. One of his boats, the schooner *Speedwell,* met with one of the most disastrous tragedies in the history of the area. Struck by a squall off the Marquesas, eighteen miles from Key West, she overturned. Nine persons were caught in the cabin and killed, three of them Collier's sons. The other six were members of the Bradley Nichols family of Bridgeport, Connecticut. Captain Collier, two deck hands and another passenger were thrown clear and saved.

In May of 1900 this enterprising man went to a wild orange grove near the Big Cypress and brought back 1500 young orange trees to set in his grove near Henderson Creek. He also had 5,000 bearing coconut trees on the island.

In 1908 he invented a clam dredging machine and had it built in Tampa. He observed that digging clams by hand limited the work to relatively shallow water, calm weather and low tides, whereas the clams were found in water up to twelve feet deep.

143

Clam dredge with load of clams alongside ready to move to cannery.

The new and important clam industry made its appearance first at Caxambas when a canning factory was established there in 1904. A second was built at Marco in 1911. This industry was based upon a large bed of hard shell clams in the Ten Thousand Islands. Collier remained interested in the problems of clam digging throughout his life and in 1920 invented a new type clam dredge that neither smashed any of the big clams nor injured the small ones.

"Captain Bill" in May 1911, having finished two new houses and with two more under way, was busy trying to run fresh water in to supply the clam factory and Marco. In 1912 the *Fort Myers Press* related a rumor that he had sold all his holdings at Marco except the clam dredge. A syndicate of capitalists was reportedly about to develop the village into a resort community. The rumor appeared again in 1917 when on December 27 the *American Eagle* reported that Collier had transferred his holdings to Mr. Edward C. Warren of New York and Sarasota.

But in 1921 he was still actively working at the development of Marco. Florida was on the eve of the land boom of the nineteen twenties when even remote Marco was to feel that stirring impulse to growth. Collier cut a road to the south beach about a mile from Marco for bathing by tourists and homefolks. Next year he was reported shelling streets and the road to South Beach, and doing much repair work on his houses. He also found time to represent the lower part of Lee County on the Board of County Commissioners.

When Barron G. Collier purchased the greater part of the island in 1922, he apparently refused to pay W. D. Collier his price for the Marco townsite. W. D. did get his price later, however, from a Mr. Buchanan of Tampa who optioned it to W. G. Williams.

Steps in the development of Marco continued. The *Fort Myers Press* reported on July 12, 1923 that a high fill had been dredged in around the shoreland fronting the store and the hotel which until then was a low mud flat, submerged at high tide.

While W. D. Collier was busily engaged in working for Marco's future, others also came to the island where they played important roles in its development. Sam E. Williams arrived in 1882 and established mango and citrus groves a mile north of the old ferry landing. He also built boats and by 1915 had taken over the Collier boat yard. His expanding enterprise included a new boat shed that would handle anything from launches to boats of considerable size. In 1916 he was reported laying the keel for a seventy-five foot houseboat for a Miamian. In 1917 Williams moved his growing business to Fort Myers, and the Daniels brothers built boats at Marco until they too moved to Fort Myers. Old timers recall that small water craft were often constructed out in the swamp conveniently near the building materials and water in which to launch them. The builders simply cleared a space, cut dogwood for the framework, and brought the other materials to the spot.

J. H. Doxsee came to Marco in November of 1910 upon the invitation of Captain Collier to look over the prospect for a clam cannery. The Doxsee family had begun to can hard or quahog clams at Islip, Long Island, in 1867, and had been in the same business in North Carolina since 1900. The year following Collier's invitation, the Doxsees moved to Marco where five generations of the family participated in the operation of the Marco cannery before it closed in 1947. The J. H. Doxsee who still resides at Marco became the first chairman of the Board of Public Instruction and later a county commissioner of Collier County. He also served as first and only mayor of the short-lived Collier City.

Another islander, Albert "Judge" Addison, arrived at New York in 1889 from Portsmouth, England, a mere lad of 19. He ventured down to Davenport, Florida, and by 1894 was at Marco. Among his memoirs is a description of an eighteen day journey by ox team to Alva, to Fort Myers, to Bonita Springs, and to Henderson Creek where he stayed two years before he moved to Marco. There he worked for Bob Everett who had a farm and grove. In 1896 he married Charity Newell who had come with her family, the J. H. Newells, from Texas in 1889. Hiram Newell, fourteen when he came, recalls running boats for Ed Watson, Bill Collier and John Gomez, whose drowned body he helped retrieve in 1900.

Chance sometimes landed people at Marco who remained to become permanent residents. Mrs. Florence E. Cannon, a 1900 "by-accident" arrival, related such a story to D. Graham Copeland in 1949, when she was living in Fort Myers. On July 15, 1900, Mr. and Mrs. Cannon, who had set sail from Crystal River, were cruising past Little Marco Pass on the schooner *Lettie* when it lost its rudder in a sudden squall and overturned. The entire family was thrown into the surf. Fortunately it was shallow and the parents waded ashore, carrying their children with them.

On shore were a Mr. Harris and several members of the Robertson family, who lived on an island just inside the pass. The Cannons remained for some time with these hospitable people. They then made their way overland to Royal Palm Hammock where they built and lived in a palmetto shack for a short time. But before the year 1901 ended they made their way by skiff down Royal Palm Hammock Creek to the Grocery Place and thence again to Marco. Here they lived until Mr. Cannon's death in 1920.

In the optimistic twenties and for a time thereafter Marco Island had a railroad. The Atlantic Coast Line and the Seaboard Airline were extending their lines southward along the coast, the Seaboard stopping at Naples, the rival line reaching Marco. The first locomotive steamed across the pass June 27, 1927, and for a time the islanders had two trains daily. The station was near the center of the island and the railroad grade may still be seen about a mile west of Marco village. Boatmen recall that pilings for the long bridge across the bay were removed only a few years ago.

Speculation as to what the railroad might portend for the region was almost without limit. Perhaps Marco would become a harbor city; perhaps it would be a way station on a line that would extend down to Cape Sable and Key West. But such development for the island was premature and the Great Depression stopped it. Since there was never traffic enough to operate the extension line profitably, it was abandoned in 1942, though trains ran intermittently for another two years to pick up shipments of clams from the cannery.

The most ambitious plan to develop Marco was initiated by the

San Marco Corporation which began operations in 1927. This was a New York Syndicate with ample financial backing from such men as George Ebret, Jr., George E. Ruppert, younger brother of Jacob Ruppert, of beer and baseball fame who was thought to be the principal investor, William B. Anderson, Walter Bolz, A. H. McKay and George Von Polenz, who became resident manager of the corporation's activities.

The corporation had grandiose plans for the development of the entire island. As described by Ed Scott, then a resident there, they were "just a little short of the blue print stage." The railroad was about to be completed to the island. A new road from the Tamiami Trail at Royal Palm Hammock had been surveyed to cross the channel just north of Goodland Point. It would include a railroad grade, suggesting the possibility of a second railroad or possibly an extension of the ACL to Everglades and Miami.

On March 2, 1927 a full page ad in the *Fort Myers Press* announced that the San Marco Corporation had 525 lots for sale to the public at Marco townsite. The prices ranged from $6,000 to $10,000.

As part of a plan for the development of the island, the State Legislature agreed to incorporate the entire island as Collier City, named for the pioneer W. T. Collier family. The center of the proposed new city was to be near the crossroads and not far from the terminus of the railroad. The Barron Collier interests, who owned the greater part of the real estate, constructed a central electric power station in the northeast quadrant at the crossroads, installed a 240 horsepower diesel engine powered generator, and strung lines to Marco and Caxambas. The building was a substantial structure with room for several larger units. But the real estate boom collapsed and the machinery was never used. The transmission lines were sold to the telephone company and the machinery was removed. Best known as a good place to catch bats, the building stood until about 1952, when Bud Kirk of Goodland purchased it. He planned to dismantle the structure and had hauled away only one load of the timbers when the remainder mysteriously burned. Thus ended a dream that is sure to rise again in one form or another.

Before the corporation gave up the effort, the Marco townsite part of Collier City had been further improved and advertised far and wide. The corporation had offices in New York and Fort Myers as well as Marco. The local managers staged huge sports events such as the Marco Regatta of May 1, 1927, for which a record crowd gathered. How many lots were sold is not recorded, but there were tarpon fishing contests, races, swimming and the like with prizes for all events.

The Marco Island Inn changed hands in 1950 when J. K. Dillon of Minerva, Ohio, and E. F. "Woodie" Woodall leased it, the latter to continue its operation. In 1955 Roy Edenfield and an associate purchased the property.

In 1922 Barron G. Collier had acquired all of the land on Marco Island except the Marco townsite and a few small parcels of land at Caxambas and Goodland which the owners chose not to sell. He bought most of it from the L & N Railroad which had received it from the state as a subsidy, but he also bought the property and claims of most of the residents, many of whom had only squatters' rights. They were all to continue to live on the property rent free until Collier was ready to use it.

Barron Collier's principal efforts were not to be spent in the development of Marco Island, however. Perhaps that fact helps to account for the "Marco War" in 1925, three years after he bought the property. The issues raised concerned the interests of squatters, homesteaders, and the holders of an option on the Marco townsite.

There had been an error in the 1876 Federal survey of the land on the island which underestimated the acreage by what proved to be 2444 acres. Collier claimed the land under the "more or less" acreage claim of his conveyance. Earlier efforts to homestead had failed since there was no record in the land office of its existence, and persistent efforts to get a resurvey had failed. Meanwhile, in 1924 President Coolidge had withdrawn all such coastal lands in Florida from entry.

Supporters of the Collier claim maintained that the owners of the Marco townsite stirred up the controversy to force him to buy them out. They had encouraged some of the same persons who had three years ago sold out to Collier to put up fences and buildings to establish intent to homestead the land.

The controversy gave rise to some highly imaginative stories. It was reported that all of the island, except the two settlements at opposite ends, was fenced, and only the road of the mail route was left open, other roads being closed by gates held fast by twisted wire. "No trespassing" signs bearing Collier's signature were reported everywhere, and most absurd, were the tales that there were several guard houses inside the fenced area and beaten paths along the fence where Collier guards patrolled.

Though it is true that many persons and interests resented the new-

Photo by J. M. Coleman, Naples.
Marco from a mile high, looking westward, 1956.

comer who threatened to interfere with their free and easy life and though a few people were arrested and fined lightly for trespass, the Marco War was largely a fabrication. The *Fort Myers Press* reported on August 18, 1925 that Marco was peaceful and that there was no evidence of other than legal battle. The United States Department of Interior a short time later ruled in favor of Collier and ended the legal controversy.

Marco Island, now one of the most attractive and least developed parts of Collier County, will certainly one day be restored to something like the relative importance it once had in the area.

The Little Marco and Henderson Creek areas on the mainland north of Marco Island also attracted settlers. The creek received its name from a surveyor of that name who had a camp there in the 1870's while running township and section lines. The settlement at Little Marco was near the high beach point, on Calhoun Island and back on what was called Hall Bay. Chester Pettit remembers going to school there at what was sometimes called the Walter Collier

School, and so does Forrest Walker. Alfred Weeks recalls that possibly sixteen pupils attended. Others who lived there for a time were Eugene Johnson, Obie and Isaiah Hall, Charles Rawls and the Harris and Robertson families who gave succor to the Cannons in 1900.

In 1928 Little Marco appeared in the news in a fashion to suggest that a development was planned there. The press reported Coconut and Australian Pine trees being planted on lots that extended a thousand feet from Gulf to bay where yachts could be anchored. Plans called for a community yacht and golf club on the north end. It could be reached from Naples by boat via the outside or the inside passage, and the Tamiami Trail and the ACL Railroad were only a mile away. But the area remained completely unoccupied until very recently.

On Henderson Creek up toward Belle Meade there was a considerable settlement around the turn of the century that included some names later well known in the history of the county. In 1894 Dr. and Mrs. Newton of Fort Meade decided to move further south. Mrs. Newton's son by an earlier marriage, James Madison Carroll, and his wife joined them as did Frank Richards and his family. Dr. Newton had a team of horses which he drove and a team of oxen which Mrs. Carroll drove, her husband walking alongside. At night they camped in the woods, cooking in Dutch ovens and over open fires, the Newtons and Carrolls in one camp and the Richards in another. When a wheel broke down south of Arcadia young Carroll rebuilt the hub and the party went on its way. They ferried the wagons across the Caloosahatchee on a lighter and swam the cattle and hogs which were being driven to the new home.

At Henderson Creek they found John and Mary Prine and their three children living in a small board house. J. J. Whidden, who later moved to Corkscrew, Jim Walker, Resee Kirkland and their families were also settled there. The Richards and Newton families stayed only briefly and with the Walkers went home to Fort Meade. The Walkers later returned to Henderson Creek and stayed until 1922 when they moved to Naples.

These pioneers lived in palmetto shacks until they could bring in lumber to build homes. As early as 1894 they had a school which met in a building with thatched walls and roof over a board platform floor. Not until about 1905 did the little community have a board schoolhouse. The lumber was purchased up on the Caloosahatchee and formed into a raft to be towed by way of the Gulf to the building

Courtesy of Mrs. Noah Kirkland, Naples

Mr. and Mrs. Noah Kirkland and their children on Henderson Creek.

site. When there were not enough children at Henderson Creek to maintain a school there, Lee County gave J. J. Whidden a contract to transport the children to Little Marco school, paying a dollar and a quarter a month for each pupil. Graham Whidden rowed his classmates to and from school each day in a skiff.

Though these settlers were hunters rather than farmers, all did some gardening and farming. Mrs. Jessie Walker Kirkland recalls that they had a farm six miles away from what they called home where they built a twenty by thirty thatch house to live in during the farming season. It was not unusual for settlers to make such living arrangements as they moved from one season or occupation to another.

In time all these settlers abandoned their places on Henderson Creek but like so many pioneers they remained nostalgic for the free and easy good old days. Little Grandma Carroll wished she could leave her neat, modern cottage in Naples and live again in a palmetto thatched house. Mrs. Kirkland, now living in Naples, raised eight children on Henderson Creek. She thoroughly enjoyed hunting, and recalls that her husband liked her for a hunting companion, for when she found a gator he never got away.

151

Caxambas and Goodland: *Now United*

WRITING of these two communities together is more than an author's device to get them into a single chapter for eight years ago the two were in a sense physically merged. Most of the people from Caxambas came to Goodland in 1949, literally bringing their houses with them. But that story will be related later.

Two giant shell mounds, one ancient and one modern, on the shore of Caxambas Pass at the south end of Marco Island, mark the place where the village of Caxambas once stood. Calusa Indians began the formation of one of these shell mounds nearly two thousand years ago. The E. S. Burnham Packing Company built up the other with clam shells as they did the piles of shell across the channel dumped there from lighters. Concrete foundations and remains of cisterns also mark the place where as many as 150 people once lived.

Caxambas is one of the oldest place names on the coast and quite likely the oldest in Collier County. It appears on the William Gerard De Brahms chart of southern Florida in 1771 as "Caxymbas Espanolas" and has sometimes been spelled Caximbas. It is apparently of Arawak origin from the word casimba or cacimba used in the Antilles to mean a hole dug in the shore for drinking water. This has given rise to the conjecture that there was an Arawak colony there, but the name was more likely brought to Florida from Cuba by the Spaniards. Cuban fishing smacks often filled their casks with water there. Local residents have always understood that it means place of wells or springs. One legend has it that a Franciscan monastery once stood there and that monks dug the well. There was a

Mr. and Mrs. James Madison Barfield.

waterworks of sorts at Caxambas in modern times that supplied "relatively fresh" water, but reliance for drinking water was principally upon rain water caught in cisterns. The "wells" at Caxambas were probably shallow depressions in beach sands which yielded surface water.

As in all but a few of the islands fresh water supply is a problem not yet solved on Marco Island. For the clam cannery at Marco, water for the boilers and the cooking vats was piped in from two miles south where surface well water was usable.

The first settler at Caxambas of whom there is any record or recollection was Tony Roberts. He was followed by Captain Charles Johnson "living high on the hill" when the Coast and Geodetic Survey measured and mapped the area in the 1870's. A white marble marker located near what was the Barfield Heights Hotel indicates the location of "Johnson" station.

But Mr. Johnson left little impression on the development of Caxambas. Like other early Collier County communities, one family more than any other came to be identified with its history. At Caxambas it was James Madison Barfield, and even more so, his wife Tommie Camilla Stephens Barfield.

Barfield was born at Sunnyside, Georgia, in 1867 and in early 1891 went to Alabama. A year later he joined his brother Benjamin at Caxambas, and with him became associated with Mack I. Smith in growing vegetables for the Key West and New York markets. James bought Smith's interest the next year and some years later bought out his brother. Thereafter he continued to add to his landholdings in the vicinity of Caxambas.

Tommie Camilla Stephens was born at Cordele, Georgia, in 1888. Her family moved to Inverness, Florida, then to Homosassa where they remained four years. They next journeyed to Fort Myers and Estero and in March, 1901 to Caxambas. They came from Estero with Frank Green with whom they farmed at the extreme southwestern end of the island. In 1906 Tommie married J. M. Barfield and together they played the most prominent role in Caxambas until Barron Collier bought them out. The Barfields had three daughters, two of whom, Elsie Ray (Mrs. Kenneth Vogstad) and Elva Lee (Mrs. R. A. Griffis) still live on the island. The third is dead.

Accounts of two journeys by Barfield in the early days provide an excellent commentary on travel in southwest Florida in the late nineteenth century. When he made the initial trip to Caxambas in 1892 he went by rail to Arcadia, continued by narrow gauge railway to Punta Gorda, and by boat on to Fort Myers. At this point he sailed with Captain Nick Armeda who carried the mail by way of Punta Rassa and Naples to Marco. His brother met him at Marco and rowed him down to Eubanks Landing, whence they walked across to Roberts Bay, took another skiff and rowed to the Ludlow Place, from which they footed it across the sandhills to Caxambas.

A few years later Barfield set out to acquire a mule. He located one at Bartow, 160 miles away. He rode the mule to the Caloosahatchee River at Fort Myers, ferried across and rode southward along the ocean front. When he reached Gordon's Pass just south of Naples there was no ferry. Though he could not swim, the mule could. The pair also swam Little Marco Pass at low tide and crossed Big Marco Pass in the same way.

Residing at Caxambas besides Barfield when the A. T. Stephens family arrived in 1901 was Frederick Ludlow who had come from Toledo, Ohio, and married Emma Collier, daughter of W. D.

Collier, at Marco. Ludlow was working twenty Negroes on his pineapple plantation in 1901 and had a 25 x 130 foot packing house on the shore of Ludlow Bay. The farm occupied the high hill on both sides of the road leading to Caxambas. The old Scripps School, abandoned in 1956 for the new school near the center of the island, stood on the site of the Ludlow home.

Barfield became the first postmaster at Caxambas on August 3, 1904, and A. T. Stephens was the first mail carrier, making the trip to and from Marco by water in good weather and on foot in windy weather. Shortly thereafter Caxambas was on a regular mail delivery service that started at Fort Myers and touched at Naples, Marco, Caxambas, Everglade and Chokoloskee.

The Barfield couple kept the general store which James had built on the wharf in 1904, ran the post office and enlarged their home from time to time to accommodate guests. By 1908, it was known as the Heights Hotel and could accommodate twenty guests. They also grew pineapples and did what they could to attract settlers and business. Mrs. Barfield, in whose honor the new "Tommie Barfield School" is named, became the best known figure on the south end of the island.

In 1904 when the E. S. Burnham Packing Company became interested in the clam resources of the region, Barfield gave five acres of waterfront for the factory which operated there until 1929. In 1921 the Barfields were offering lots for sale in the Heights subdivision on the bayfront at prices ranging from $200 to $350. While tourists came for the winter season, year 'round residents were fishermen, farmers, hunters, employees of the clam cannery, or a combination of these.

The Burnham clam cannery supplied much of the economic stability of Caxambas and it never recovered after the plant closed in 1929. For by that time farming and hunting had both ceased to be important means of livelihood and the once diversified occupations were reduced almost entirely to commercial fishing. Mrs. Chester Pettit recalls that her widowed mother came from Cardenas to Chokoloskee in 1903 hoping to find a refuge with her brother only to find little opportunity on that island for herself, nine daughters and one son. But the cannery at Caxambas built houses for workers and the Rojas family found a place for themselves there. Five of the daughters remained in the county.

Precisely when the first school was established in Caxambas is not

Goodland looking NNW from a mile high. 1957.

clear. A news item in 1892 reported the schoolhouse as needing paint and equipment which suggests that it might have been new. Mrs. Pettit recalls going to school in the kitchen of the old Barfield place, and another account indicates twenty pupils in school in 1908. Chester Pettit recalls that at Goodland his father had a tutor for his sons for a time and that he attended school on Horr's Island as well as at Little Marco. School seems to have been kept for a few months at a time whenever a sufficient number of pupils could be assembled and a room and teacher provided.

Until 1928, when the Scripps School became the central school for the island, there had been a three-teacher school at Caxambas and a two-teacher school at Marco. But ten years later the population at Caxambas had fallen below that at Marco. At Caxambas were thirty-one homes with 114 people plus twenty single men living on boats, while at Marco there were thirty-five homes and 143 persons plus an uncounted number of boats. The location of the Scripps School nearer to Caxambas had been in recognition of the large number of pupils from that area in 1928.

In school matters as in many others there was always intense rivalry between the two communities. Thus when the Caxambas population fell below that of Marco, the citizens of the now larger

Courtesy of the Collier Development Company.
Road to Marco three miles north of the ferry in 1921. Road was later shelled.

place demanded that the school be moved to the crossroads at the center of the island. When officials wouldn't even consider such a possibility, some Marco citizens boycotted the school. Attendance fell off from seventy-three in the 1928-29 session to fifty-seven in 1932-33, a low of thirty-nine in the next year, and then gradually rose to fifty-four and sixty-three in the next two years and back to a normal seventy-nine in 1939-40.

The old schoolhouse at Caxambas became for a brief time a movie house, the only one the island ever had until M. C. Johnson began to operate one at Goodland in 1952. Later it served as a community house. The old Marco schoolhouse was first converted into three efficiency apartments but finally served also as a community house.

Mrs. Barfield worked energetically for the development of Caxambas, and indeed the whole island, being especially anxious for the community to emerge from its isolation. She is credited with almost singlehandedly inducing Lee County commissioners to authorize a road from Naples to Marco, a ferry across the channel, and a road from Marco to Caxambas, and with supervising the building of the roads when the county authorities finally yielded to her demands which she made regularly every month at their meetings. A road of sorts was completed in 1912 and a one-car ferry began to ply the channel. In 1925 the new county authorized a four-car capacity, self-powered ferry which was built in the Sam Williams boatyard at Fort Myers.

These improvements she achieved only to find them inadequate. The first road from Marco to Caxambas ran only five miles, through mangrove swamps and sandhills, but residents often took to water to make the trip, since the north end of the road was bad in wet weather and the south end a sand bed in dry weather. The mail was carried first by wagon and then by Ford automobile, the condition of the road permitting. In 1918 the editor of the *American Eagle* reported after a visit to Marco Island that there were on the island fifteen automobiles in spite of the only five miles of road and that bad. Fourteen of the autos were Fords.

Mrs. Barfield found time and energy for many other enterprises. In the thirties she operated in association with George Lowe one of the largest apiaries in southern Florida, reportedly shipping 60,000 pounds of honey in 1942. Other bee and honey producers in the county were J. E. Burney, near Miles City, and W. A. Gardner, near Naples.

Ship Ahoy at the end of the highway bridge is another of her ventures. The 36 x 125 foot houseboat had been used to house workers on the Overseas Highway roadbuilding project after the 1935 hurricane had put an end to the railroad there. The boat sank and had been abandoned in the harbor at Marathon when Mrs. Barfield saw it and perceived a possible use for it. With J. H. Doxsee to supervise the operation she set out to have it raised and towed to Marco Island. When four gasoline powered pumps mounted to remove the water failed, the crew stuffed the hull's cracks with cotton from old mattresses or nailed boards over them. After this procedure, the pumps could keep the water out. Captain Ferg Hall undertook to tow the unwieldy craft to Marco with the schooner *Eureka*. A northeaster very nearly wrecked the enterprise. But the navigators were able to hold the barge in the lee of the schooner for four hours until the blow had passed and finally made their slow way to their destination. A part of the housing on the boat was removed and set up as a house to be rented. The remainder was towed to its present location where Mrs. Barfield's daughter and her husband, Ken Vogstad, dispense hospitality and good cheer to visiting sportsmen, mostly fishermen.

Because she was always energetic in her support of schools, Governor Carey A. Hardee appointed her the new Collier County's first Superintendent of Public Instruction. She was later elected to this office in the first general election in the county, but retired to membership on the Board of Public Instruction after one term as superintendent. She remained an active member of the school board until she resigned in 1949 because of ill health. Governor Fuller Warren appointed her daughter Elva (Mrs. R. A.) Griffis, aiso active in civic affairs, to fill her unexpired term and she has been reelected to the post since that time. Mrs. Barfield was farsighted enough to demand that adequate grounds for schools be set aside in developments while land was still plentiful and cheap, envisioning a day when the island would be fully developed and school lands hard to find and costly to purchase.

In the early nineteen-twenties she met Barron G. Collier, then starting to acquire land in the area. He too saw the possibility that this island far south on the Florida peninsula might attract settlers. When he inquired of Mrs. Barfield what she could see in the future for these rugged hills of cactus covered shell, she replied, a railroad, hotels and fields. She worked with Collier to secure the new Collier County, going to Tallahassee to lobby for the necessary legislative action. When she died in 1950, pallbearers at her funeral were the principal citizens of Collier County: Ed Scott, D. W. McLeod, Louis Thorpe, J. L. Howell, Leslie Bronson and John Ludlow.

Goodland started as early as Caxambas but grew very slowly until 1949 when almost overnight it absorbed most of the population of Caxambas. The first settler on this corner of the island was Johnny Roberts who named the place for its characteristic feature. At Goodland Point was a forty-acre shell mound on which early settlers planted vegetables and fruits. Marco channel provided it with a deep water passage to the north or to the south.

Roberts sold his squatters' rights to Samuel Alexander Pettit who farmed there with his five sons, two daughters and wife. Harry Pettit remained to carry on the family role as chief proprietor and when the highway bridge reached the island just north of his property he built the road to join it almost single-handed. Later the county improved and hardsurfaced the short piece of road, following the curving lines Pettit made as he moved from one low shell mound to another, filling in the low intervening spaces.

The big shell mound at Goodland supplied road building material for the county and revenue for the Pettits. The shell top on the road to Royal Palm Hammock, completed in 1938, came from that source. Workers loaded the shell on barges and towed it up the canal dredged beside the roadbed to provide fill.

This road had been first designed in the expansive days before the 1929 crash. Goodland Bay was to be spanned by a hydraulic fill 1500 feet long and wide enough to accommodate a railroad as well as a highway. A bridge from the fill to the island would be 1490 feet long, with a 1350 trestle and a 140 foot swing span. The bridge was to have a clear width of twenty-five feet to make it possible to build a railroad on one side and allow ample width for the highway.

The national financial crisis brought this and other projected developments to an abrupt halt for the time being. Not until a bridge to Marco Island was approved as a Public Works project in 1936 did hopes rise again. A wooden trestle type bridge was built with a swing span over the channel. This still serves automotive traffic and the railroad dream has not been revived. The swing span came from a Caloosahatchee River bridge at Fort Myers that was being replaced by a concrete structure. It was loaded on a barge and towed to the new location where it has served very well the traffic needs there. It was Sunday, April 24, 1938, that Marco Islanders and their Collier County neighbors celebrated the opening of the new highway bridge and the discontinuance of the ferry operating from the island to the old Marco road that reached the pass opposite Marco.

The old Marco road was a narrow, winding shell road from Marco Junction on the Tamiami Trail, the reward for island support of Trail building bond issues. The Isles of Capri development across the Marco end of the old road may revive its importance. The developers plan to rebuild a part of the road and add a new connection to the Trail.

When Barron Collier purchased most of the island in 1922 he started making changes that indicated an intention to transform Caxambas into a port of some importance. He had the general store repainted inside and out and it became number three in the Manhattan Mercantile group. A substantial dock, platform and warehouse also appeared and the post office was moved to one side.

The history of the Caxambas store had never been a happy one, and it was not soon to be much improved. A news item in early 1921 reported that Captain J. C. Rye, failing to sell his stock, had moved it to Marco leaving Caxambas without a store. But, one report stated, Thomas Curry was going to purchase a stock of goods for a new store in which he would sell only for cash—"Thus he hopes to stay in business." Captain Rye at Marco would also operate on a cash basis.

Collier's plans for Caxambas did not materialize and the store stood empty and abandoned until A. P. "Bud" Kirk rented it in 1944 and operated it until it was moved to Goodland. There Lloyd House bought and operated it for a time, and then gave it up. In 1952 the old Caxambas store again came into possession of the Barfields when the Griffis and Vogstad families bought it. They remodeled and reopened it after it had been closed for about a year.

The Collier interests had since 1922 owned most of the property at Caxambas but had allowed the tenants to remain in the houses rent free. In 1949 they decided to move the entire community across the island to Goodland where at the time there were only a few houses. Goodland was considered a better location for the fishing village and the Caxambas site had interesting possibilities for development. The company agreed to give the houses it possessed at Caxambas to the occupants who would purchase lots at Goodland, and for good measure also agreed to pay the cost of moving the buildings to the new site.

A professional moving firm loaded the houses on big trucks, hauled them to Goodland, and set them up there. In late September everything was gone from Caxambas except the schoolhouse and the dwellings of several families, none of them near the old site on the Pass. The road is still there, and so are the rotting timbers of docks and wharves, the concrete floor of the old clam cannery and other structures and a cistern or two. But Caxambas is at the moment dormant. For how long nobody knows, but probably not for long.

On the Islands and on the nearby mainland south and east of Marco Island small settlements appeared, flourished for a time, and died, often leaving little trace of occupation. On nearby Horr's Island to which he gave his name lived John F. Horr with his wife, sons and daughter. He had been a United States Marshall with headquarters at Key West and Jacksonville, and had used the island chiefly as a vacation resort. A caretaker managed a small citrus grove and a larger pineapple plantation. Enough people lived on the island to maintain a school there for a brief time, and Captain Horr took the Federal Census in that region in 1880. Mrs. Mata Partrick, a New Yorker who has wintered there for eighteen years, is now the sole resident.

The Roberts brothers reportedly settled on Fakahatchee Island as early as 1870, and later moved about to various other locations. Numerous others farmed and fished there. There was never a store or a post office but in 1912 Mrs. Claude Storter was teaching a school

Photo by J. M. Coleman, Naples.
Site of old Caxambas settlement on Caxambas Pass. Ideal Fishing Camp in background left, 1957.

of thirteen pupils there. Ada Knowles, who went there forty-seven years ago as the bride of Phineas Daniels, still lives there with four of her ten children. Her son-in-law, Clifford Daniels, and his family live in what was the schoolhouse.

John Gomez of Panther Key, down the coast about two miles from Marco Island, was by all odds the most famous character to settle in the Islands. He claimed to have been patted on the back by Napoleon Bonaparte, to have been cabin boy to the pirate Gasparilla, to have fought with General Zachary Taylor at the battle of Okeechobee in the Seminole War in 1837, to have been a slaver and a Civil War blockade runner. He said he was born in 1778 and claimed to speak seven languages. Local residents remember him always as an old man wearing a heavy white beard.

Pinicher and Brown, two plume hunters, he said, gave him the small home he lived in. He called himself a farmer in the census of 1880 and he reportedly attempted a goat ranch in partnership with Captain Horr, but panthers ate all the goats.

Hiram Newell who sometimes worked with him, recalls that people, intrigued by the story of Gomez's association with pirates, came to Panther Key wishing to dig for treasure. Old John told them to dig to their hearts' content. He pointed out that pirates never buried their treasure in low lying places near the seashore, but carried it back to higher ground. Nevertheless, treasure hunters dug up great areas of the key.

Old John died on July 12, 1900. He had gone out in his skiff as usual to net some fish. Apparently he caught his foot in the anchor line or in the net and was dragged overboard, or possibly, as some

Courtesy of Mrs. Chester Pettit, Caxambas.
Captain Horr's home on Horr's Island with pineapple packing shed on waterfront.

conjecture, he was knocked over by an overhanging bush as the current swept the skiff under it. Newell has another theory. He thinks John might have committed suicide. He had been despondent, his wife reported, and tired of living. He regularly wore a dirty white canvas cap and, clamped in his teeth, a short, broken stemmed clay pipe, a "nose warmer." He was never seen without them. Yet when they found him the cap and pipe lay on the boat seat where, says our theorist, John had placed them before stepping overboard. Perhaps this theory arises from the doubt that an old hand like John would become tangled in a rope or net.

Old cisterns and bits of rusty iron testify to at least temporary occupation of other islands to which people often gave their names. Christ Johnson came in 1872 and stayed in various locations, finally settling on Johnson Key where he gardened for years and became expert at budding and cultivating mangoes. His wife was well known for the tropical trees and flowers she grew about the house. Other places more frequently mentioned were Pavilion Key where people lived temporarily while they gathered clams, Dismal Key, Mormon Key, and so on. Clam diggers camped on the higher keys and worked the nearby waters. The 1910 hurricane caught twenty-two men camped on Plover Key which stands seven or eight feet above normal high tide. When the storm had passed, all but three of their boats were gone, and it was with difficulty they made their way back to Caxambas. Joe Dickman who has lived on Kice Island for twenty-five years, and who gathers shells for a living, is a hermit not by choice but because all others have deserted the keys as a home.

163

Another center of settlement for a time was up Royal Palm Creek and at Grocery Place in the bay of the same name. This was rather wild country and Mrs. Florence Cannon reported bears and panthers too plentiful there in 1901 to make her feel comfortable living in a palmetto shack. James Cannon and Frank Futch first hunted the territory for furs. In the nineties of the last century farmers settled on the river beginning at the first high land and extending to the saw grass at its source. Jim Daniels grew sugar cane and was reported to have the first cane mill in the entire region. The remains of an old twenty foot barge used to move produce to market lie stranded up the river. The stream is now so overgrown that it is hard to believe that it was once navigated.

12

Naples I, "Crackers" and "Colonels"

THREE different groups, each giving it distinctive characteristics, have combined to make the Naples we know today. The first permanent white settlers—until recent years the only year-round residents—came in 1876. Left to their guidance alone, the area would probably have assumed much the same character as the other coastal communities in Collier County. But ten years later a second group, who built winter homes and became seasonal residents, discovered Naples and controlled its destiny down to about 1915. The third and last formative group came with the highway and railroad age and gave finishing touches to its present character.

The physical setting of Naples is unique in the county. Unlike other communities with sandy beaches on the lower west coast, Naples is situated on more than a narrow sandstrip, backed with mangrove swamp and lagoon. The land is sandy, with pines down to the edge of the water of the Gulf and an elevation up to ten feet within a hundred yards of the water.

Instead of low, swampy regions inland there is Naples Bay, which also gives the city a character all its own. Naples is on a long peninsula of land which lies between the bay and the Gulf and meets the outside waters at its south end near Gordon's Pass, named for Roger Gordon who had a fishing camp there about 1874.

Early comers to Naples found a wide shallow canal, apparently man-made, extending a little over a mile across the peninsula between the bay and the Gulf. All evidence of it is now gone, but the first plat of the townsite made in 1887 pictures it running just

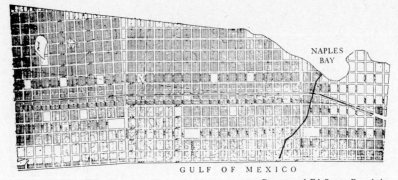

NAPLES
BAY

GULF OF MEXICO

First plat of Naples showing course of canal from Gulf of Mexico to Naples Bay.

south of the Naples Hotel block in a direction slightly north of east to the bay. Lucien Beckner, who spent the winter of 1889-1890 there, recalls that at about its middle course there used to be some timbers standing in it, probably the remains of a gateway.

On the plat the canal is described as being fifty feet wide. Other sources describe it as a thirty foot canal three feet deep. T. S. Stearnes, running section lines in the Federal Survey in 1874, recorded in his field notes that at the highest point of land it was about twelve or fifteen feet deep and apparently partially filled up, "as it was a work of great antiquity." Forrest Walker, who first came to Naples in 1904, recalls that boys had to scramble up the sides of the canal. He also remembers that the bay end held water and was bridged at what is now Twelfth Avenue and that there was an oyster house at a pier on the Bay side.

There has been much speculation about the origin of the canal, but who dug it, and why, is not entirely clear. It is almost certainly of Indian origin. The Bernard Romans map of 1775 calls it a haulover, but that may indicate only that the beach end tended to fill up with sand and that no effort was made to keep it open. There was a small midden near the mouth of the canal, similar to others found near Indian canals. These are quite common and range up to six miles in length. As there is no record of activity there by the Spaniards, they may reasonably be ruled out.

That pirates dug it, as is sometimes conjectured, seems unlikely as there is an outlet to the Gulf three miles south at Gordon's Pass.

Some maintain that this pass is of comparatively recent origin, perhaps opened up by a storm. Whatever its origins, before its existence, the only outlet from the inland waterway would presumably have been down at Little Marco. It is not unusual for storms to alter the shoreline and open or close small inlets. After the 1910 hurricane, for example, Captain Stewart of Naples reported Gordon's Pass entirely changed; it was broadened out to a half mile in width and so shallow that he touched bottom several times while coming out at high tide.

Andrew Weeks, still living in Naples, recalls going there from Wauchula with his father, Madison Weeks, and his father's brother, John, in 1876. They settled at Gordon's Pass at the "Old Shell Pit," but later sold their squatters' rights to the Naples Company and moved further down the coast. John Weeks is elsewhere described as a Union sympathizer who took refuge in Key West during the War between the States. He was among a number of persons who located at Cape Sable to produce vegetables for the town of Key West. Reported still there in 1866, he may have gone to Wauchula before the 1876 date when the Weeks family became the first settlers at Naples.

These early arrivals were all squatters. How many of them came in the next ten years is not known. But they were sufficiently numerous to protest when the land became the property of Hamilton Disston in the early 1880's. And they protested even more loudly in the late eighties when the Naples Company acquired the townsite and began its development. Squatters could have purchased the land on which they had taken up residence and constructed improvements, for such a provision was made in the Disston contracts. But the early settlers believed they should each be permitted to homestead 160 acres of high and dry land. They had not been able to do so because the land was designated "swamp and overflowed" and title to it had been transferred to the state. It may be added that squatters rarely made any move to secure title until their possession was threatened.

In the 1880's the lower Gulf coast of Florida was attracting an increasing number of tourists, principally sportsmen who came to hunt and fish. Many of them made their homes on their yachts. They usually based at Punta Gorda, the nearest rail and telegraph head, or at Tampa. At Marco, Caxambas and Everglade small hotels grew to serve these seasonal visitors, but Naples was to prove different.

Courtesy of Mrs. N. Ernest Carroll, Naples.
First office of the Naples Company, Louisville Courier Journal print, 1888

Influential families, principally from Kentucky and Ohio, conceived the idea of building homes there to which they might return each winter. To these people the city owes much of its development.

Walter N. Haldeman, owner and publisher of the *Louisville Courier Journal,* is usually considered the founder of Naples. Actually he did not take control of the enterprise until 1890. Together with nearly a dozen others Haldeman was first associated as a partner in the Naples Town Improvement Company founded in 1887 to develop the community. Officers of the company were General John S. Williams of Mt. Sterling, Kentucky, president; R. G. Robinson of Zellwood, Florida, vice-president and general manager; C. W. Jacobs of Orlando, secretary-treasurer. Others interested in the enterprise were W. T. Grant, Charles D. Pearse, Dr. C. G. Edwards, W. R. Fleming of Louisville, the Hon. Thomas G. Stuart of Winchester, Kentucky, and I. Oscar Loraine of Zellwood, Florida.

Naples seems to have been promoted by the original company as a venture in real estate and tourism. If so it was premature. The combine purchased 8700 acres of land from the Florida Land Company which had been organized to market the lands acquired by Hamilton Disston and his associates. Disston had received 1,250,000 acres in 1885 as a result of a drainage contract. But the Trustees of the Internal Improvement Fund could not give clear title as the lands were pledged to guarantee payment of principal and interest on railroad bonds. The bonds were in default and the fund was threatened with bankruptcy which would have forced the public sale of the pledged lands. Disston thereupon purchased four million acres of the state lands at 25 cents an acre to enable the trustees to pay off the obligations and clear any claims on the lands. Only thus could he get title to the lands due him under the terms of the drainage contract.

Disston was accused of fraud and unduly high profits on his land deals. Squatters maintained that he disregarded their rights. Some of them had planted crops and built homes and they claimed the right to homestead their lands. Disston answered his accusers in the *Fort Myers Press,* January 17, 1889. He had given settlers who had gone there before he acquired title one year to purchase deeds at one dollar an acre and had even extended the time, he said. Disston also said his company had offered 30,000 acres at $1.25 per acre. In smaller amounts the price was $1.50. The founders of Naples purchased 8700 acres for $13,050, or $1.50 an acre.

Some accounts say that a Major Champney, a French engineer, platted the early subdivisions of the new town-to-be. He accompanied the "prospectors" when they chose the site and he gave his name to a bay. He may have been responsible for the general planning of the town, but the actual surveying and platting seems to have been done by Ed Scott, an uncle of the Ed Scott who is Collier County Clerk of Court, since his name appears on the plats filed at the Lee County Courthouse in Fort Myers. Copies of the plats may be seen at the Collier County Courthouse in Everglades.

Major Champney did plat another subdivision, for the Kentucky gentlemen were not the only ones who had discovered Naples. J. M. Raleigh had come to Florida from Connecticut because of weak lungs for which the climate was recommended. He had secured a position with the Coast and Geodetic Survey men working on the Gulf Coast. Like others, he was charmed with certain spots on the coast and marked them for purchase from the government.

A year after the new enterprise was launched Raleigh, then living in Orlando, heard of it and came to Naples. After the Naples Company lines were located he engaged Major Champney to plat certain subdivisions on his own. In doing so, Champney discovered the lake and waterway now bearing his name. The lake was later called Grand-dad's Creek until E. W. Crayton and his associates discovered the earlier record. Raleigh's project probably inspired the note in the 1888 advertising booklet of the Naples Company which read: "Not responsible for places advertised as North, East, or South Naples or so-called Additions to Town of Naples."

The Naples Town Improvement Company sold lots in considerable number in 1887, deeds to eighty different purchases being dated May 31, 1887. This suggests that they were not ready to give title before that date. In June of the same year twenty-six other deeds were recorded.

Lots appear to have sold at ten dollars apiece. Modern day legend relates that a shotgun was once traded for three lots that eventually sold for $5,000. The company numbered its deeds. Number 47 deeds two lots (13 & 14, Block 17, Tier 3) to Rose Elizabeth Cleveland, sister of President Grover Cleveland. The price is recorded as twenty dollars. On June 15, 1887, a deed recorded sale of 64 lots to General John S. Williams for $640. And in April 29, 1889 the General acquired another 32 lots for one dollar and land certificates for $200. The first deed to W. N. Haldeman, dated July 25, 1887, was for the 24 lots in Block 3 Tier 3. The price was $240. But on June 15, 1889 he paid $480 for the twenty-four lots in Block 1 Tier 1.

Stockholders and directors may have been purchasing lots to provide the company with working capital. Presumably the "land certificates" referred to in some deeds were given to raise money on lots to be located later if not redeemed in cash. W. T. Grant received a deed for 42 lots on February 22, 1889 for the recorded price of one dollar and land certificates for $218.33.

The company had extensive plans for the development of Naples. A small hotel which forms the center section of the present Naples Hotel was to accommodate tourists. A general store to sell supplies made its appearance. The first version of the Naples Pier was thrust out into the Gulf to accommodate boats rather than fishermen. The original pier was a wharf 600 feet long extending out to water 18 feet deep. A sloop and a schooner to maintain contact with the outside world were provided.

The pier has been a Naples institution from the beginning. At first it served as a freight and passenger dock as well as a place from which to fish. At the height of its importance Claude M. Storter, who operated a boat service on the coast from 1912 to 1919, recalls that it was a hundred feet longer than now and had two wings form-

View looking east from the fishing pier in 1906, showing board walk and car tracks with Naples Hotel in the distance.

ing a "V" at the outer end. A narrow gauge tram road of wood rails ran from the hotel onto the pier and out to the end of both wings where porters pushed small cars carrying freight and baggage unloaded from passing steamers.

The 1910 hurricane almost completely destroyed the pier, but it was immediately rebuilt. In 1922 a carelessly dropped cigarette started a fire that burned the post office and almost twenty feet of the pier which had to be replaced. The 1926 hurricane did some damage to the famous landmark. Since then it has lost its freight and passenger function to land based carriers and serves only as a recreation base. Hopeful fishermen—and women— vacationing in Naples, now line it throughout the year!

In the early days individuals built their homes in a cluster around the hotel and pier. The first home was built for General John S. Williams and later acquired by the Haldemans. The second was later owned by Rose Cleveland. Henry Watterson of *Louisville Courier Journal* fame occupied a cottage. Writing in 1906 he said: "Rose Cleveland has a cottage here. Grover ought to come down and try his luck. I promise to receive him with a deputation and never to utter a word about the tariff . . ."

The *Fort Myers Press* watched the goings-on at Naples with interest and apparently with some envy. On December 15, 1887 it reported

171

the Naples Company was to put up a forty-five room hotel and some cottages, and added, "Fort Myers will trust to luck as usual." On August 2 of the next year the *Press* reported seventy or eighty people in Naples. Shacks and tents had housed them at first. Now there was a hotel for twenty or thirty people, a store, an office building, and several cottages. Three concrete houses were reported contracted for. In January of 1899 the newspaper reported that the Naples Company had prevailed upon the H. B. Plant Steamship Line to have the *Olivette* call at Naples. Three years later in its March 10, 1892 issue, the *Press* reported the season at Naples a success. The Plant steamer *Tarpon* was making two trips a week from Tampa during the winter season. It left Tampa Wednesday and Saturday nights with persons who had left Louisville on Mondays and Thursdays.

But all had not gone well financially for the company. In 1889 it had mortgaged its properties to W. N. Haldeman for a loan of $45,000. In the same year a number of judgements in favor of the First National Bank of Orlando added to the company's troubles. At a meeting of stockholders called in Louisville on October 15, 1889 and adjourned to the 16th, The Naples Town Improvement Company, which had now shortened its name to The Naples Company, decided to sell its property and wind up its affairs. Public sale of its assets was advertised in Jacksonville, Orlando, and Louisville papers to take place in Naples on January 30, 1890.

At one o'clock on that date, the appointed hour for the sale, W. N. Haldeman was the only bidder present. The sale was postponed to five o'clock in the vain hope that the steamer *Fearless* might bring in other bidders. At five o'clock the property was offered separately and Haldeman's bids totalled $49,500. It was then offered in a single bid and Haldeman, still the only bidder, offered $50,000.

For that sum W. N. Haldeman acquired the town lots and property of the company which included the Naples Hotel, hotel fixtures, office equipment and furniture, docks, machinery, the sloop *Edith,* the steamer *Fearless,* all small boats and lighters and about 8,600 acres of land outside the town.

On April 21, the stockholders approved the sale and the terms, one-half down and the remainder in two payments in six and twelve months. When these payments were duly made, W. N. Haldeman became sole owner of the company's assets. He and his sons, W. B. and Bruce, owned the enterprise until 1914 when E. W. Crayton,

Beach at Naples looking south along the "Gold Coast" from the Espen-
hain house in 1906.

an Ohio real estate executive, organized the Naples Improvement
Company and launched the program that has grown into present-day
Naples.

The town was fortunate in its connection with the *Louisville
Courier Journal.* Colonel Henry Watterson was a regular visitor and
he wrote enthusiastically about the place and its advantages. "Naples
is not a resort," he reported in a story reprinted in the *Fort Myers
Press* on February 16, 1906. "But to the fisher and hunter Naples
is virgin; the forests and the jungle around about scarce trodden, the
waters, as it were, untouched. Fancy people condemned to live on
venison and bronzed wild turkey, pompano and sure enough oysters—
and such turkeys! and such oysters!"

On the previous day he had described Naples in these words:
". . . sea washed stretch of sandy beach, white as snow and gently
firm, like a paving asphalt, North to South from Doctor's Inlet to
Gordon's Pass, seven miles. Eastward a trellis work of orange groves,
palm gardens and orchards of coconuts, pineapples and mango,
interlaced by tropic flora. To the west an endless girdle of wave and
sky. Midway, a long wooden pier, with a group of cottages nestled
about, and embowered in the setting a larger and more pretentious
edifice, technically described as the hotel, but looking the house of
a gentleman. And this is Naples . . ."

Andrew Weeks recalls that he hunted for the hotel and was paid
seventy-five cents for a hen turkey and a dollar for a gobbler. Weeks
also received two dollars a day to serve as a fishing guide, which
meant rowing a boat all day. He was also first to run a gasoline
powered boat for fishermen, but had to guarantee a larger catch of
fish for the four dollars a day he received.

Lucien Beckner, who spent the winter of 1889-1890 in Naples,
returned sixty-five years later and in 1955 wrote some of his recollections and impressions in a letter to Marjorie Stoneman Douglas.

He recalled, "When I was a boy at Naples there were only eight or ten houses there and it was startling to see how the town has grown; and delightful to see how beautiful a semi-tropical town can be built the American way. It has grown to the south down to Gordon's Pass; and to the north some distance into what were wild woods in my day. The sea-wall, thrown up by an earthquake wave in 1874, has been cut down in places so it seemed to me . . . The Bay of Naples has been partially filled with sand dredged from the bay itself and houses and streets occupy what was once good fishing water. The vast number of birds, geese, ducks, curlews, fish crows and others, which would line the beach in the morning for miles so numerous that the sands could hardly be seen, are gone and the flocks of curlews which flew steadily over the town for an hour or more every evening are no more.

"The founder of Naples thought he could grow Cuban tobacco there and had a camp of Negroes grubbing up the scrub-palmetto from a tract in which they were going to experiment (they were all from Kentucky tobacco country). I presume the experiment was a failure as it was abandoned.

"The winter I was there Miss Rose Cleveland, sister of the President, was living at the hotel. She purchased a tract of land several miles south of town and set out a coconut plantation. She had delivered on the pier several hundred coconuts by the little steamer *Pearl,* which ran from Punta Gorda to Naples; they were taken south in the little sloop *Enid,* Captain Lide (or Lloyd) skipper, a South Carolinian. An old Kentuckian named Taylor was employed by her to plant the coconuts . . . He took a liking to me and I stayed several nights in his shack on the plantation and helped him dig holes for the first coconuts . . .

"We were running into Little Marco one evening in the little *Enid,* seeking refuge from a 'nor'wester.' I was swept overboard just in the mouth of the harbor but swam ashore and we camped that night on the sand. There were seven of us, four ladies and three men. The next morning the storm having blown out we proceeded to Caxambas which was the nearest place to Naples where vegetables and fruits could be bought. I was told that it was (now) no longer inhabited. The beautiful little county seat of Everglades was a surprise to me. I remember when there was nothing there . . ."

Another pioneer, Captain Charles W. Stewart, came to Naples in November of 1900 to be superintendent of the Haldeman estate and operate the Haldeman boat during the season. In 1908 he moved into a small cottage at the foot of the pier and became postmaster, succeeding Will Pixton. The post office dated back to April 8, 1888, making it the first in the county. Stewart later moved the post office to quarters on the pier, and again in 1929 he moved it into the old Haldeman store where he was also storekeeper. In 1925 the Crayton interests built a post office down near the Naples Hotel which served until early 1957 when the present site was occupied.

The birth of the first child born in Naples is recounted in a letter appearing in the *Collier County News*. It names Pearl Ethel Maynard, now Mrs. Pearl Gesheidt of Oakland Park, Florida, as the first white girl born there. Mrs. Maynard, now dead, had related the following story to her daughter in a letter dated in 1930:

"Your father, Verne, and I came to Orlando in 1887 . . . After we left Orlando your father bought a lot in Naples. We left Orlando on a narrow gauge road and landed in Pontorassa (Punta Gorda?) where we took the sailboat to Naples . . . The Gulf of Mexico was rough. There was no wharf so Dennis Sheridan took me in his arms and waded ashore with me . . .

"When we got to Naples there were no houses, just two tents for sleeping and one for cooking. The men moved further down the beach and built a palmetto shack and your father and I moved into it.

"A short time before we went down there a boat stopped and a woman came ashore so Dr. Green of Cincinnati, Ohio, who was one of their group, could wait on her. She stayed long enough to have a baby boy, then left on the same boat . . .

"You are the first white baby born in Naples whose mother lived there. You were born on Wednesday between 11 and 12 at night on December 19, 1888. Dr. Green brought you into the world . . . Six months after you were born, a Mr. and Mrs. Brockman from Dade City, Fla., became the parents of a son born in Naples . . . The place you were born in was near the beach. The sides were boarded up for a ways and a tent put on top of that. It also had a board floor."

While attending to its physical developments, the early Neapolitans did not lose sight of the educational needs of the community. The minutes of the Lee County Board of Public Instruction for September 17, 1888 record the appointment of T. T. Ebney as trustee of the Naples School District, and Miss Annie Metcalf as teacher in the Naples school of fourteen pupils. On October 5, of the same year, the board agreed to rent Dr. Green's house as a school. On May 3, of the following year the board accepted a deed from the Naples Company for a lot for public school purposes, but in November the matter of a building was laid over for future consideration. Andrew Weeks and Captain Stewart built the first public school. Support was partly by private funds but Lee County contributed twenty-five dollars a month. Another structure on the same site followed the abandonment of the Weeks-Stewart building. Still later a one-room school was constructed on the present school grounds, a second room being added almost immediately. The school plant now in use was started in 1925 and later expanded.

Until after World War I the population of Naples remained small, being made up of a few fishermen, farmers, and cattlemen who stayed the year around, and the winter residents and a few guests. The lack of any adequate roads limited travel almost entirely to water. There was, of course, the overland sand trail called the "Surveyor's Trail" to Fort Myers which might be negotiated in good weather. In 1909 the *Fort Myers Press* reported General Haldeman ready to pay one third of the cost of a hard road from Naples to the county seat, but the other two-thirds was not forthcoming.

In the winter of 1914-1915 an auto bus was being operated from Fort Myers but was taken off at the end of March as it had not proved profitable. Part of the explanation was certainly the condition of the roads over which it was driven. The *American Eagle* had reported on January 21, that the bus was temporarily out of commission, roads, not the car, being the cause. The rear wheels had twin tires and tracked a little wider than the average car. At several points along the route the tires had been badly snagged by roots or stumps which it was hoped would soon be grubbed out. Apparently the tires were of solid rubber for it was announced that new cushion tires, claimed to be puncture proof, had been ordered.

Nor were "average" cars always able to negotiate the distance safely. Captain Stewart recalls meeting the train in Fort Myers in the summer of 1914 and bringing a passenger to Naples over a sand road made fairly firm by a recent rain. But when he drove the visitor back to Fort Myers a few days later it had been raining and water came up to the floor boards in places. Stewart made it to the train, but had to leave his car and return by boat to Naples where he waited three weeks before the water fell enough to drive his car home.

This was the Naples that "Southern Crackers" and "Kentucky Colonels" had built in a generation. Only their unusual enterprise was responsible for the progress made. Nonetheless, Naples had a population of less than 200 even at the height of the season. But a combination of circumstances was about to rescue it from isolation and give it a push forward that would in another generation transform it into the Naples of today. That combination was improved transportation and a new group of men not satisfied for it to remain a rather exclusive winter resort for part of its population and just another coastal farming, fishing and hunting village for its year-'round citizens.

Naples II, Fastest Growing

T HE MAKING of the Naples we know today began in about 1915.
It is usually attributed to the efforts of a small group of men,
and particularly to one of them. Prior to their coming the few
permanent residents and winter visitors who made up the population
seemed not too much interested in having Naples break from its
isolation and obscurity. It should be said in their defense that there
was not much they could have done about it. Certainly the newcomers
had advantages denied to the earlier generation. Roads and railroads
were reaching down the coast far enough to offer some hope that
Naples might be freed of its dependence upon water transport. No
amount of money or effort would make much difference until these
facilities became available.

In 1913 the heirs of Walter N. Haldeman transferred their
Naples property to the Naples Development Company of which they
were members. They retained only a few homes and tracts valued
chiefly for sentimental reasons. The new company was headed by
a group of Ohio business men who were to succeed the Kentuckians
in guiding the development of Naples. They were E. W. Crayton and
J. S. Ralston of Columbus, J. K. Hamill of Newark, and George W.
Cassingham of Coshocton. The directing genius of the group and of
most Naples activity for the next twenty-five years was Crayton, who
left his name and stamp all over the new Naples.

When Crayton died on December 21, 1938, the *Collier County
News* summarized his activities and achievement. Principal among
them were promoting the building of roads, helping to bring two

railroads to Naples, influencing Allen Joslin to build a fine golf course, financing five miles of sea wall to protect beach front homes, making more land available by dredging, working to sell a $35,000 bond issue to improve Naples Bay, and obtaining funds up to $50,000 to guarantee an extension of Naples Bay by dredging to Marco Pass.

Early in 1916 the company opened a forty room addition to the Naples Hotel, which up to that time was frequently referred to as Haldeman Club House. Guests could make the trip to and from Fort Myers in a ten-passenger bus that met the trains. This was but the first of a series of expansions of the Naples Hotel property.

In 1922 John S. Jones, a coal and railroad man from Granville, Ohio, bought a controlling interest in the company and injected new energy and capital into its activities, sharing the control with E. W. Crayton. They installed the first central electric power plant which the Florida Power and Light Company took over in 1929. Up to that time home owners had their own power plants, principally the popular Delco type. They also took the first steps toward a central water system, sinking a half dozen wells where the small lake is now located. This was primarily to serve the Naples Hotel but citizens who wished could buy the water service. The water was unfiltered and unmetered, but passed all tests for purity.

They constructed the building in which the Naples Company offices are now located. In the center was a small auditorium which served as a community hall in which all religious groups were encouraged to hold their services. They were instrumental in getting the railroads to extend their lines to the city. And they built a small laundry and a ten ton ice plant to serve the needs of the hotel.

Jones died after only four years in Naples and for a time development by the Naples Company, and that meant for practically all of Naples, was paralyzed to such an extent that the hotel did not open for a season. As soon as the Jones estate could be settled Crayton carried on as agent for the heirs and growth continued. The city bonded itself and did its first street paving. It had a newspaper for a time when Vernon Lamme was publishing the *Naples Transcript*. The hurricane of 1926 and the subsequent collapse of the Florida land boom slowed, where it did not stop, expansion in all parts of the state. Yet Naples' recovery was more rapid than some for it got a real boost in 1928 with the opening of the Tamiami Trail.

In 1928 Naples also had its first try at a Chamber of Commerce with J. W. Chatterton as president, J. K. Hamill, Jr., as vice president and Lamme as secretary. On November 10 they adopted a constitution and by-laws based upon a model supplied by the state chamber. The directors agreed upon a five dollar membership, but expected each businessman to take at least five. In the next month Judge Wilkerson, chairman of the Channel Committee of the Chamber, reported that his committee had made soundings and had concluded that deepening of the pass might not be as formidable a task as had been supposed. This promising start was cut short by the national depression which began in the fall of 1929. And though the Naples Chamber had begun to function shortly before that date, it was not formally incorporated until 1951.

The same state legislature that created Collier County in 1923 authorized the incorporation of the City of Naples. The citizens seemed not to have been in any hurry as they did not complete the process until August 13, 1925. The first town council met in the Naples Improvement Company offices, rooms 5 and 6 being designated the Town Hall.

Speed S. Menefee was the first mayor. He had come to Naples twenty years earlier, had worked for the "company" and had been employed on down the coast at various jobs, places and times. He liked to recall that he came to the community when it was little more than a clearing in the wilderness, and claimed to have caught thirty-six wildcats in his chicken yard. He said he came with seventeen dollars and ten cents in his pockets—more than many who came—and had a guitar. He could sing a few tunes like "Casey Jones" and he roamed all over the area, receiving a generous welcome wherever he appeared. Judge E. G. Wilkerson succeeded him as mayor and held the office for many years.

L. W. Tuttle, C. W. Stewart, E. W. Crayton, Andrew J. Weeks, and E. G. Wilkerson made up the first town council. In February of 1926 they approved a tax roll of $170,000 and a budget of $8500, and borrowed $375 from Crayton to pay the town marshall, Thomas J. Weeks, his salary for three months. Councilmen received one dollar for each meeting and a year later they began to pay the mayor a hundred dollars a year. Also in 1926 the city council appointed William Cambier town engineer and thereby secured the able and devoted services of the man for whom Cambier Park is named. Veteran members of the city government today (1957) are Mayor Roy Smith, just re-elected after twelve years of service, and councilman Claude M. Storter, who has served seventeen years. Other members of the council are Archie Turner, Theron Ridge and William W. Berry. Fred M. Lowdermilk is City manager. Cale Jones, now fire chief and police chief, began his association with Naples in 1928 as town marshall: Naples did not become a city until 1949.

Apparently the first public building the city fathers put up was a jail on Tenth Avenue. It was a two-cell concrete structure costing $381.68 and, though long since abandoned, it stood until 1954 when it was broken up and piled along the beach as an auxiliary sea wall. Law enforcement has never been a serious problem in Naples. Even now, the police force numbers only ten. The present city hall, built in 1940 and expanded in 1953, is already outgrown. The building department moved across the street in September of 1956.

Naples has had a volunteer fire department since 1934. The building that now houses the fire fighting equipment and the jail (two offices and two ten by ten cells) was built in 1949. This fifty-one by ninety-one foot structure is expected to be doubled in size within the next year in an effort to keep pace with the growing need for floor space to accommodate municipal services.

The Crayton group made the first steps to improve Naples Bay and the approaches to it. This was no new problem, as it was essential that easy and relatively deep access to a protected harbor be provided for both pleasure craft and the fishing fleet that the city hoped to attract. Gordon's pass was shallow, with a constantly shifting channel so that only boats drawing up to five feet could use it with safety. The first effort was to improve the inside passage to Marco where there was a deeper channel and ample protected anchorage. The first Crayton dredge was a shovel type that dug away the oyster bars on the Marco passage. In 1935 Claude M. Storter operated a dipper dredge over the same route to deepen the passage over oyster bars and shallow places.

A continuing effort to get the Federal Government to aid in harbor improvement failed to get any help for deepening Gordon's Pass, but Uncle Sam did aid in the improvement of the inside passage. Not until 1946 was Gordon's Pass dredged out, only to have the hurricane of that year fill it with sand again. The Marco Passes have also filled up to some degree and many boats come in at Coon Key and make their way to Naples. Naples Bay also presents some serious dredging problems as a rocky bottom makes it difficult to provide the eight foot depth deemed necessary for the industrial purposes of the city. In the summer of 1956 Army Engineers approved further study of a project to provide and maintain an adequate ship channel at Naples and Fort Myers Beach. Neapolitans hope that Gordon's Pass will again be deepened and that provisions will be made for keeping it clear.

In the optimistic boom days following the Broward Administration's drainage efforts it looked as if Naples might get an electric railway from Fort Myers. In October of 1915 the Lee County Commissioners authorized such a project and H. E. McCormick of Birmingham, Alabama, announced that work would start in six months. But in February of the next year the *American Eagle* reported that a party surveying the right of way for the proposed interurban service had quit the job short of Naples by a good many miles, and raised the question whether it had even been more than an effort to boom real estate values.

When Naples did finally get railroad service it came in a double portion. The Atlantic Coast Line and the Seaboard Air Line both reached the city within ten days of each other, the ACL on December 27, 1926 and the SAL on January 7 of 1927.

S. Davis Warfield, president of the Seaboard, was completely sold on Naples and joined forces with local developers to make it the "Seaboard's Miami." He purchased 2645 acres in Naples for right of way, terminals, station, and development. His faith in Naples survived the Florida depression but his death ended the Seaboard's active interest in Naples.

In 1942 the Seaboard pulled back to Fort Myers, selling its real estate to the ACL and others. The ACL took over the Seaboard right of way and tracks seven miles north of Naples where the two lines paralleled, and moved its operations to what had been the Seaboard station. The Coast Line had been equally ambitious, for it had run its line on down to Marco. But as Marco failed to become as important as had been hoped, either as a deep water port or a local development, that extension was given up in 1942. Trains ran intermittently for another two years to pick up shipments from the Doxsee Clam cannery, but in 1944 the tracks were taken up back to the point where the Seaboard right of way was taken over.

The original Coast Line station was at what is now the Naples Airport. It may have been located there on the assumption that the Tamiami Trail would eventually be routed that way. Or, as others suggest, to obtain the right of way and land for development in Naples they may have had to place it on Crayton property. O. L. "Kit" Carson, well known local representative of the Coast Line, served two years at the old station before it was moved to the present site.

Itinerant ministers, who usually made a circuit of the coastal settlements, preached in Naples as early as the eighteen nineties. The Reverend George Gatewood was among the first, and in 1926 the Reverend James L. Glenn was still at it, preaching once a month at Marco on Wednesday night, at Naples on Thursday night, and at Caxambas on Friday night before returning to his post in the Community Church at Everglades. When there were no church buildings services were held in schoolhouses, community houses or even in private homes.

In 1927 and for a short while thereafter Naples had a Community Church which, like that at Everglades, was under the nurture and support of the Presbyterians. The Reverend Alexander Linn organized the congregation and Reverend J. G. Knotten became its resident minister. As they had no building, they met in the Community Hall.

The community church idea did not take hold in Naples, perhaps because it fell between already existing cleavages in a population that was part year-'round and part winter visitors. The Methodist Church South had begun at about the same time and also served much as a community church until members of other denominations became numerous enough to launch independent organizations.

In the late twenties there was also a small Church of God in East Naples and a Catholic congregation, which shared the use of the Community Hall with the Methodists and the Community Church. Within the last ten years, as the population has increased rapidly in number and religious diversity, a comparable number of churches has appeared. Presbyterians, Trinity-by-the Cove Episcopal, and St. Ann's Catholic all have their own buildings. St. Ann's started a parochial school for 160 children in the Naples Hotel in the fall of 1956. They planned a school on Eighth Avenue to be ready before the hotel opened for the season, but the building was delayed until the summer of 1957 and the pupils occupied rooms in scattered places after vacating the hotel. The Christian Science Church began services in 1956 and the Lutherans are holding services in a store building until they can complete a religious edifice on a lot north of the golf course.

Until their church was ready the Baptist Congregation met in the former Woman's Club building. This was an old converted residence on Eleventh Avenue, South, contributed by E. W. Crayton and

William L. Clarke, Jr. The Woman's Club is now housed in a modern building across from City Park.

A distinguished Naples pioneer was Dr. Henry Nehrling, ornithologist, botanist, and plant breeder extraordinary, who was born in Sheboygan, Wisconsin, in 1853. He began to experiment with tropical plants in Houston, Texas, in 1879 and took his interest with him to the Milwaukee Public Museum of which he became custodian. In 1883 he purchased forty acres of land at Gotha near Orlando and began to make preparations to move to the more nearly tropical climate where he could grow his plants in their natural habitat. He made his first trip to Florida in 1886 and spent a month or two each year on his new project until he was able to move permanently to the state in 1902.

In 1917 a severe freeze killed most of his tender tropical plants. At sixty - six years of age Nehrling decided to pioneer in yet another place and moved to Naples in 1919. The change from high, dry pine to the high water table in South Florida frustrated many of his early efforts and he died in 1929 before having time to fully develop his botanical experiments in the new location. The Caribbean Gardens is a restoration and expansion of his garden.

Nehrling was especially famous for his breeding of many beautiful strains of amaryllis and caladiums. He kept painstaking and exhaustive records of all his experiments. It is to the everlasting credit of Allen H. Andrews of the *American Eagle* that he induced Nehrling to write extensively about horticulture in Florida. The articles have since been published in book form under the titles: *The Plant World of Florida,* in 1933, a condensation of them, and *My Garden in Florida* in 1944 in two volumes, a more nearly complete edition.

Naples winter residents who inhabit the "Gold Coast" north along the beach from the municipal pier have long been noted for their civic mindedness. When Naples was new and small they provided employment for a goodly number of the town's citizens. During the depression years winter residents created a fund to employ them at public works during the summer. A local committee administered the project and paid out wages of $1.50 a day for a four day week.

Though differences of near serious nature have arisen from time to time, it has always been possible to maintain a working agreement between them and the town's permanent residents. Apparently the latter have often suspected that any new scheme is designed for the benefit of the part-time residents and their estates and that possibly they don't pay their share of the costs. The winter residents, who might argue that they had more to do with starting the town which they looked upon as a retreat from what modern Naples threatens to become, are interested in zoning regulations to permit them as much privacy as possible and in municipal improvements for their end of the town.

If it may be said that the estate owners look askance at taxes, it cannot be said that they are unwilling to participate in community ventures aimed at improvement of the city's services. And they are willing to pay their share of the costs. But they seem to prefer giving to a community fund rather than supporting bond issues and new taxes. Some have given freely of their special skills to various projects.

W. B. Uihlein, president of the Schlitz Brewing Company, divided his time between Naples and Milwaukee. He was an able engineer, and undertook to provide the city with plans for an adequate water system. Naples got a water supply but at a cost

Photo by J. M. Coleman, Naples.
The Naples Pier, 1957.

that brought protests from users and the charge that Uihlein had personally profited. After eight years of service, he resigned.

The *Collier County News* of May 20, 1949 in an editorial on "The Price of Water" offered the following defense of Mr. Uihlein's work. "At the bottom is the price of water in Naples. We have a fine plant but we also have a fine debt to pay off. Money which might have been used to reduce the debt has been needed to expand the plant in the face of increased consumption during the winter dry season. Naples has been forced to build and maintain a water plant whose capacity for nine months of the year is much larger than is needed. Naples is also spread over an area seven miles long and from one to four miles wide. Distribution costs are almost prohibitive . . . except for the very rich and the very foolish, a private well is the only practicable way to water lawns, shrubbery and gardens."

The city laid eleven original water mains with proceeds of a bond issue. Individual property owners and real estate developers paid for additional lines and fire hydrants as well as streets. The *Collier County News* noted in January 4, 1952 that $100,604.90 worth of such improvements had been accomplished in five years under the cooperative plan.

Like all other expanding communities, Naples was suffering from growing pains. Uihlein and others actually planned well, if inadequately at times, for the city's future. The water plant constructed in 1946 has already had two additions, the first in 1951. The second, called Uihlein Plant Number Two and located in the northern part of the city, was ready in 1954 to serve a part of the anticipated winter demand. On October 8, 1954 the editor of the *Collier County News* reminded citizens that Mr. Uihlein had commented shortly before his death that Naples would soon need a sewer system. The time had now come, said the editor, since "growth demands action."

By far the most ambitious project in community development was the Naples Plan, launched in 1947. The plan provided for the raising of $300,000 in cash and pledges for new streets, groins to restore the beach, a park-playground and a mosquito control program. The editorial announcing the plan called the projects "Improvements for which municipalities ruinously bond themselves, tax away new residents and impoverish old, or wait for years in hope of a miracle that never quite comes off."

The plan originated in an informal meeting of representative Naples businessmen with Major Roy Smith and members of the town council in December of 1947. They agreed that Mr. Cambier, city engineer, should be in charge. They proposed four 700 foot groins of creosoted piling to check erosion and suction dredging to start rebuilding the beaches. The United States Government had refused to assume the obligations for the dredging and beach restoration on the ground that there was not enough commercial use made of the waters involved. Selected streets would be paved according to SRD specifications. A 10 3/4 acre park was to be located across Eighth Street from the Town Hall. At the meeting three individuals present pledged $70,000 in cash. Another offered the entire tract for the playground contingent upon the success of the fund raising. A letter explaining the project to all citizens and soliciting contributions was to be prepared.

An editorial appeared January 2, 1948 on "The Congenital Gossipers," warning that a whispering campaign was endangering the Naples Plan. It was the same old mistrust of the Gold Coast people by the townspeople who saw a scheme to make them pay for improving the Gold Coast. And, said the editor, there was also some such talk from wealthy individuals who opposed the project. He deplored anything that would "increase the area of misunderstanding between winter residents and townspeople." The gossip was widening the breach, having reached proportions that could threaten the future of the project. There had never been any hope of success if the plan even seemed to benefit any one area at the expense of another. The editor pointed out that wealthy property owners, primarily on Gordon Drive, were planning to raise $250,000 of the proposed $300,000. Construction of the Gold Coast groins and the rebuilding of Gordon Drive would actually cost under half what that area's residents expected to pay.

Two weeks later the newspaper announced that the park was to have top priority in the Naples Plan. Next in order were mosquito control, four open groins on the beach, repairing Gordon Drive from the post office to the Myrin property, repairing First Street to the town pier, repairing Gordon Drive from the Myrin property to the Pass, and finally sand dredging between groins if necessary to start building up the beach. The committee already had $66,000 in cash and $100,000 in pledges.

On February 6 the ground was broken for the New Naples Park Playground. A week later the local paper was denying the rumor that tax money was being used to make the park. The Committee, headed by the Chamber of Commerce, was speeding up the drive for funds. They now had $175,000 in cash and negotiable notes. The Lee County Bank at Fort Myers agreed to take enough of the Naples Plan notes to complete the street, park and beach groins jobs. On June 18, however, the bank was reported refusing to honor the notes, the fund was dwindling, and the town could not legally guarantee the

The Naples Community Hospital.   Photo by Thomas McGrath, Naples.

notes. But money and credit were still forthcoming and the work went on. On July 5, 1948 the new $60,000 Cambier Park was dedicated.

Neapolitans apparently liked doing things the Naples Plan way. In 1954 they announced a similar drive to raise $108,000 for a new hospital and other civic improvements. Original plans called for an emergency clinic-infirmary type of hospital, but the conviction grew that Naples needed a more complete hospital service if it was to attract the needed physicians and surgeons to serve such a rapidly growing community. Accordingly the hospital project was separated from the others and became the principal activity of civic minded citizens until it was completed two years later. It is a $750,-000 fifty-two bed, fully equipped and accredited hospital, all paid for by public subscription. And it is maintained partly by the services and money of these same citizens as a community service, essential but not yet completely self-supporting.

Naples has had two golf courses, and a third is projected. The first was a small nine-hole course built and maintained by the Naples Company. It lay between Fifth and Eighth Avenues and between Third and Eighth Streets. The small lake in the center of that area was a marshy depression at the time and the course lay around it. The house now occupied by city commissioner Claude M. Storter stands on the site of a small greenskeeper's cottage.

The present Naples Golf Course, a one hundred and twenty acre, eighteen-hole course was first used in the fall of 1930. Crayton, acting

188

Photo by J. M. Coleman, Naples.

Naples looking north from Gordon's Pass. Note land development on shores of Naples Bay. 1957.

for the company, induced Allen Joslin of Cincinnati, Ohio, to build and operate the course as a private venture, reportedly giving him the land for the course and a half interest in the blocks adjoining it north and south, excepting beach front. Joslin also built the Naples Beach Club, but Larry McPhail and associates built the Beach Apartments and operated them for two years before the Naples Company acquired the golf course, the club and the apartments.

The latest version of the Naples Company came in 1946 when H. B. Watkins and W. D. McCabe of Columbus, Ohio, and their associates formed the company to purchase the holdings of the Naples Improvement Corporation, the Naples Development Company and the Naples Tropical Realty Company. The new owners immediately planned twelve new homes, renovated and redecorated the entire Naples Hotel building and converted the adjoining Hendrie property into a twenty-room hotel annex. They announced plans to renovate the Naples Golf and Beach Club.

The rapid expansion of Naples at the present time renders futile any attempt at description. A few statistical measures will indicate the accelerated pace at which it has been growing since 1950. Building permits, which first passed the half million dollar mark in

189

Photo by J. M. Coleman, Naples.

Naples' unique Swamp Buggy Race in a mile of mud.

1948, reached a million and a half in 1950, and by 1955 almost reached the five million mark. This was passed by October 1, 1956. In the five year period, 1950-55, the assessed value of property rose from $4,828,715. to $24,419,060. and postal receipts rose from $20,000. to $72,000. Charles W. Stewart recalls that when he first took over the office of postmaster in 1908 the receipts were about fifty dollars a quarter.

Public utilities provide another yardstick for measuring growth. The Inter-County Telephone Company reported 621 phones in 1950 and 2539 five years later, while Florida Power and Light Company meters increased from 821 to 2554 in the same period. City water users, however, rose from 447 to only 1275, indicating that many residents have their own wells and pumps. The city's population, including suburban areas was 1450 in 1950 and estimated at 5500 in 1955.

Naples had no bank until the Bank of Naples opened in 1950. In August of 1953 the Naples Federal Savings and Loan Association began to do business. And on April 1 of 1956 the First National Bank of Naples joined the financial fraternity in the rapidly growing city.

Naples has made an increasingly successful bid for tourists. Dan House and associates built the Naples Tourist Court in 1932 and the Naples Trailer Court appeared shortly thereafter. But the beginning of the modern motel building era came in 1949 when four went up simultaneously, the Motel Naples, The Sea Shell, the Siesta Terrace and the Trail's End. The Naples Chamber of Commerce lists a dozen others in 1956 besides three dozen apartment buildings, numerous duplexes, guest houses, trailer parks and fishing camps.

Naples also has its own unique festival, "Swamp Buggy Days." This unusual event was started in 1949 by hunters and sportsmen who got together to put their rigs through a gruelling test on a mile of mud track. The original swamp buggy was an ox-drawn cart or wagon. The modern version mounts airplane tires on all four wheels, has a souped up power engine and usually uses chains. The festival has grown from a one-day to a three-day affair with numerous contests, parades, and special events, all full of fun and frolic.

Communities have grown on either side of Naples. William Weeks and Harrison Nash first settled in East Naples in 1925. In 1927 Noah Kirkland owned the oldest home in the village and was operating the Gordon River Fish Company. W. H. Surrency started the first development when he built a home for himself and induced others to do so. He also operated a garage and filling station on the Tamiami Trail. In 1931 the *Fort Myers Press* reported a general store, a garage, a barber shop, a restaurant and a filling station in East Naples. All houses were occupied and there was demand for more.

More recently North Naples developed to the point of considering incorporation. A published story said that North Naples residents were planning incorporation "before Naples gobbles us up and saddles us with high taxes." In the *Collier County News* of July 27, 1954, it was denied that Naples had such designs on her younger neighbor. And from that embryonic city came the statement that the residents had nothing against Naples, they just wanted a community of their own.

Immokalee: *Ranch and Garden*

IN 1923 the only non-coastal settlement in the new county was in the Immokalee and Corkscrew area and Immokalee remains the only community of considerable size in the interior. Lying in the extreme north central part of the county, it is the center of a nearly square area of Collier County that reaches up into Hendry County. Fort Myers lies thirty-five miles to the northwest, LaBelle twenty-two miles to the north and Everglades forty-one miles due south.

The Immokalee area has the highest elevation in the county other than the limited sand dune area on southern Marco Island. It is a high hammock, some of it more than forty feet above sea level and none of it below twenty-five, and it was originally covered with hardwood forest. This elevation is in sharp contrast to the lower elevation of the Everglades, some thirty miles to the east, and the Big Cypress, about half that distance to the south, and is slightly higher than the lands between it and the Gulf Coast.

Immokalee is surrounded by natural features only slightly less well known than those of the Everglades and Big Cypress. To the north in Hendry County is Devil's Garden, once a famous Indian and white hunting ground, now largely given over to ranching and farming. The Okaloacoochee Slough lies to the southeast, roughly parallel to and east of the highway and railroad and extending southward about fifteen miles. Directly west are Lake Trafford and Corkscrew Marsh, in the south end of which is Corkscrew Island, and west of which is the Corkscrew settlement. Here also is the famous Corkscrew Cypress Rookery now assured of preservation where all may see virgin bald cypress and the ibis rookery.

Calusa Indians made their way along these marshes and sloughs and have left their mounds and middens to mark the courses they followed in their canoes. The Seminole Indians who, unlike the Calusa, were not a coastal dwelling people, discovered the Immokalee area's advantages long before the white man came there. To them it was an important camping and resting place from which they went on hunting expeditions in all directions. From the Seminoles it received the name "Gopher Ridge," there

Courtesy of Mrs. Irby Johnson, Fort Myers.
William "Billy" Allen, who gave his name to the Allen Place, now Immokalee.

being an unusual number of land turtles or gophers there which were an important part of their diet. Immokalee is still closely associated with these Indians as the Federal Reservation in Hendry County is nearby and they frequently come to trade. Others live in nearby camps in Collier County, but find employment in Immokalee, trade there and send their children to the Immokalee school.

White hunters, cattlemen and Indian traders first found their way to Immokalee around the middle of the last century but no permanent settler appeared before 1872. Temporary camps may have been visited by hunters with some regularity before that date. The Charles Hendrys lived there in 1872 but, when a daughter died there, they returned to Fort Myers. Then came William Allen, known familiarly as Bill or Billy. During the twenty-five years he lived there, it was known as "Allen's Place." Allen was a Confederate veteran from Arcadia who built a log house where the Roberts Grove now stands. When W. L. Apthorp ran the township and section lines in 1873 and 1874, he mentioned the Allen home in his field notes as unoccupied at the time, suggesting that Allen,

Courtesy of the Museum of the American Indian.
Bill Brown's trading post at Boat Landing. Mission hospital to the right.

like many others after him, did not at first spend all his time there.

In 1885 William H. Brown, whose family has been closely associated with its history, came to live there. He had visited the area on trading expeditions and for a few years thereafter divided his time between the new home and Fort Myers. At that time he found three other families living there: the Wilkersons, Fred and Webb; the Currys; and the Allens. Robert Carson came shortly afterward. Brown gave his name to the hammock, where he settled, about seven miles west of present day Immokalee.

Brown became actively engaged in the Indian trade, working at first out of the H. P. Parker Grocery Store in Fort Myers, where he secured his trade goods and sold his hides and feathers. His next move was to a bay hammock three miles farther east, to which Indians came in increasing numbers and where Mrs. Brown taught Johnny Osceola to read English through the first grade reader. Brown also did some extensive gardening and hunting, particularly for egret plumes.

He moved again to a homestead of one hundred and sixty acres still further east, but his next move by-passed the present town-site and landed him nearly thirty miles to the east at Boat Landing, later known as Brown's Landing. His homestead was three miles short of the landing and, after a few years, he made the final move that placed his home and trading post at the head of canoe navigation on the western edge of the Everglades. There, with the assistance of the Indians, he built a home and store with a platform at which the Seminoles could tie up their canoes and unload the items they brought to trade, and added a shelter under which the visitors might sleep.

Their source of trade goods and their market were still at Fort Myers. Mrs. Rose Brown Kennan, the eldest child, recalls the trips they made by ox-team. She began driving oxen at thirteen and, when she turned the job over to her brother Frank five years later, she could handle three yoke of the critters. She would drive one team while her father drove another and the mother and other children followed in a horse and buggy. In 1908 Brown sold the store to the Episcopal Church which incorporated it in the mission there and operated it until 1914. Brown returned with his family to Immokalee and ran a store there until his death in 1927.

Frank Brown remained for some years at the Boat Landing mission where he learned the Seminole language. He is one of the few white men who can communicate with them in their own tongue. As a result he has learned more of the Seminole lore than anyone else in the county. Frank also learned to know the country unusually well and in 1910 guided one of the trips made by William A. and Julian Dimock into the Everglades.

The first post office at Immokalee opened October 9, 1897, and was presided over by Mrs. Alice Platt. It was located, as was the entire settlement, nearly two miles west of the present location which did not become important until the railroad came in 1921 creating a new center of activity. The carrier brought the mail overland in saddle bags, and later by horse and buggy, from Denaud on the Caloosahatchee River where the mail boat stopped.

The naming of the post office, as is often the case in pioneer communities, changed and fixed the name of the settlement. The "Allen Place" now became Immokalee, meaning "my home." The name was suggested by Bishop William Crane Gray who argued that it should be a Seminole word with pleasant associations. The building now housing the post office was put up in the summer of 1956.

The first church in Immokalee was intended for the benefit of the Indians but served the Whites instead until 1924. It was part of the Episcopal Indian Mission that became the Glade Cross Mission at Boat Landing. The first service was held in it in 1896. The bell was so heavy that it was mounted on a separate platform.

Josie Bille and Frank Brown in 1908. Vest and hat from Brown's store.

196

Old settlers recall that a double row of bamboos lined the approach to the church until recently. The building was badly damaged in the 1910 hurricane and partly restored, but so complete was the destruction in 1924 that no effort was made to rebuild it. The number of Episcopalians proved too small to maintain a church. Even before 1924 there had not been a resident pastor; a visiting minister from Fort Myers or a bishop had held services about once a month.

In 1914 Bob Roberts came to the old Allen place and added another family well known among the pioneers. He and his sons are still prominent ranchers. In 1916 the Roberts family was one of four that made up the small Baptist congregation, meeting first in the schoolhouse and later in a small building near the cemetery. Still later they moved the building to the lot where the new Baptist church rose in 1952. The Baptist Home Mission Board maintains the old structure on the east side of the new one for the benefit of Spanish-speaking people who come in the winter, principally Puerto Rican and Mexican migratory workers.

Reflecting the rapid growth in population in recent years are a half-dozen other denominations now maintaining services. The Methodists have a new and modern structure on the north side of town. The Roman Catholics have acquired a building site but are now meeting in the Kent Theater. The Church of God, the Church of God of Prophecy, and the Assembly of God have churches in widely separated parts of town. A Mennonite mission, established principally for migrant workers' children, completes the list of religious organizations.

The first school at Immokalee was also part of the mission for the Indians, but actually taught only Whites as no Indians came to it. In 1891 Lee County agreed to pay twenty-five dollars a month for the support of the school and Mrs. Clara Brecht, wife of the missionary, was the teacher. When the mission moved out to the edge of the Everglades, the county apparently rented the building, for the minutes of the Lee County Board of Public Instruction show fifteen dollars paid to Dr. J. E. Brecht for the church in 1893 for its use. Three years later the county built a schoolhouse on a piece of land donated for that purpose and in 1897 Miss Mattie Vivian Lybass, now Mrs. Sam Thompson, was the teacher. The Collier County School Board still owns this piece of land but can use it only for a school; otherwise it reverts to the heirs of the giver, now over a hundred in number.

This building sufficed until after 1921 when the school population began to grow. In 1926 there were forty-three pupils and a new frame structure replaced the thirty-year-old edifice of learning. Repeated additions have been necessary to keep pace with growing needs. In 1926 rooms were added; in 1942 a separate two-room structure was built; and in 1952 a one-room portable was added. In that year officials also took the first steps to move the entire school location from down near the railroad out to the new location north of town. The first unit was a high school building, and in 1956 the move was completed. The new site is large enough for expansion and free from the noises and dangers of railroad and downtown traffic.

In 1896 there were enough settlers out near Lake Trafford to have a school there for a few years. It opened as district number 22, with J. R. Burnett as supervisor and R. A. Kennon as teacher at thirty-five dollars a month. There was never a schoolhouse there, classes being held in a private building.

Another settlement intimately associated with the early history of Immokalee was at Corkscrew, eleven miles away. This may have received its name from a winding and twisting creek of that name as is sometimes stated, but the name is much older than the settlement. William Swinton's *Grammar School Geography,* first published in 1880, identifies the Imperial River on which Bonita Springs is located as "Corkscrew." Later it was known as Survey or Surveyor's Creek and was finally named Imperial River in 1912. The post office called Survey when it was established in 1901 was also changed in 1912 to Bonita Springs.

The source of place names is a fascinating study. They do not necessarily have any relation to natural features even when they appear to do so. Green River Swamp south of Corkscrew Marsh is so named because of a pile of nearly a hundred Green River whiskey bottles accumulated at a nearby hunting camp visited regularly by a party with a liking for that brand.

J. J. (Jehu) Whidden came to Corkscrew from Henderson Creek in 1911, bringing to the north end of Collier County yet another name destined to play a prominent part in its history. He found the families of Joe Carson, Abel Lamb, Jake Taylor, and J. C. Keen living there and sustaining themselves mainly by hunting. The Whiddens had lived at Bonita Springs from 1893 to 1905 during which time another prominent Collier County family, that of Jim

The J. J. Whidden family at Henderson Creek prior to 1911. Pet deer belonged to Graham Whidden.

Walker, also lived there. The two families helped to found the first school at Bonita Springs and the post office.

At Corkscrew the Whiddens added farming and ranching to the hunting being done by the earlier comers. Lumber for the Whidden home was brought overland by ox wagon from Alva. Though Corkscrew grew into a community of twenty families and had a school, it never had a store or a church. The people traded at Immokalee eleven miles away, where Charles Hadley and Bill Brown had stores at a crossroads just west of the present city limits. Only in the last ten years have Corkscrew residents had a dependable all-weather road out to the highway. They recall a protracted wet spell when it required the efforts of six men to get a Ford truck out to the road and into town for supplies.

In 1923 the Corkscrew community had its first school. Each family paid five dollars and the county aided with thirty dollars a month ostensibly for rent, but actually to help support the teacher. The following year the county assumed full responsibility for the school and provided a schoolhouse which served until 1946 when the pupils began to travel by bus to Immokalee. Mrs. Mary Christian, who was the first teacher at Corkscrew, moved to the Immokalee School after two years and was still teaching there in 1957.

Immokalee had all the natural endowments for a flourishing community, but no adequate means of transportation or communication with the outside before 1921 when the Atlantic Coast Line Railway Company extended its line south from LaBelle and broke the isolation.

The enterprising Koreshans, who founded Estero, sought repeatedly to have the Lee County commissioners build a road from their town to Immokalee. Allen H. Andrews, who edited the *American Eagle* at Estero, campaigned for that road for years. Andrews first visited Immokalee in 1906 and described it as a settlement of a few farms and groves with a school, a church and a store. But the observant editor recognized the potentialities of the place, and perhaps at his insistence the Koreshans took the first step to open a road. In 1906 they employed Steve Crews from Bonita Springs to cut the road at eight dollars a mile. His principal task was to blaze a trail along a route that would avoid all natural obstacles, removing only those trees and palmettos which he could find no way around. Later, Lee County threw up a sand grade and built some bridges, straightening the road somewhat in the process. But water washed out the roadbed and fire burned the bridges and the road was abandoned for many years. A road is now projected along the same route to open up the area between Corkscrew and Estero.

The lines of travel and trade did not flow to Estero. The residents of Immokalee wanted a road to the county seat at Fort Myers. In September 1909, the *American Eagle* reported that a Good Roads "Congress" was to meet at Immokalee on the 12th to try to find a way to improve the condition of roads to Fort Myers. At the time the "road" to Fort Myers was a sand trail easily followed in high places but branching into innumerable trails in the sloughs and low places as drivers sought firmer footing for their ox teams and heavy wagons.

Out of the conference came a public letter from Adolphus Carson in favor of bonding for county roads and a committee of four organized to secure support in all parts of the county. Perhaps as a result of these moves the county commissioners did appropriate $2,000 for the Immokalee road in 1910. But this was far from providing the needed road. The *Fort Myers Press* announced that the Immokalee road would be graded "so that it will permit a land trip during wet season, rather than the water voyage it has been in the years past." To be hard-surfaced later, it would meanwhile be a "good road except in the driest season."

Road-building was by no means a simple task. Ed Scott, referring to the effort, described the result in these graphic terms: "Enterprising county commissioners . . . advocated a road across the undrained sloughs and pine and cypress land intervening. They purchased a tractor and a huge grading machine. They felled the pine and cypress trees, dug the palmettoes, burned the stumps and generally cleared the right of way. The tractor and grader bogged down completely in a watery slough. Oxen hauled in timbers and excavated the machinery. Thereafter they built corduroy span over the bog. The first heavy rains washed out the fill across the slough, and floated off most of the corduroy timbers. So vehicles again took to the winding paths through the sand flats."

When it became a part of Collier County in 1923, Immokalee still did not have an adequate road to Fort Myers. Captain Bill Tolles had graded part of the trail in 1917 and a few miles were hard-surfaced, but when he died the project was dropped. In good weather it was usable, being corduroyed over low places and having bridges with frame made of logs and poles for cover. In wet weather it was necessary to travel by LaBelle and along the river.

Becoming a part of Collier County in 1923 did not immediately improve the situation of Immokalee's seventy-four citizens; rather it made it worse in one respect. To reach the new county seat at Everglades they still had first to go to the county seat of Lee County, Fort Myers, and thence by boat to Everglades, or they could drive south along a not so good road to Marco Island and continue from Caxambas by boat. Barron Collier and his associates were well aware of the importance of opening a direct route from Immokalee to Everglades. While pushing the completion of the Tamiami Trail, they made equally strenuous efforts to open a north-south road and to induce the ACL to extend its lines to the county seat town.

The two projects proceeded simultaneously and brought to Immokalee in late 1925 an already well known southwest Florida pioneer, Sam Thompson. Earlier, he had recruited Indian labor to clear the Everglades town-site of mangrove, rebuild the Deep Lake Railroad, help install the power plant and string the wires in part of the town Collier was building there.

Thompson came to Immokalee to tackle the problems of overland communication and transportation. Adolphus Carson was then stringing a telephone line from Fort Myers, mostly from tree to tree. Collier bought this, finished it, and tied it into the Fort Myers exchange which he later bought from the Heitmans. Carson got the first telephone in Immokalee, Charles Hadley the second, and Kennedy Carson the third, which served not only his meat market but his ranch eighteen miles away. When Carson left the market he switched the service to the ranch until his return.

Thompson's immediate business was to get a line through from Immokalee to Everglades. Though Everglades had local service, it had no outside connections until the line from Fort Myers with its long distance connections came through. With a crew of Indians, Thompson cut and set poles and strung the wire for the line. He had already set up a makeshift switchboard in his home to serve until a better one could be acquired and brought in. A venerable sage ready to discuss the early days in the new county, Thompson retired after thirty-two years with the Colliers and is now residing in Immokalee.

Of more interest to the citizens generally was the progress of road-building. A giant steam-powered dredge came by railroad to Immokalee in parts to be assembled there and put to work. Few believed that it would ever move a yard of dirt, but with its boom extended to one hundred and twenty-five feet it was soon moving southward, digging a drainage canal and building a highway and railroad grade in a single operation. The machine was so large that there were living quarters on top of it for the eight-man crew. A smaller dredge had already started from the south end and the two met near Miles City.

This did not solve the transportation problem, however, as it did not become a completely adequate highway until it was rebuilt and resurfaced a second time in 1955-1956. An equally good road to Naples is now under construction as are others to Fort Myers and LaBelle. This growing system of county and private roads is rapidly making Immokalee the hub of a wheel of roads leading in all directions, with a railroad to carry heavy and long distance freight.

Meanwhile, farming and ranching were beset by difficulties other than lack of transportation. Ranchers in particular, and farmers who kept livestock, suffered from depredations of wild animals. The *Fort Myers Press* reported in April of 1915 that C. B. Douglas,

Courtesy of the Collier Development Company.

Immokalee in 1957 looking east. Bob Roberts grove in foreground.

owner of a large ranch at Immokalee, had been in town organizing a party to assist him in destroying some of the bears and panthers of the Big Cypress that had lately been doing considerable damage to his young stock.

As late as 1953, panthers were reported as still numerous. They were killing deer, cattle and hogs. The State Conservation Department had approved a plan to hunt them and O. M. Harrison of the Department and J. R. Barnes, Collier and Lee County game warden, went along to see to it that only the declared objects of the hunt were molested. The party travelled on horseback and used dogs to locate the animals. The hunt was organized at Leesburg at the home of Dave Newell who had hunted panthers in Mexico and South America and owned a fine pack of dogs. It included Prentice Grey, another hunter and author, who came in by air from Guatemala to Miami to join the party. Vince and Ernest Lee came from Paradise, Arizona, and John McKeel from New Jersey. The hunting party rendezvoused at Fort Myers. The actual hunt began south of Immokalee, and Seminole Indians served as guides when the horses and ox carts left the beaten path.

Farmers and timber owners suffered also from cattlemen and hunters who fired the woods with resultant burning of rail fences around their fields as well as many trees. Hunters started the fires to drive out alligators or other game, while ranchers burned the range in the mistaken notion that the new grass thereby produced justified whatever destruction the fire wrought.

The Immokalee area is a graphic illustration of the conflict of interest between hunter, rancher and farmer, as well as that between civilization and the forces of nature. Farmers, if they come in sufficient numbers, spell the end of the open range cattle industry and severely limit the chances of the hunter. The hunter, be he Indian or White, sees a mortal enemy in both the others, and particularly the farmer. To the rancher the farmer's fences and the wild animals are equally a menace. As always where the land is fertile, the farmers have won the battle down to the rim of the Everglades and the Big Cypress. The open range cattle industry is no more. Many cattle are raised but under fencing and controlled conditions. Even in the Big Cypress country much of the higher land is surrounded by barbed wire within the confines of which cattle graze. Hunting lands have also become more and more restricted.

The railroad in 1921 and the highway developments in the next

Right to left: W. H. "Bill" Brown, Frank Brown, Sheriff Tippins of Lee County, Water Turkey, Billy Roberts, and John Bowman early in this century.

ten years resulted in progressively more rapid growth around Immokalee. Despite the conflict of interests, it has become a thriving center of ranching, farming, and lumbering. Little of this is obvious to one driving along the highway as most of the activity is far back from the road. Ranches are located south, east and southwest of the Corkscrew Island area. Farms extend ten miles west and south and thirty miles east to the edge of the Everglades.

C. A. Johnson, writing in the *Collier County News* of April 26, 1928, sang the praises of opportunity in the new place and recalled that, when he arrived in December of 1921, the ACL had just finished its tracks, section houses and depot. One and one-half miles west of the depot was an eight or ten family settlement. There were two small stores hauling their merchandise from Fort Myers. Mail came twice a week by Star Route from LaBelle. And Mr. Adolphus Carson was building a house near the depot. Johnson then cited his own experience to show how things had moved thereafter. On March 22 he had rented the building being erected by Carson, and had put in a $400 stock of general merchandise. At the time of writing he owned a hotel, a drug store, a barber shop, seven residence buildings, a garage, an electric power and light plant, and thirteen building lots. The land boom, he said, had come to but never left Immokalee. Bill Brown's store and the Manhattan Mercantile Corporation were also operating. Two years later Mr. Johnson might well have been somewhat less exuberantly optimistic.

Immokalee's pioneer families have witnessed many changes and are to see many more. The Browns, Whiddens, Robertses, Hadleys, Carsons, Thompsons and Crosses have watched an increasing number of newcomers play important roles, particularly in the newly burgeoning vegetable-growing industry.

Each winter a veritable horde of migrant workers descends upon the town, doubling its population and creating as yet unsolved problems of housing, sanitation, schools, morals and policing. These are but the growing pains of all such communities. Since 1949 there has been talk of incorporating the "town" and turning the task over to the city fathers. But the idea is repeatedly voted down, partly by pioneers who resent this invasion of their Eden which brings with it problems not of their own making. Immokalee citizens are organized after a fashion for fire protection but the absence of a central water service is a handicap. More recently its businessmen organized a Chamber of Commerce. So, the unincorporated community finds itself acting in some respects like a city. Meanwhile, Immokalee grows in every direction, and county, private and denominational agencies struggle with the new order and its potentialities and problems.

15

Thirty-Five Years Of Collier County

I N 1923, when the Florida Legislature met, Barron G. Collier was ready with a plan for the creation of a new county. In southern and eastern Lee County there was strong support for county making. There was some talk of a new county with Naples as the seat of local government, but interest had centered upon a proposal to create Hendry County with LaBelle as the county seat. No mention had been made of a county in southern Lee, but division had been an issue of the race for state representative in 1922. Robert A. Henderson, Sr., of Fort Myers favoring county division won the Democratic nomination over H. A. "Berry" Hendry by the narrow margin of 723 to 704.

The distribution of the vote reveals sharply divided opinions throughout the huge Lee County that was shortly to be divided into three units. Henderson lost Fort Myers by 173 to 319 but won Marco by 26 to 6, Immokalee by 21 to 6, LaBelle by 158 to 6, Naples by 61 to 6 but, interestingly enough, lost Caxambas by 21 to 1. Everglades showed little interest in the election, only ten votes being cast, 6 to 4 against the candidate supporting county division.

Residents of the Fort Myers area had led the movement that created Lee County in 1887. The community was beginning to grow. In 1884 it had its first newspapers; the next year it was incorporated. But the county seat of Monroe County was at faraway Key West where those who controlled county affairs knew little and cared less about the small settlements on the mainland. The

Fort Myers Press maintained that New York would be a more convenient county seat.

The reasons for dissatisfaction with Lee County in 1922 were now almost identically the same. The county was for practical purposes pretty much Fort Myers and its immediate environs. Residents of the southern end of the county were no closer to Fort Myers than they had been to Key West, and they had much closer commercial ties with the island city. But the principal grievance was the failure of Lee County to provide roads. Barron Collier argued that Fort Myers had isolated itself by refusing to open up the back country east and south. Local road and bridge districts had exhausted themselves financially and roadmaking had come to a dead halt. What good were Model T's if the roads were fit only for ox teams?

When a bill to create two new counties instead of one came before the legislature, it occasioned some surprise, but it won approval in the state capital and in the newly divided areas. The principal argument in favor of Collier County was the promise that Barron Collier would complete the unfinished work on the Tamiami Trail and construct roads between all the towns in the proposed county. His supporters also spoke of electric power plants, a boat line along the coast and, if necessary, a railroad, and talked about the possibilities of drainage. The vote in the Senate was 19 to 5 and in the House 53 to 27.

Opposition to the creation of the new county was partly sentimental. Lee County, named for the illustrious southerner of the same name, was said to be the largest county in the United States east of the Mississippi River, and feeling existed that it should be maintained as a memorial to the general. Actually, its size was another measure of the undeveloped character of the region.

As related elsewhere in this volume, Barron Collier and Collier County did move at once to accomplish the things that had been promised. That they did not all come to pass immediately was not altogether the fault of the man who promoted county making. The Florida depression followed by the national depression dried up the financial resources with which they were to have been accomplished.

And as he extended his operations northward to Tampa and eastward to Miami and the Palm Beaches and organized telephone, bus, boat and highway services for the whole southwest coast, most of his critics joined the chorus of general approval.

Only once was the management of county affairs by his associates seriously questioned. In 1927 the Lee Cypress Company, which owned the best of the cypress stand in the county, sued the Tax Collector and the County on the ground that it was being unfairly assessed and taxed. After seven years of litigation, the Cypress Company lost the case, the assumption being that if Collier had enough influence to secure tax favors he had instead allowed the assessment on his own lands to be raised at least as much.

The first Board of County Commissioners of the newly created Collier County met on the afternoon of July 7, 1923 in the annex of the Rod and Gun Club in Everglades. Four members of the Board, long established as leading citizens of the districts they represented, have appeared prominently in this narrative. They were George W. Storter, Jr., of Everglades who became chairman, James Madison Barfield of Caxambas, William D. Collier of Marco, and Adolphus Carson of Immokalee. The fifth member, Jack T. Taylor, manager of the Deep Lake Fruit Company, was the only newcomer to the county.

In most of the principal county offices the tenure has been long and the total number of holders of the position has been small. Only in District No. 1 has there been a large number of holders of the office of County Commissioner. George W. Storter, Jr., resigned after two years to become county judge. He was succeeded in turn by Fred Phillips, F. Irwin Holmes, F. C. Morgan, C. M. Collier, Jr., Joseph M. Bryan and E. B. Nichols. In October of 1942, the present chairman of the Board, J. M. Davidson, began his tenure of office.

In District No. 2, Taylor was succeeded by Barron Collier's brother, C. M. Collier, for a four-year period, after which he resigned to enter the state House of Representatives. F. Irwin Holmes then served only four months before he was succeeded by David Graham Copeland, who served until 1948 when he went to the state House of Representatives for a term. Winford Janes of Copeland has represented the district since that time.

In District No. 3, J. M. Barfield resigned because of ill health on December 7, 1942. His son-in-law, Robert A. "Grits" Griffis, was appointed to fill out the term and elected regularly to the post until 1956 when he chose not to be a candidate after the district lines were changed. R. H. "Dick" Goodlette of Naples now represents the district.

Courtesy of Mrs. D. W. McLeod, Everglades.

Daniel W. McLeod, the county's first and only tax assessor.

In District No. 4, W. D. Collier resigned after two years, after which J. H. Doxsee had a four-year term. William L. Clarke, Jr., of Naples then represented the people of the district until J. Lorenzo Walker succeeded him and held office until he resigned in 1956 to enter the state legislature. H. B. Watkins, Jr., now represents the district.

In District No. 5, Robert Roberts followed Adolphus Carson for a term and gave way to Graham W. Whidden four years later. D. C. "Doc" Brown was next elected to the office but resigned after a few months to accept a state office. Ewell W. Moore, the present incumbent, has held the office since.

D. Graham Copeland, serving from May 1929 to 1945, and J. M. Davidson, since 1945, have had the longest terms as Chairman of the Commissioners. Jack T. Taylor, C. M. Collier, and F. Irwin Holmes held the position only briefly.

Daniel W. McLeod, another newcomer, became the first tax assessor and has been regularly re-elected to the office since that time. He is also the only one of the original county officials now living. McLeod came from Arcadia, Florida, where he had an abstracting business which he has continued since coming to Everglades. Until recently only the Clerk of the Circuit Court, the Sheriff, and the Superintendent of Public Instruction have been full-time employees of the county, the others all supplementing the meager income of the county offices with business or other activity, and often leaving the details of the office to deputies or clerks.

The first Clerk of the Court was W. B. Lanier, a newcomer from Tampa, who remained only a year and was succeeded by E. W. Russell who died after eight years in the office. His son, J. W.

Russell, who had been deputy clerk, held the office for two months until Ed Scott, the present clerk, took over in May of 1932.

C. M. Collier was the new county's first tax collector. When he resigned after two years, John Henry Fears, then cashier of the Bank of Everglades, succeeded him in the office for part of a term, but resigned to go to LaBelle and later to Fort Myers. Charles H. Collier, a cousin of Barron Collier, was the third tax collector and served until 1953 when A. P. Ayers took office. Ayers is the first collector to operate the office himself. Mrs. Lucy I. McLeod had been deputy collector during all the years but one of the previous terms.

Captain W. R. Maynard was the first sheriff, holding the office until he resigned in April of 1928. Louis J. Thorp then became the chief law enforcement officer in the county until his death in 1954. His chief deputy, Roy O. Atkins, was appointed to serve until an election could be held, when he won a two-year term, but he lost to E. A. "Doug" Hendry in the 1956 election.

After one term as Superintendent of Public Instruction, Mrs. Tommie C. Barfield retired to membership on the Board, yielding the superintendency to Mrs. Wallace Alderman, who served only briefly. She was followed in turn by John Hinton, T. George Walker, Ernest Bridges, Ernest W. Hall, and the present holder of the post, W. D. Reynolds, who has held the office since 1953.

The first members of the Board of Public Instruction were Ira Hancock of Chokoloskee, J. Harvey Doxsee of Marco, and P. P. Schutt of Naples. The members of the Board at this time, their number being raised to five in 1947, are Clyde L. Clifton of Deep Lake, Mrs. Elva B. Griffis of Marco, W. M. Littlefield of Immokalee, C. L. Strandberg of Everglades who is the chairman, and Leo Chickering of Naples who replaced Mrs. Geraldine Smith of the same place upon her retirement after sixteen years on the Board. As related elsewhere, Mrs. Griffis has been a member of the Board since her mother, Mrs. Barfield, retired.

From the Rod and Gun Club the courthouse was moved to the Manhattan Mercantile Building, one of the first new buildings in Everglades. Then, for a short time, a small building directly across the street became headquarters for both the Bank of Everglades and the County Court House. The present courthouse, occupied since 1928, has been enlarged twice to accommodate increasing county business and personnel. In late 1956 and early 1957 it

This building housed the court house operations as well as the Bank of Everglades in the very early days of the county.

received a complete face-lifting and additional floor space, but not enough as some county offices are still housed in nearby buildings, and there are plans to establish branch county offices in Naples.

Since the late thirties, population in the county has grown at an increasing rate. The state census in 1925 fixed the number of residents at 1256, and the federal census in 1930 showed an increase to 2883. Five years later it was 4792, with only slight growth to 5082 in 1940. In 1950 the census takers counted 6488 inhabitants and the rapid increase since then has already more than doubled that figure.

The assessed value of property in 1923 was $1,653,360, the county debt $347,357.45, and the tax levy $125,296.42. As in all other counties in the booming twenties, Collier County's bonded debt grew faster than the value of property and capacity to pay taxes. This dilemma was due to the many financial needs of the new county for public buildings and roads. By 1929 the assessment had risen to $3,614,306 and the debt to $1,577,826.93, and the tax rate to 100½ mills.

Collier County bonds were never in default but one hundred dollar bonds did drop to less than fifty in 1931 and the county was nearest in its history to bankruptcy. But after that low point the financial picture improved steadily. Relief came first when the county began to benefit by new state legislation which provided for the distribution of the gasoline tax on a basis of area and miles of highway as well as gasoline sold in the county. Its share rose from a little over $15,000

Photo by George C. Trabant, St. Petersburg Times.

The County Court House at Everglades, 1957.

a year to more than $100,000 in each of the succeeding years. The county's share of the state racing tax has also increased steadily, easing the local tax burden.

Systematic efforts to put the county on a sound financial footing have characterized the years since 1929. The debt and the tax levy have been steadily reduced while the assessed value of property for tax purposes has been rising, reaching the ten million mark in 1943. In 1941 the bonded debt of the county was down to $385,899.40 and a tax levy of only 5.8 mills sufficed to cover the county budget.

In 1946 and 1947 the county's citizens were in the enviable position of paying no taxes whatever as the county's share in such resources as the racing and gasoline taxes yielded more than the county budgeted. In response to the needs of a rapidly growing population and the demands for services, the county tax rate in recent years has increased moderately as has the bonded debt. The assessment for tax purposes in 1956 was $24,627,561 and the tax rate 30 mills. But Collier County is still considered to be a model in financial matters.

The county fathers may have overreached themselves when they refused to ask for any Federal aid during the depression. They chose instead the commendable slogan and policy "Collier County takes care of its own," and pointed to the small number of unemployed in the county. But in so doing the county lost what might have been worthwhile relief projects, though the county commissioners were always careful to point out that these economies and efficiencies were achieved without depriving citizens of any essential social services.

In an effort to improve the management of county business, the Board of Commissioners made Ed Scott an unofficial county manager. As the elected Clerk of the Circuit Court, Scott is by law the ex-officio clerk to the commissioners. He is without any authority except that given him by the commissioners, and he may plan and recommend only. The strength of his position derives largely from the fact that he is a full-time employee of the county, and that he thinks and plans county-wide. His duties, according to the commissioners, are "to generally coordinate the functions of the various public offices, with a view toward attaining cooperation between the several offices and the Board in the management and operation of county government."

In this capacity Scott may be called the head of the planning department. He determines the needs of the county, prepares the budget, and makes recommendations to the Board. One of his first assignments was to make a survey of the county's financial obligations and recommend ways and means to get the county out of debt. He is also the official spokesman of the Board in dealings with the State administration and with the State Road Board. He and others from the county have been active organizers and supporters of the small (in population) county bloc in the Florida Legislature which has been responsible for such financial bonanzas as equal distribution among the counties of the revenue from the state racing tax.

The informal arrangement has worked very well, but it depends entirely upon the willingness of those involved to work together. Few men know Collier County as does Ed Scott, and the county might not find another clerk who could double as chief executive assistant of the Board. Perhaps that is the reason that there has been no move to formalize the arrangement or to adopt the county manager plan of government.

County officials in 1926 attacked the problem of surveying lands and properties in the county, which until then were not much more than half com-

Ed Scott in Circuit Court Clerk's Office he has held since 1932.

pleted. This work was necessary both to get the lands on the tax rolls and to prepare the way to bring in settlers who might wish to buy the land. In May and June of 1926 the Wallace Engineering Company resurveyed the line between Collier and Monroe counties, camping at Ted Smallwood's store on Chokoloskee Island while they worked at it. Local legend has it that the men who surveyed the line between Monroe and Lee counties a generation earlier had sat in a camp at the head of Turner River and run a fictitious line, naming the physical features that did not even exist. If true, it had made no difference in the intervening years when the line was unoccupied and the matter of taxes unimportant.

In 1928, recognizing that much of the interior could not immediately be reached by surveyors, the county had a mammoth aerial survey made, on which it based a map. Captain W. R. Maynard, then sheriff of the county, did the job. He served in the flying corps in World War I. Flying a specially equipped Curtiss "Oriole" Maynard shot 4400 feet of film from an altitude of 10,000 feet, covering eighty townships and 2880 square miles. The map, put together by experts from the Army War College in Washington, D.C.,

Courtesy of Mrs. M. K Ashworth, Ventura, Calif.
Home of Ed Watson on Chatham River about 1917. Only a part of the dwelling remains.

was eighteen feet square, being scaled to three and three-eighths inches to the mile. In 1947, the county published a remarkable topographical map of the county's area under the direction of engineer David Graham Copeland. It included so much historical data that the *Florida Historical Quarterly* carried a review such as is usually written only for books. Aerial timber cruises coordinated with ground work were employed in the appraisal of timber lands of the Lee Tidewater Cypress Company, both for litigation with the county and for a loan from the R.F.C.

Law enforcement in Collier County has posed some difficult problems. Before the establishment of the new county brought the institutions of government and law to the area, the citizens had by necessity been compelled to make and enforce their own law. Key West and Fort Myers were a day's journey away and relatively uninterested in what the scattered population around the Ten Thousand Islands might do. The remote region, of course, attracted refugees from law and order who had enraged citizenry in other places. One is amazed at the references of violence in the reminiscences of old Ted Smallwood, himself a mild, peaceful and law-abiding man.

The most famous of the local renegades was Ed Watson, who farmed on a shell mound near the mouth of the Chatham River just below the line in Monroe County. There are many versions of the Watson story, but even his friends conceded that he had a penchant for trouble. He reputedly gathered other bad men around him, and paid them off with death rather than the promised wages; nor were they always bad men. In 1910 a gathering of men at Smallwood's dock on Chokoloskee Island shot Watson when he appeared with gun in hand, gave his version of goings-on at Chatham Bend, and apparently challenged any who doubted him.

In 1915 four men reasonably well known on the southwest coast, and of generally good reputation, robbed the bank at Homestead and fled to the swamps east of Chokoloskee. One of them, Leland Rice, went to the island for supplies, and was shot resisting arrest. His brother Frank swam out to the island to discover what had happened. On learning Leland had been killed and the money taken out to a fish boat, Frank went out to the boat, was shot as he came aboard, and fell back into the water. He was rescued and held for authorities. A third member of the robber gang, known only as Tucker, drowned in an effort to swim to the island in search of the Rice brothers. The fourth member, Hugh Alderman, made his way around the shore to Turner River where he gave himself up and asked to be taken to Fort Myers to the sheriff. He and Frank Rice, who recovered from his wounds sufficiently to stand trial, were given long prison terms.

Legend added fiction to fact and made good stories. A law enforcement officer at Key West got his job on a promise to bring in a law breaker whose description sounds suspiciously like Ed Watson of Chatham Bend. Gone a month on the man hunt, he returned without a prisoner and it soon became known that he had been forced to work that month in the cane fields of the man he sought to arrest. And there was the even more fantastic story of the Hermit of the Ten Thousand Islands who had a hideaway, complete with slaves and a harem of beautiful women, and who occasionally brought to his place an unsuspecting wayfarer to satisfy his hunger for the company of another white man.

Though there was less of violence in the new county, the problems of enforcement of law were numerous. These grew chiefly out of efforts to enforce the laws prohibiting the sale of liquor and protecting wildlife. The many channels and passes among the islands made it an ideal place for rum runners to operate. One hears of a boat builder in a respected family who developed a fast shallow draft type of craft with which to bring in the cargo from larger vessels beyond the twelve-mile limit. There are also tales of boats wrecked and cargo scattered to be collected by thirsty natives who preferred it to the local brands of moonshine described by Charles G. McKinney as unusually deadly in their effects. It is easy enough now to hear the names of the violators who reputedly reaped huge profits, but arrests at the time were rare indeed. Nature and human nature in the region favored the rum runner and afforded him protection.

The same combination has made the enforcement of game laws difficult. Old timers and some newcomers were long accustomed to hunt and fish where and when they willed. It must be said in their defense that they killed only for food or for sale and never, like some sportsmen, merely to kill. They have tended to look upon game laws as unwarranted interference with their inalienable natural right to use what nature provides. The area is enormous, and much of it is without any means of direct access, so that even spotting from the air has not made it possible to catch offenders with the goods. An uneasy truce exists between them and the law, and any one of them who becomes a wildlife officer is likely to be looked upon with suspicion.

For a time Collier County had a unique agency in the Southwest Florida Mounted Police, whose role was nowhere near as colorful as the title suggests. At ten-mile intervals along the Tamiami Trail, Barron Collier built stations at which travelers could buy gasoline and food and drink. The proprietors, deputized by the county sheriff, doubled as police and once each hour mounted their motorcycles and patrolled the road, riding each way to check with the rider from the next station. In November of 1928 the *Collier County News* listed James Laury at Belle Meade, J. A. Pike at Royal Palm Hammock, S. M. Weaver at Fakahatchee or old shell camp, Charles B. Waltz at Turner's River, William Irwin at Monroe, and E. T. Bayman at Paolita on the county line. D. Graham Copeland, also a deputy sheriff, was in charge of the project.

Their function was not so much to arrest lawbreakers as to aid motorists in difficulty. Their distinctive uniform and the name gave them some prominence, but the idea was dropped along with many others when the Great Depression dried up the sources and taste for such frills. Some of the early stations are still operated on the same sites.

Collier County's problems today arise principally from a growing population and an expanding economy in a still relatively undeveloped area. Roads, streets, utilities, schools, law enforcement, public health, social services, water supply and water control all require planning and foresight as well as money. The example of school needs points this up sharply. Early in 1957 the School Board estimated that it

218

would require $2,800,000 for the next five years. The 2506 pupils enrolled that year was up 21.52% over the previous year which had shown an increase of 18.79%. A comparable increase for the next five years would require 124 new classrooms, 124 new teachers and twelve new buses with drivers. The county's history to this time gives promise that the issues will be faced and the money provided so that the plans may be executed.

16

Tamiami Trail:
Collier County Life Line

LOCAL ROADBUILDING PROJECTS and plans for long distance highways to the North and East got under way at about the same time in Collier County. By 1915 hopes for a long distance road northward to Tampa along the Gulf Coast and across the Everglades to Miami were centered in the proposed Tamiami Trail. Such a road would leave only Immokalee and Chokoloskee off its route since plans included a spur which would reach the channel separating Marco Island from the mainland and the town of Everglade was only four miles south of the route.

In the generation since the beginning of modern day settlement literally no steps had been taken to open up the interior by improved roads. From Fort Myers sand trails fanned out in easterly and southeasterly directions to lose themselves in the vast uninhabited wilderness. A sand trail from Naples to Fort Myers was usable in good weather, and a narrow winding road southward to Marco Pass was open at times, but travel was pretty much limited to water courses and led always toward the sea. The widely scattered settlements, the small populations, and the undeveloped economy together with formidable problems of construction precluded any effort being made.

Who first conceived the idea of the Tamiami Trail is not likely ever to be known. Certainly it was expressed by several people at about the beginning of World War I. Dr. John C. Gifford of Miami,

Hard rock made Trail building slow and expensive.

whose fertile imagination was quick to recognize the potentialities of the region, gave early if not first written expression to the idea. Writing in *Tropic Magazine* for July 1914, he said in part: "According to many reports Chokoloskee Bay on the west coast has a great future. A city will in time develop there . . . There is rock all the way. There is a good hard bottom to build on and material can be quarried here and there along the whole route . . . It seems to the writer that a road across the state would do more good than a road along the canal to Okeechobee. The canal affords ample transportation northwards . . ."

Reference to the alternate route suggests that the proposition of a cross state road was already being widely discussed. In 1914 plans for the Dixie Highway to be extended southward from Jacksonville down the east coast to Miami stirred interest in a "loop road" across the lower peninsula to connect with a west coast branch of the same highway. Newspapers on both sides of the peninsula gave wide publicity to the idea.

J. F. Jaudon, tax assessor of Dade County, was the most active promoter of the Tamiami Trail route at a good roads meeting in Orlando in 1915, one of the first such meetings in the state. It was E. P. Dickey who formally suggested the name of "Tamiami Trail" at this first meeting of the State Road Department. The name was such a natural that it was almost immediately accepted. The *American Eagle* at first objected that it sounded "like a bunch of tin cans tied to a dog's tail and clattering over cobblestones," and queried, "Why not call the Jacksonville to Miami Dixie Highway 'Jackiami Joypath' and the road through Arcadia to the east coast 'Pair-O-Dice Loop'?"

Consideration of the location of the proposed highway was to produce considerable rivalry among real estate groups as well as among the several communities that might be touched by the magic of the new road. Some interests supported a suggested route from Fort Myers to Immokalee, from there to Sam Jones' Old Town or possibly Brown's Landing on the western rim of the Everglades, on by way of LaBelle eastward to the Miami Canal, and then along the canal to Miami. The other route, approximating the one finally followed, received more support from all points on the west coast south of Fort Myers and from most Miami interests. As most of Lee County's citizens lived in the Caloosahatchee valley they favored the more northerly route. Only eight or nine hundred persons resided in the district from Fort Myers to Marco, and there was not a white man living along the route from Marco to the Dade County line.

The problem of financing the construction of the Trail made all others appear insignificant by contrast. As it turned out, the road through the areas least developed and least able to pay proved most difficult and expensive to construct. All early discussion exhibited more enthusiasm than realism and certainly plans were based on a blissful ignorance of what was to be involved. It must be conceded, however, that standards of highway construction had not then been established, much of the proposed route had not been surveyed, and only experience would reveal the difficulties.

Meanwhile each community voted itself a Road and Bridge District and bonded itself to finance roadbuilding. This might have proved adequate in fully developed areas where property values were higher. But even when the districts south of Fort Myers bonded themselves to the limit, the funds thereby raised proved only enough to start the work. The distance from Marco to Miami was nearly a hundred miles, almost completely uninhabited.

However naive it may appear at this distance in time, initial steps for construction were taken in 1915. In May Road and Bridge District #1, representing the area from Fort Myers to Marco, bonded itself for $177,500 to acquire a fifty foot right of way for building a hard surfaced road from Fort Myers to Naples and a graded road from Naples to Marco. Later in the same year the

Everglades section provided $125,000 for their segment of the Trail from Marco to the Dade County line. And in 1916 Dade County voted $175,000 to build the road from the county line to Miami.

It immediately became clear that an approach from Naples to Marco involved some difficult and expensive construction problems. It had been necessary to assure citizens of Marco that they would be served by the road since they had to be induced to approve the bond issue. But the route at first proposed, down the beach from Naples, crossing Gordon's Pass, New Pass, Little Marco and on down to Big Marco Pass, had to be abandoned. All interests agreed that the new road must be located further inland, and should turn east across the peninsula before reaching as far south as the island. The islanders would reach the Trail by a short spur.

In 1915 and 1916 the several Road and Bridge Districts began hopefully, one might almost say naively, the task of building their segments of the Tamiami Trail. Nobody dreamed at the time that a war would intervene to raise the cost of labor and materials, that Florida would experience a "boom and bust," that a new county would be born, and that thirteen years would pass before the road would be declared finished. Nor did the pioneer builders foresee the engineering and financial difficulties that would multiply the cost by many times the original estimate.

Standing in the trees to the right of the road entering the Barron G. Collier Memorial Park is the skeleton framework of the old Monegan walking dredge which started the work of throwing up a sand grade east of Marco Junction. The steel beam structure weighed nearly twenty tons and had a dipper capacity of one cubic yard. It straddled the canal and ran on its own track of steel rails. The tracks were twenty-nine feet apart, making possible a canal source of fill twenty-four feet wide and twelve feet deep.

There was little rock to contend with in this part of the road but swampy areas posed serious problems. Captain K. B. Harvey, in charge of the operation, described the work in the *American Eagle* of November 30, 1916, as follows: "We began cutting through the swamp, dumping the mass of marl and sand, etc., to one side. This dump is leveled down to grade and surfaced by hand with big heavy hoes and rakes. Through Williams Island Jungle, which is truly jungle in every sense of the word—a mass of trees of all kinds and sizes, thousands of switches, poles, brush, ferns all woven together

223

with bamboo, rattan and vines. Perhaps several hundred would be chopped off at the ground before the mass would fall, so that it could be chipped apart with brush axes."

In another instance he related: "It was scrub and mangrove and grass muck. Think of leaves on the trees shaking and trembling and the whole mass of muck and sand for hundreds of feet in each direction quivering and shaking like a mass of jelly with each vibration of the dredge engine. Then think of putting a 40,000 pound engine across it . . . with muck and marl twelve feet deep and chancing the slightest mistake or error of judgement would make a buried and tangled wreck of 40,000 pounds of steel and machinery . . . (we) tried plank and log cribbing but this was too uncertain and treacherous."

Finally brush mats piled up four feet high, with the track laid on them proved most practicable for the machine to travel over. Even so, the mats often worked down into the mud until the track layers had to fish to their shoulders in the mud to retrieve the rails and cross ties.

On September 6, 1917, A. H. Andrews of the *American Eagle* set out to walk from Naples to Marco along the right of way. He described the condition of the roadbed and the sixteen bridges north of Henderson Creek which was crossed by a high wooden bridge. It seemed to him that this part of the road could never withstand the pressure of water that was washing out parts of it. Across Henderson Creek where the tides controlled the water level, such drainage was less apparent.

In the Spring of 1921 Charles Torrey Simpson described a trip on the mail bus from Fort Myers to Caxambas. He declared that on the lower end of the route the track had been cut only wide enough for passage of one car and commented, "In all my life I have never seen a narrower or more zigzag road. Deep ruts change direction about at right angles. The ferry to Marco was just barely large enough for one car with not an inch to spare."

By that date work on the Lee County end of the Trail had stopped. The contractor had given up in 1918 and the county had taken over the work but for lack of funds the tired old dredge had come to a final stop several miles west of Carnestown at the end of a road that led nowhere and was aptly described as two ruts on a slight elevation. Much had been learned by experience, but the financial resources of the thinly populated and undeveloped area had long since been exhausted. The grand design of a road across the peninsula was sound enough, but the planning and execution had fallen far short.

Perhaps it was too early in the automobile age for road builders of the horse and buggy era to realize what the requirements of heavy and fast travel would be. The road bed was too narrow and too low and the hard surfacing of limestone rock topped with shell would not withstand the wear imposed by heavy traffic. Bridges were too few and too narrow to handle either the flow of water beneath or the flow of traffic over them.

But the idea of completing the Trail was nowhere given up and demands grew that broader financing by county-wide or state aid get the work going again. In the summer of 1921 George W. Storter, Jr., of Everglades and J. F. Jaudon walked over the unfinished portion of the Trail along a route for a temporary road they hoped could be made usable by January of 1923. They started out on Saturday afternoon, July 30, and worked their way to Turner River. Sunday they continued in an easterly direction, camping Sunday night in about the southeastern corner of Lee County after covering twenty-five miles. Monday they struck an Indian trail and went to the camp of two Seminoles, Captain Tony and Billie Buck, where they found magnificent crops of sugar cane, oranges, bananas, grapefruit, lemons, limes, corn, peppers and sweet potatoes. From this point they proceeded southward hoping to intersect the line of a survey crew, but missed it and finally made camp five or six miles south of the Lee County line. On Tuesday, their fourth day out, they made slow progress over rocky prairie and saw grass sloughs to a point on the Trail about thirty-five miles west of Miami, and walked along the survey line to the dredge on the Dade County end of the Trail. Operations were shut down but they reached the camp of Argyle Henry where they spent the night and on Wednesday completed the trip by auto. They concluded that distance between the dredges could be reduced to twenty miles and a temporary road built by winter of 1922.

In the spring of 1923 the "Trail Blazers," a self-styled group of promoters of the Trail, made a dramatic effort to revive interest in finishing the Trail. They attempted to navigate by automobile the thirty-five or forty mile gap between the Dade and Lee County ends of the Trail, following the route Storter and Jaudon had laid out two years previously. Jaudon warned that the most difficult part might be a tidal marsh of two miles between the terminus of the Lee County road and the Deep Lake Railroad. W. Stanley Hanson of Fort Myers and two others made a reconnaissance of the area two weeks in advance and were able to walk through dry shod. They believed that Ford cars could make it if the wheels were roped.

With two Indians to guide them through the unmarked cypress strands, the "Trail Blazers" left Fort Myers on April 4, with seven cars and picked up three more along the route southward. All but two were Fords. The twenty-six men lunched at Royal Palm Hammock and then moved eastward on a road grade so overgrown with tall grass, weeds and bushes that the car ahead could not be seen. They found a dozen washouts to be bridged, filled, or detoured and found frequent use for the heavy planking they carried with them. One mile before the end of the grade George Dunham's car quit. It needed a new engine.

The first night out they made camp at the end of the grade, about two miles west of the point where the road was to cross the Deep Lake Railway. Some high tides had lately made the marshy two miles much wetter than they had expected. Two scouting parties set out on the second day, one to cruise out a feasible route to higher ground, the other to walk to Everglades, a distance of seven or eight miles, for advice, gas, oil, food and other supplies. A. H. Andrews and two others set out for Carnestown, a lone warehouse where the highway now crosses the railroad, and walked the cross ties into Everglades where they met George W. Storter, Jr., who proposed that the small Caterpillar tractor at a logging camp up the railroad be used to get the cars across the marsh. They then returned to Carnestown by railroad.

Several of the cars had made the plunge from the grade into the mud and by keeping to the tall grass had made a half mile or so before bogging down. The others were soon scattered over a wide area where they remained until the tractor arrived to round up and haul seven of them to fairly firm ground by nightfall, leaving two still some distance in the rear. They camped Thursday night a mile or more west of the railroad, broke camp early Friday and with much lifting and pushing reached the railway grade toward noon where the train from Everglades met them with gas, oil and provisions. After bridging the ditches with cross ties, all but four accepted the invitation to spend the night at the Collier Hotel. The four remained to assist Giles and Smith in raising Mr. Giles' 3200 pound Elcar out of an open slough where the tractor was already bogged down in the effort. The big car was left in the bog, however, its owner being told the party could not wait for him. The Collier Company later agreed to send the tractor, an operator, and men and equipment to put the Elcar back up on the grade, headed back westward.

The party on its fourth day out headed southeastward across open marl prairie to the camp of Abraham Lincoln, one of the Indian guides. For several miles they were able to follow an Indian oxtrail by cutting some stumps, though one car smashed a wheel and was abandoned. On Sunday, the fifth day, they were off again, men and baggage for ten cars now in seven Fords. After four miles they encountered Gator Hook Cypress strand or Rockwell strand and much black muck.

They corduroyed more than half way through with sticks, branches and cabbage palm leaves and made three miles in the afternoon across open marl prairie to another cypress strand, beyond which they found a survey stake of the Trail and three more miles across open prairie.

On Monday, the sixth day out, they proceeded several miles before sending out scouts to find a way through the cypress, there being no more Indian trails to follow. They were soon hewing their way into Garnett Cypress Strand in which they stayed all night and finished cutting their way out on Tuesday, the seventh day. That night they stopped at the entrance of Roberts Lake Strand, a most formidable two-and-one-half miles wide.

On Wednesday morning, the first day of the second week out they discovered blazed trees and surveyor's stakes on the Trail right of way in northeast Monroe County. They sent a guide and two members of the party ahead on foot to Miami where they were to report to anxious families and forward gas and food to the main party not yet out of the woods. The advance guard reached the edge of the grade late that day and were in Miami by one o'clock Thursday afternoon. Meanwhile those left behind cut their way one mile into the cypress and camped there for the night. After supper Porter Richards came in from Everglades and reported Joe Taylor and Mr. Giles at the edge of the cypress about a mile back having progressed that far with the Elcar which Giles was determined should go all the way with the Fords, though it be escorted by two tractors, one of which had broken down.

Shortly before noon Thursday they got out of the cypress where they met a rescuing party bringing gasoline and other supplies on a stripped down Ford truck with dual wheels. That night they camped five miles short of the dredge at the Dade end of the Trail, with two cars in camp and five scattered behind in the swamp waiting for the tractor to provide assistance in getting out. By 3:15 p.m. Friday all cars were in camp but they decided to stay the night at that point, and at 5:25 Mr. Giles arrived, nearly famished, his Elcar still twelve miles back.

Saturday morning, the eleventh day out, they tackled the last five miles of swamp on foot while the tractor rounded up the cars at a spot three and one-half miles from the dredge where they remained until the following week. The men walked to the road's end and thence to Miami on the eastern end of the Trail. What they had proved was not too encouraging, but they made national publicity for the uncompleted trail and for Model "T" Fords.

Having tied his fortune to this area, Barron Collier required the completion of the Tamiami Trail for his purposes. The new county had been created partly on his promise to complete the project that had now been at a standstill for four years. How much of the credit should be given to Collier for the completion is a matter of some difference of opinion. The possibility of local road and bridge district financing was already exhausted. County-wide, or state, or federal financing were already being argued as the only feasible means to raise such sums.

Meanwhile, Collier County undertook to go ahead with the work, bonding itself for $350,000 in 1924. It was Barron Collier's backing that gave the county most of whatever credit it now had. John W. Martin was elected governor of Florida on a platform promise to complete the work of Trail building, but before that promise could be redeemed the proceeds of the bond issue were swallowed up and there was the usual resort to time warrants which Collier picked up as needed. It was not until August of 1926 that the state road department took over and finished the last twelve most difficult miles. At the same time the state also took over the work from Naples to the Lee County line.

The base of operations was set up at Everglades, the county seat and center of Collier's activities, which was conveniently located on a waterway just four miles south of the Trail. A newly organized construction firm, Alexander, Ramsay and Kerr, began operations in October, 1923, with a one-yard Marion floating steam dredge

*Marion Floating Dredge builds highway and railroad bed on Immokalee
Road, floating in canal it digs. Service road alongside used to move fuel,
dynamite and supplies to blasting crew ahead.*

starting from the point of crossing at the Deep Lake Railway and
working westward to where the old Monegan dredge had come to
rest some four years earlier.

This was purely a dredging proposition, throwing up a sand base
thirty feet wide and about four feet high. On this a lime rock
wearing surface nineteen feet wide and compacted to eight inches in
thickness was laid. This involved regrading and finishing much of
the old narrow, low grade thrown up earlier.

In January of 1924 a one-yard Bay City crawler type dredge
started east from Carnestown headed for the Dade County line along
the route followed roughly by the Trail Blazers a few months before.
How difficult this part of the road work was to be nobody at the time
guessed. Within two miles of Carnestown the soil formation was
largely sand and could easily be scooped up by dredges, the most
difficult problem arising from mud and water in swamps. But from
that point to the Dade County line (and in Dade also) the road-
builders encountered rock that required extensive blasting operations
and they were soon purchasing dynamite by the car load.

229

Oxen haul dynamite to blasting crews on Trail.

C. G. Washbon, supervising engineer, has told of the all out attack on these natural obstacles that were to require nearly five years to overcome. He described the terrain as largely saw grass prairie covered with muck eight inches to four feet deep, underlaid with sedimentary lime rock in two strata, under which was a stratum of marl, sand and shell from twelve inches to three feet thick. Under that the harder rock averaged three feet thick. The way was largely through scrub cypress growth but also crossed cypress strands and water courses in large numbers.

Transportation requirements on the project were staggering. A weekly boat service from Everglades to Fort Myers and Tampa brought in machinery and supplies. A tugboat and seagoing barge handled dynamite and other large shipments. A tanker with a capacity of 10,000 gallons made weekly trips to supply the 1200 gallons of gasoline burned in daily operations. All supplies were loaded on barges and floated to the dredges. From that point they were hauled to blasting and drilling crews by ox cart.

Two teams of oxen, each with three yokes, drivers and helpers, were attached to the drilling and blasting crews to haul the gasoline and dynamite ahead to them. No less than forty oxen were available at all times. Only on the last two miles was the muck and water so deep that boats pushed by men were required for the moving.

The need for vast quantities of lumber for bridges and buildings led to the establishment of a saw mill, not by any means the first in the area, but the first since the founding of the new county. It

Courtesy of the Collier Development Company.
Workmen lived on the job building the Tamiami Trail in Collier County.

was first located at Port DuPont but the need for lumber on the Trail induced a move out on the Trail a mile east of Turner River. When high water and an inadequate timber supply made this site unsatisfactory, the mill was relocated two miles north of Carnestown. The logging camp at the head of an extensive strand of pine was connected to the mill by a logging road eleven miles long. The log train, drawn by locomotives of a converted Fordson tractor with a standard railroad driving gear design, averaged three carloads a day to the mill, which had a capacity of 10,000 feet.

To maintain equipment a large warehouse and magazine at Carnestown stocked twenty thousand dollars worth of spare parts for all machines. For emergency repairs not covered by spare parts, machinists and blacksmiths at shops in Everglades stood ready to make them. Ordering parts from distant sources of supply was a disastrously slow business. All phases of the operation kept in close contact with the central office by telephone, lines being strung as the operation moved forward.

To care for the crews the company maintained three messes on the east section with portable bunk houses and kitchens and one mess for the sixteen men working on the west end. A hospital with a doctor and a trained nurse at Everglades looked after the health of the men who were given a medical examination and typhoid shots when they were hired. For recreation there was a pool room and bowling alley at Port DuPont, open evenings and Sundays, and motion pictures, usually followed by a dance, twice a week in the clubhouse at Everglades.

The Trail was officially opened with ceremonies at Fort Myers on April 25, 1928, nearly thirteen years after the first shovel of dirt was turned. On the following day a gala celebration at Everglades marked the event with a county fair and an invitation to all Seminoles to assemble there for the occasion.

The completion of the Trail, together with a north-south road from Everglades to Immokalee, provided the new county with the economic life line necessary for opening up the interior. Since then, roads from the Trail to Marco Island and to Chokoloskee Island, from Immokalee to Fort Myers and from Immokalee toward Naples have been added to provide the county with its trunk line highways.

17

Pioneer Economy:
Living Close To Nature

EARLY SETTLERS in Collier County earned a livelihood in ways more varied and quite different from those of more recent days. The transition from old to new ways came in the nineteen twenties when roads and railroads began to open up the interior of the Florida peninsula.

The earlier life was more self-sufficient and the techniques comparatively primitive, being in large measure the gathering of what nature provided. The principal investment was the labor usually supplied by members of the family without benefit of many mechanical aids. A bountiful nature afforded the first two generations of white residents a varied if somewhat limited way of life, most aspects of which have ceased to exist.

As indicated in the accounts of early settlement in preceding chapters, the newcomers found life easiest in the same areas that Indians before them had found attractive. This was largely in coastal areas reached by water only, where abundant wild life was close at hand. White settlement did not at first involve the displacement of any occupants as the Calusa had long since departed and the Seminoles lived mostly in the interior.

It is noteworthy that the first permanent settlers came as farmers. Hunters and fishermen had preceded them, but they came and went without establishing anything more than temporary camps. It is also remarkable that, where early settlers grew so many fruits and vegetables, there is today scarcely a vegetable garden or a fruit tree, the farming activities having since passed to more favored areas. Visitors to Chokoloskee Island, Marco Island, Turner River, Half-Way Creek or Everglades will find it hard to believe that they once were relatively prosperous agricultural communities.

These first farmers were usually squatters on the land they tilled. They settled wherever they found the soil sufficiently fertile and high above sea level. Hence they found the shell islands in the Ten Thousand group most attractive. On the nearby mainland they found shellmounds, high hammocks and long and narrow ridges along the rivers excellent places to plant their crops. This was particularly true from Gordon's Pass at Naples on down the coast at Henderson Creek, Little Marco, Big Marco, Royal Palm Creek, Allen's (now Barron) River, Half-Way Creek, Turner River, Lopez River, and further down the coast to Chatham River and other points south of Collier County all the way to Cape Sable. Only at Immokalee was there any farming in the interior, except the little around Indian camps, and it was almost exclusively for local use as there was no way out to market.

In the coastal and island settlements, farming had large commercial importance almost from the beginning. The market was Key West, a rapidly growing community that produced almost none of its food. Its population grew from two thousand in 1850 to near ten thousand in 1880 and to almost eighteen thousand ten years later. By the end of the century, some of the produce was also finding its way to the New York market from Key West by way of the Mallory Line steamers. After 1904 some of it went by boat to Fort Myers, then north by railroad.

The method of soil analysis was simple and primitive, but effective. Heavy natural vegetation attested its fertility and, if the soil was not salty to the taste, it promised good crops. Commercial fertilizers were almost unknown, though farmers did sometimes move in rich muck to fertilize trees or small areas. When the original fertility was gone, the land was abandoned until nature restored it. Modern farms, by contrast, have been called hydroponic tanks without bottoms, in which any native fertility is supplemented with chemicals.

On the lower lands there was always danger that storms or hurricanes might inundate them with salt water which killed most of the growing crops and salted the soil until rains leached out the salt. This was not all loss, however, as the floods often left an enriching

Pineapple plantation on the sand hills of Caxambas about 1900.

deposit of silt. The 1910 hurricane left such a layer a foot deep at places along the river where Everglades now stands. This may account for the fact that the Storter brothers could grow sugar cane there for twenty years without replanting and without fertilizer.

There was a considerable amount of local specialization in crops. Tomatoes grew best on the shell mounds and were the most important money crops. On the heavier bottom lands, sugar cane was the most common and profitable crop, notably at Everglades, Half-Way Creek and Chatham River. The cane might be made into syrup or sold by the stalk in Key West. Cane chewing is familiar to every Florida Cracker for every farm had at least a small cane patch. In chewing, the joint of cane is peeled and cut into convenient sized blocks for putting into the mouth to press the juice from it. Many a Cracker has waited expectantly for the inevitable Yankee question, "How long must I chew this before swallowing it?", whereupon he is told merely to spit out the fiber.

Less important but quite common vegetables, both for table use and for market, were beans, cabbage, cucumbers, eggplant, melons, okra, onions, peas, peppers, potatoes and pumpkins. All these vegetables grew along the coast or river banks, on hammock and island, but in greater extent and abundance in the lower part of the county. By contrast, they are now concentrated in the upper interior part of the county.

The following list of produce sent by Adolphus Santini from Chokoloskee Island to Key West in 1880 is probably incomplete

235

but it gives some measure of both variety and price.

Jan.	19	300 & 20 cabbages shipped per "Laura" .... net $	7.00
Feb.	2	243 cabbages & 500 cane per "Fanny" .... net	30.90
Feb.	12	453 cabbages 160 cane per "Fanny" .... net	35.93
March	9	418 cabbages 5 pumpkins per "Fanny" ..... net	29.41
April	14	65 cabbages 5 pumpkins per "Fanny" ..... net	2.03
May	13	403 cabbages 4 sacks potatoes	
		3 bunches bananas per "Fanny" .... net	19.50
June	12	638 cabbages 28 chickens	
		25 melons 1 lot peppers per "Fanny" .... net	25.07
July	8	117 cabbages 190 melons .... net	26.11
Aug.	6	22 melons 3 B. bananas	
		12 egg plants shipped per "Laura" .... net	2.22
Sept.	6	300 cane 5 B. bananas	
		48 egg plants shipped per "Fanny" .... net	14.16
Oct.	13	32 egg plants 1 lot peppers .... net	2.19
Oct.	19	13 pumpkins per "Laura"	
		500 cane per "Laura" .... net	5.04
Nov.	19	298 cane 37 pumpkins	
		44 egg plants per "Fanny" .... net	4.18
Dec.	4	576 cane & peppers 1 lot .... net	14.67
Sept.	20	400 cane 40 egg plants per "Laura" .... net	6.36
June	29	374 cabbages	
		2 B. bananas 60 melons per "Laura" ...... net	13.42
July	21	50 melons 1 B. bananas	4.02
Aug.	2	173 melons 17 cabbages	
		4 egg plants 1 B. bananas per "Fanny" ..... net	15.68
			263.38

Marco Island was best known for its fruit growing, though it by no means had a monopoly, nor was it less a vegetable growing center. Pineapple growing was once a big industry on the sand hills of Caxambas where the Ludlow family had as much as two hundred acres and a packing plant on Ludlow Bay. On nearby Horr's Island, Captain John F. Horr had considerable acreage and a packing plant, and for a time he also had a canning plant. The Barfields also had quite a field of pineapples but did not specialize as much as the other two.

Pineapple growing was quite general all up and down the sandy coast, east as well as west. One writer noted that everybody had at least a backyard patch of them, and when Fort Myers adopted a city seal in 1885 the symbol engraved on it was a pineapple. This has long since given way to a graceful palm and a leaping tarpon. But Florida pineapples could not long compete with imports from other areas.

On Marco Island one may still see remnants of the once extensive palm, mango, and avocado groves, and on Chokoloskee Island, when most other farming and fruit growing had ceased, one avocado grove extended all the way across the island. The trees grew to enormous size and height, many 100 feet high and 30 feet across. But the 1926 hurricane broke them up so badly that no effort was made to restore the groves.

Adolphus Santini, whose role looms large in this story because he left such a complete record of it, experimented in true farmer fashion with fruit trees on Chokoloskee Island. In 1884 he listed 217 alligator pears (avocados) of which sixty-five were bearing, seventy-five sugar apples, sixteen Jamaica apples, fifteen sour oranges, twelve sweet oranges, 300 bananas, and 125 guavas. Ted Smallwood, on the same site, maintained 250 avocado trees. He packed the pears in barrels and shipped them to Fort Myers and Punta Gorda where he received as much as five cents apiece for them.

It may be said that "everybody" grew citrus fruit, but it grew well only in the upper part of the county. Early reports from Naples refer to oranges and grapefruit in abundance, and there were small groves on Henderson Creek and at Marco, where there were 350 grapefruit trees on the Georgia Fruit Farm on the eastern neck of Marco Island. The severe freeze in the winter of 1894-95 sent citrus growers into the Collier County area seeking more frost free land. Groves were also associated with the early development of Estero and Bonita Springs in the nineties. But the most ambitious project was at Deep Lake, where Walter Langford of Fort Myers and John Roach of the Chicago Street Railway Company planted some two hundred acres of grapefruit. There was also the smaller Welch grove in the same vicinity near Miles City.

The Deep Lake fruit growers probably hoped for early highway or railroad development to get their crops to market. When that did not materialize they constructed in 1914 a railroad from the grove to the head of navigation on Barron River from which the fruit went by barge to Fort Myers where it was packed and shipped.

Barron Collier knew Roach through the streetcar advertising business, and the Deep Lake grove may have been one of Collier's earliest purchases in southern Lee County. He made considerable efforts to develop the grove, but without satisfactory results. The rocky soil was difficult to fertilize and cultivate and it never produced a profitable return. In 1929 Collier invested in a canning plant but the grove was not productive enough to keep it running very long and there were no other citrus sources nearby. Now one must search carefully to find the old trees at either of the Deep Lake groves. Other groves in the county at Naples and Immokalee today appear flourishing but they are small and Collier County is not yet a part of the citrus belt.

The writings of C. G. McKinney, who came to Chokoloskee in 1886 to farm with Captain Richard Turner, reveal some of the trials and tribulations of farmers. The danger of frost was almost negligible, but there might be too much or too little rain. At the head of Turner River just north of Tamiami Trail, McKinney cleared and planted several acres in oranges, grapefruit, pumpkins, sugar cane, rice and cabbages. The crops started out well but soon turned yellow and ceased to grow. The imaginative McKinney called the place Needhelp. He had discovered what many another pioneer farmer in South Florida was to find. While the soil was full of humus and organic matter and looked black and rich, later scientific experiments found it lacking in certain minerals essential to the production of good crops.

Commercial fishing steadily became more important in the pioneer economy and soon became the principal means of livelihood in the county from Naples southward around the coast. This was no new industry in that area as Cuban fishermen and so-called "Spanish Indians" had continued extensive fishing operations there long after Florida became a part of the United States.

The early day fishermen prepared salt fish, chiefly mullet and kingfish, for the Key West and Cuba markets. Boats from Key West began to come regularly in the early nineties to pick up the fish. By the end of the nineties, boats from Punta Gorda, and shortly thereafter from Fort Myers, began carrying ice and hauled away to market the iced fresh fish. Fish and ice houses appeared all along the coast and boats brought ice and other supplies and carried away the catch. Some commercial fishermen maintained their own crews and supply boats based as far away as Punta Gorda.

Mullet was the staple fish of the area, and though the price fell to three cents or lower, fishermen still went out with their nets, catching in their season mackerel, kingfish, pompano, weakfish or sea trout, snapper, redfish or channel bass, and snook. Fishing was done on large and small scales. It might be one or two men in a skiff with cane poles or handlines, or a larger outfit with nets and

The Doxsee Clam Cannery at Marco about 1925.

gear of all sorts. Oar and sail and tide and wind moved the boats until the advent of steam and gasoline power at the end of the century. Steam played an unimportant role in small craft, though some had a small boiler heated with a gasoline burner. Fortunately, at that time the source of fish was nearby so that the equipment was more adequate than now seems possible.

The waters of the Ten Thousand Islands once produced oysters and clams in great abundance. The clam beds extended from Chokoloskee and Rabbit Key to below Harney River, with the largest and richest off Coon Key from Rabbit Key to Pavilion Key. A clam cannery began operations at Caxambas in 1904 and a second at Marco in 1911. Neither community has entirely recovered from the closing of these plants, each of which employed forty to fifty people to handle the canning and an equal number to collect the clams.

At first clams were gathered by hand, or perhaps one should say by foot. The digger located the clam by stepping on it with his bare foot, then reached down to slip a two-pronged clam hook under it, place his thumb on it, bring it up and drop it into a skiff which floated beside him. The diggers worked in water not much more than knee deep and at low tide, but a man might sometimes gather nearly thirty bushels on a single tide, for which he received twenty-five cents a bushel.

Since this limited operations to shallow water and calm weather, it is not surprising that the enterprising Captain Bill Collier invented a dredge that mechanized the process of bringing the clams up from the bottom and made it possible to find clams in water up to 12 feet deep. As the picture indicates, the dredge was a large flatboat or barge with housing for the machinery and twenty-five men who made up the crews. The machine could gather five hundred bushels of clams in a twelve-hour shift. Each of the canneries operated a dredge until the Doxsee Company bought the rights to the Collier invention and the Burnham cannery ceased to use theirs after it sank in a storm in 1929. Doxsee once reported a record day in which his plant canned eighteen hundred bushels of clams.

Turtling was also once an important part of the sea food gathering. Although Adolphus Santini was a farmer and operator of a boat service, his brother Nicholas, better known as "Tino," spent most of his time hunting and netting turtles. Charlotte Harbor was the favorite hunting ground but some of the passes in coastal Collier County were also regular "sets." Santini brought the turtles to Chokoloskee where they were kept in crawls until he was ready to carry them to market in Key West.

In season, people all along the coast gathered turtle eggs and when they found turtles on shore, turned them over, a favorite method of capturing them. Now almost extinct, turtles once came ashore in great numbers in the spring to lay their eggs on the sand beaches. As they left clearly marked trails from the nests back to the water, it was relatively easy to locate the nests. Adolphus Santini records that, on the morning of April 14, 1882, they dug nine nests and on the following morning five more. Since each nest had upward of a hundred eggs, this was gathering eggs wholesale for the turtle egg market.

The large flocks of wild birds that fed and nested in the Collier County area were another important source of income during the last half of the nineteenth century. Hunters and traders in bird plumes preceded permanent settlers there. To be near the rookeries, they established themselves temporarily at various places along the coast and in the islands. The feathers they gathered, sometimes worth twice their weight in gold, were sold in large quantities to agents in Miami and Fort Myers representing New York firms. Most sought after was the plume of the egret, although the Roseate Spoonbill was almost as much in demand and some herons provided marketable feathers.

The ruthless method used in gathering the plumes was ruinously destructive. Because the plumage was most brilliantly colored at nesting time, hunters "shot-up" the rookeries and took the feathers of the nesting birds, leaving eggs unhatched and young birds a prey to starvation or predatory animals and birds. As a result, the flocks that produced the feathers were soon in danger of extermination.

Not until 1901 did the Florida Legislature enact a law forbidding the killing of wild birds at nesting time for their plumage. Enforcement was all but impossible, and to make matters more difficult, the legislators appropriated no money for it. The National Audubon Society undertook to provide wardens to guard some of the rookeries and at least two lost their lives at the hands of illegal hunters.

The traffic was almost impossible to break up. In 1910 the state of New York prohibited trade in domestic wild bird plumes, whereupon feathers from Florida found their way into New York from Cuba and European ports, and Florida hunters went as far afield as British Honduras to find new sources of plumes. Not until the United States a few years later stopped the import of plumes did the industry cease. And perhaps more important, new fashions in women's hats and an aroused conscience had much to do with it.

The demand for wild bird plumes produced a unique experiment on Chokoloskee Island designed to domesticate the birds and produce the feathers. The Lopez brothers were reported in 1915 to have a bird ranch. They had captured nestling birds and were feeding them, hoping to tame them. McKinney reported in his news column that he found the bird ranch a fine sight. The birds were afraid of strangers but knew those who fed them. He saw a lot of them feeding in Mrs. Howell's field where they seemed to be catching grasshoppers. The experiment was abandoned because, among other things, the birds ate too much.

As in all frontier communities, sales of hides and furs played a large part in the economy. Skins of alligators and raccoons went to market by the thousands every year. Coon skins might sell for as little as ten or fifteen cents but they were plentiful and easily caught, and killing them did not seem to deplete the supply. Alligator hides might sell for as much as a dollar and hunters pursued them until they were in danger of extinction. The furs of otter were much sought after as they brought as much as fifteen dollars apiece, but the supply was limited. Deer hides, raw or tanned, also counted in the annual income of many a pioneer.

In a day when hunting and fishing are thought of primarily as

Original type of swamp buggy with hunters and dogs on way to hunt.

sport, it is difficult to understand their importance in keeping the larder of a frontier family stocked to provide variety in the diet. Modern Collier County citizens are mostly conservation minded and think of hunting and fishing in terms of sport, but frontiersmen and sons of frontiersmen can still see meat and money in the business.

Sportsmen did find their way to the Collier County area, and by the time the county was created, catering to them was already a growing business. Naples was the leader in this respect but hotels at Marco, Caxambas and Everglades also served winter tourists who came to hunt and fish. Yachts were tied up for several months near Chokoloskee Island where visitors depended upon men from the pioneer families to guide them in the trackless woods and unmarked waterways.

Immokalee was then, as now, the center of a growing cattle industry, but with what a difference! That was the day of open range cattle roaming which produced what would now be called scrub cattle that sold for an average price of ten dollars a head. It was this grade of cattle that started the oft-repeated story of the Chicago packing house that ordered a carload of three-year-olds weighing 900 pounds. In reply the rancher offered a thousand head of nine-year-olds weighing an average of 300 pounds.

The Collier County area was one of the last stands of open range cattle growing made so famous in the seventies and eighties of the last century on the Great Plains of the American West with cowboys, cattle drives and branding irons, some feuding and rustling. All had their counterparts on Florida ranches, but not on quite such a grand scale. Generally the Collier County ranchers belonged to pioneer families of the area who knew each other and operated amicably.

Literally every frontier family claimed a few cows though they might not often see them, but it was only in the northern third of the county that operations were on a scale that might be called ranching. Indians also kept cattle on the range but as they found themselves in conflict with Whites over their rights there, they increasingly retired from the field. Most of these earlier day cattle were marketed at Fort Myers or Punta Rassa.

Members of the Brown family recall pioneer names, now well known in Fort Myers, that appeared in the cattle business in the Immokalee area before 1900. They kept an eye on the cattle belonging to Captain Bill Tolles and penned some of them for their own use. Tolles himself frequently rode out on the range. Langford and Summerlin and Frazier were other owners of large herds. Two Mann brothers from Bartow and Tom Lybass also became prominent early in this century as cattle ranchers.

Cow-penning was a common practice on the farming and cattle frontier and served several purposes. Farmers split rails from pine trees and laid up fences around patches they wished to fertilize. Sometimes it was land already used, more likely it was new ground about to be brought under cultivation. At night they drove the cattle into the pens where the droppings provided the only fertilizer they used, still pronounced the best by pioneers. By keeping the calves in the pen during the day, they induced the cows to return at night. Besides "keeping up" with the cattle, this provided an opportunity to milk as many of them as necessary to provide milk and butter for the family.

Cattle ranching was not without excitement. One rustler who had been warned by Captain Tolles to leave his cattle alone ambushed and shot the Captain late one afternoon on the range where he was looking after his stock. Tolles received part of the load of buckshot in the upper part of his body. A doctor was summoned from Jacksonville by telegraph from Punta Rassa and driven overland to Tolles' ranch in a surrey drawn by a pair of horses. Though the treatment came a bit late, the Captain survived and lived to a ripe old age.

243

In addition to farming, fishing, hunting and guiding, there were other avenues to a livelihood if not to wealth. At one time or another, nearly every man in lower coastal areas cut wood and many of them made charcoal for the Key West market. To make charcoal they cut and stacked great cone-shaped heaps of wood containing as much as ten cords for a single burning. This they covered with grass and sand to make it airtight except for a vent at the top and enough openings around the bottom to fire the wood and burn it so as to drive out the volatile gases and leave charcoal. A cord of wood produced two bags of charcoal for which there was a ready market. One may still find the burned circles where the firing took place.

When pioneers down near the coast wanted lime, they often made it themselves by firing piles of hard wood and oyster shell which produced ashes with a high lime content. These they mixed in mortar, sometimes containing additional shells for building cisterns and foundations.

In an era where all travel was by water, boat building and boat maintenance were always essential, and every coastal community had its boat designers and makers. The remains of boat ways, one of them still in use, may be seen at the Smallwood place on Choko-loskee Island, and new boat ways appeared on the eastern side of the island in 1957. George W. Storter maintained a similar business at Everglades as did Captain Bill Collier and Sam Williams at Marco. Several builders established Naples as a boating center that has continued to grow there.

Now that the pioneering days are so nearly gone, it is easy to see why old timers like to recall the good old days. One gathers they would not have sought the comforts of the towns in which they now live in exchange for the ways they love to recall. And they are not merely being sentimental. Their lives on the frontier had color, variety, challenge and even abundance of a kind that no longer exists in Collier County or, for that matter, anywhere else. If that existence also had its hardships and limitations, they are in retrospect easily forgotten, so vivid are the recollections of more pleasant and exciting features of life in that not too long ago past.

18

Modern Economy:
Pioneering New Style

THE DECADE in which the county was born, appropriately enough, bridged the gap between the old ways of living and the new. Many of the same words are used to describe the new, and many of its activities have their roots in pioneering days, but the final contrast is sharp indeed. Fundamentally, it spells the difference between an isolated community remote from the main currents of modern life and the same community suddenly transformed by highway, railroad, airplane, telephone, radio and electricity into a part of the bustling and busy modern world.

The pursuits of farming, fishing—both commercial and sports—hunting, cattle raising, wood cutting, guiding visitors to hunting and fishing grounds, and catering to winter visitors are all still there, but with differences in kind and degree. Added in this last generation were road, railroad, and airfield building, drainage, river and harbor improvement, home and city building, real estate operations of near boom proportions, lumbering and oil digging.

The scene of the farming operations shifts from the coastal and island regions to the interior, mostly around Immokalee but also at Ochopee, Copeland, and near Naples. Only now are the potentialities of this activity being realized, as new crops are produced on lands recently brought under cultivation. Though some planting is still experimental, it is big business involving careful planning, scientific management and large capital outlay. And if profits may

Action such as this brings fishermen to the Ten Thousand Islands waters year after year.

be large, the risks are comparably great and losses can be ruinous. Here farming now involves water control, both drainage and irrigation, use of fertilizers, insecticides, fungicides, and careful timing to hit the market on a date selected well in advance.

Much of the guesswork in modern agriculture is removed by the analysis of the soils of the county made by the University of Florida Experiment Station and the United States Bureau of Plant Industry. The prospective grower can study soil maps at the county courthouse, select the type of soil he wishes, and learn beforehand how best to manage it. At this time there is a great amount of land to choose from and roads are constantly being extended into new areas. More often than not the modern farmer proceeds by ditching and diking the land and installing powerful pumps to drain or irrigate as the season demands, though one may still see tomato growers planting fields in the prairies along the Tamiami Trail where nature is expected to maintain a proper balance of moisture.

The completion of the Tamiami Trail and the Everglades-Immokalee road, followed by the coming of the railroad, started the transition from old to new ways of life. The *Fort Myers News Press* on January 1, 1930 reported that a new and nameless town of 250 people had sprung up four miles east of Carnestown in the sixty days since planting time. It was a mammoth tomato farm complete with barracks for workers, store, filling station, stables, garage, tents and packing house. In 1929 J. B. Janes and E. C. Gaunt had been induced by J. F. Jaudon and the Barron Collier interests to move their tomato planting there, and Ochopee, meaning "Big Field," became its name.

Jaudon secured a post office for Ochopee in 1932 and was postmaster for a year before Sidney H. Brown took over the post. The post office was in a general store until it burned in 1953 and the present 7'3" x 8'4" structure was put up to serve both as a post office and a ticket office for the Trailways bus line. By 1935 Ochopee reached the height of its growth, boasting three stores (doubling as commissaries), two packing houses, a big garage and a restaurant. The State Road Department also had an office and camp there for Trail maintenance.

Since then the center of tomato-growing has shifted away from Ochopee, but twenty white families, thirty Negro families and Indians in a half-dozen nearby camps call it home. Farming continues but catering to travellers on the Trail is the main business of the three filling stations and three restaurants. Some of these operate only in the winter season which is also the farming season.

Copeland, two miles north of the Trail on the Immokalee road, also owes its origin to tomato farming. In 1930, the Janes brothers, J. B., Winford, and Wayne, and Alfred D. Webb began farming in the vicinity. Others joined them in extensive operations until the late forties when willow bushes began to take over the prairie lands left to rest between plantings. It was customary for growers to clear the land, plant it for two years, and then let it rest for two years before planting again.

Copeland derives its continuing growth from the location of the Lee Tidewater Cypress Company headquarters there since 1944. Winford Janes has remained there to operate a large grocery and department store business. There is some indication that farming is "coming back," as some eight hundred acres were planted in the 1955-56 season. As farming operations in Collier County expand these "farmed over" lands may all be brought back into production.

The agricultural center of Collier County is at Immokalee where there is continuing expansion both in acreage and variety of produce The land was always good, but access to markets was lacking. J. J. Whidden and his sons and Francis Hall had raised sweet potatoes at Corkscrew, and Fred Whidden, Bob Roberts and Charles Hadley had tried small truck crops with indifferent success.

Modern farming did not really begin there until 1929 when Jim Tooke and Roy Hanchey of Fort Myers planted between thirty and

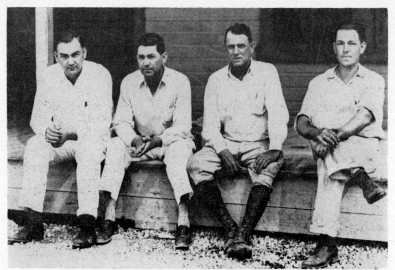

Courtesy of Winford Janes, Copeland.

These four men pioneered farming at Copeland. Left to right: Winford Janes, J. B. Janes, A. D. Webb, and Wayne Janes.

forty acres of tomatoes and eggplant, a big crop for the time. This produce was shipped out by train as there was as yet no good highway. In 1931 Dr. Spooner built the first packing house and Crawford Lee Parrish came from Parrish, Florida, to run it. In 1944 Immokalee growers organized and built their packing house, and in 1947 George Sanders added another, to be followed by C. D. Bethea of Gainesville who began operations in 1949. In 1950 Ewell Moore built for the Immokalee Packing Company, and Tip-Top Corporation, an association of farmers, built another. The State Farmers' Market began operations in 1951. In 1953, when the county celebrated its thirtieth birthday, there were nine packing plants besides the State market, and some farmers continued to do their own packing on their farms.

Tomatoes shared crop prominence with watermelons until 1939 when Jim Tooke planted his first cucumbers, and completed the list of "big three" crops that have led all others in acreage and value. Also produced are yellow crook neck, acorn, straight neck and white squash, okra, peppers, pole beans, eggplant, cabbage, black-eyed peas, green beans, cantaloupes, sweet potatoes, and strawberries. A gladiola packing plant began to operate in 1951, and in 1955 the first planting of Irish potatoes was promising enough to be continued

Bill Brown's Fort Myers-Immokalee Boat Landing "Express," 1897. Rose Brown was the driver.

the following year. A canning plant to process surplus vegetables also appeared a few years ago.

In the fall of 1949 the Board of County Commissioners first voted to employ a full-time agricultural agent. The expansion of that service has kept pace with the rapid increase in farming with its many special problems requiring expert scientific knowledge. The county agent's staff has now grown to four, with offices at Everglades and at the State Farmers' Market at Immokalee. Since October 1, 1956, Bill Wortman has been assistant to county agent Don Lander, serving the more than 100 farmers who in the 1955-1956 season planted 15,702 acres of vegetables. Large landowners and big growers are constantly experimenting with new crops and devising better methods of growing old ones.

In 1955 Collier County's commercial fishermen brought seven and a quarter million pounds of fish to a dozen fish houses, mostly to Everglades and Naples, but in lesser amounts to Chokoloskee, Goodland and Marco. Slightly more than three million pounds were black mullet and nearly a half million pounds were silver mullet. In spite of a falling price, mullet continues to be about half of the catch by weight. Other varieties of food fish that yielded 100,000 or

Shrimp boats lined up at dock in Naples Bay.

more pounds in 1955 were Spanish mackerel, sea trout, snook, pompano, red fish and common jack.

The discovery of new beds in the Tortugas area made shrimp a major part of the industry first in 1954 when, for the first time, netters brought in more than a half million pounds for a total of 1,467,409 pounds of shrimp, which rose to slightly over two million pounds in 1955. Because of their high value, stone crabs also figure prominently among the shellfish, producing 178,680 pounds in 1955.

Only slightly less spectacular has been the growth of ranching, the county's oldest industry. The principal changes were the result of the ending of the open range aspects of the cattle industry. Defenders of the old system prevented the passage of a "no fence" law for two sessions of the legislature after the new county was founded, but finally capitulated. Now all cattle graze behind barbed wire fences. Wild pasture is still the rule on many large spreads and near-wild cattle still are to be found. But improved pastures are characteristic of many new ranches and particularly some of the smaller ones without acreage enough for extensive operations. Combinations of farming and ranching are increasingly common. After a field is planted to crops for several years it may be sown in pasture grasses and used for grazing. Improved breeds are characteristic of

Steers in feeder lot at modern Immokalee Ranch.

the newer ranches. Brahmans seem to be preferred, but one also sees Hereford, Black Angus, Santa Gertrudis and Red Devon.

In 1956 Collier County ranchers withdrew from the Hendry County Association and formed their own Cattlemen's Association. The president of the new group claims more than fifty going ranches in the county, but pioneers in the business, accustomed to more extensive spreads, scoff at the name ranch as applied to small intensively pastured areas even though they may support about as many head of cattle. While a market for vegetables has grown up in the county, cattle are usually sold at Wauchula, Arcadia, Moore Haven and Belle Glade, riding to market by truck instead of being driven as in the old days.

A major problem of the industry several years ago was the battle against the cattle tick which was killing off the animals in great numbers. The prevalence of wild and semi-wild cattle made it difficult if not impossible to round up and drive them through the dipping vats. In the summer of 1948 nine riders were employed by the state of Florida to hunt wild cattle south of Bonita Springs and east of Naples. An estimated twenty-five of the critters, reported warier than deer, had eluded the owner's efforts to corral and dip them, and the hunters' orders were to shoot on sight.

About the same time, a storm of controversy was raised over the decision to kill all the deer in the woods in order to rid the county of cattle ticks. Sportsmen accused cattlemen of merely wanting to save the range for cattle and pointed out that other animals were also host to the ticks. The National Audubon Society sent an investigator who reported that killing the deer would do no good at all. Friends of the Seminole Indians wondered what they would do for meat if this principal source was destroyed. By actual count 8874 deer were killed before the tick quarantine was lifted. The remnant of deer, increased by some brought in from other areas, has gradually rebuilt a considerable herd.

For its early lumber industry, Collier County in 1923 had one of the largest remaining stands of virgin cypress and pine timber in Florida, and, indeed, in the United States. Cutting the main body of the big trees did not begin until the early forties, but they were almost all gone by 1957. The only important big cypress left are in the museum stand at the Corkscrew Cypress Rookery.

Commercial cutting of the timber began on a small scale around the turn of this century, small mills being reported at Everglade, Naples and Immokalee. Related elsewhere is the story of supplying lumber for the building of the town of Everglades and for bridges and other construction purposes on the Tamiami Trail. Any extensive cutting in the interior waited for the development of transportation. The railroad reached Immokalee in 1921, and by 1930 eight small mills were operating within twenty miles of the town. Highways running east and west as well as north and south opened up wider possibilities by the late twenties.

Two mills, one at Naples and the other at Bonita Springs, reached into the timber lands from the west coast. The Clancy Mill, located south of the Trail four miles west of Monroe Station, pushed its logging railroad down into Monroe County and cut the cypress there. At the same time, the Maxcey Mill located east of Ochopee was cutting cypress north of the same highway. Cummer and Sons carried on an extensive logging operation, cutting most of the cypress belonging to the Colliers. This outfit still cuts smaller cypress and the scattered large trees not yet reached by loggers.

The most extensive cutting of pine timber was done by the C. J. Jones Company which operated a mill at Jerome from 1940 to 1956. The principal stands of pine timber were on "islands" in the Big Cypress north and east of the mill location and the logging road was finally extended almost up to the Hendry County line. Jones

End of the logging road. Note skidder trails upper right made by logs dragged up to road.

Photo by Jack Holmes, Coral Gables.

produced finished lumber in contrast to most of the cypress loggers who sent their logs outside the county to be milled. The big trees were gone by 1956 and the owners sold their mill, buildings and equipment. While the mill was being dismantled and before all of the lumber had been moved away, a careless workman started a fire with a blowtorch and burned the remainder of the mill and lumber. At Jerome, Jones had built homes for workmen and a small church. Now that the mill is removed or burned, the church and most of the homes moved away, Jerome shows signs of returning to wilderness.

By far the most dramatic of the logging stories in the county is the cutting of the cypress of the Lee Tidewater Cypress Company which owned about two-thirds of the cypress and one-third of the best pine timber in the county. In March of 1944 the first trainload of these high grade rot resistant cypress logs left the ACL station at Copeland for the mill at Perry, Florida, 417 miles away. A Reconstruction Finance Corporation loan of two million dollars, a favorable freight rate and an about-to-be abandoned mill at Perry were put together to set up the operation. By October 1956 over nine - hundred trainloads, comprising 36,120 carloads or about 360 million board feet of cypress, had moved to the mill.

This logging operation of massive proportions and colorful drama was the subject of an illustrated article in the *Saturday Evening Post,* May 29, 1954, by Jeanne Van Holmes, "Loggers of the Unknown Swamp." Almost half the men spent their time and energies pushing the standard gauge logging road deeper and deeper into the Big Cypress and building and tearing up to rebuild at another place spur lines feeding a mainline that became forty miles long. To bring the ten-ton logs to the road the company used an overhead cable way skidder, an 800-foot cable running from the skidder tower to a back spar tree fixing the limits of the operation.

A year before the trees were to be cut down, loggers girdled the sap outer layer of the big trees to kill them and drain out some of the water weight, for otherwise the trees might break into pieces when they fell. After the lapse of a year the saw crew cut them down and sawed the hundred foot high trunks into thirty-two foot lengths to be loaded on the cars. In extremely wet weather excessive water hampered the loggers but. in season of drouth, fire was a great menace for there might not be water at hand with which to fight it.

In the course of operations, the cypress company built a complete community at Copeland. In addition to the offices and warehouses,

Photo by Jack Holmes, Coral Gables.

Felling trees in the Big Cypress Swamp. Splash made by falling tree.

there are today houses for twenty-nine families of white workers and, nearby, homes for fifty families of Negro workers. Seminole Indians who make up part of the crew live in a large camp they built for themselves. At the height of logging activity in the early fifties, two hundred men, White, Negro and Indian, rode the train out to the swamp each morning. The payroll then was fourteen thousand dollars a week. By 1956, the payroll had dropped to ten thousand dollars a week, giving rise to the rumor that the big cypress is about gone and that the mill will shortly close.

This does not mean the end of sawmilling in the county, but it marks the end of the big virgin timber era. Cypress requires generations to grow back, but smaller cypress left behind and scattered large trees will continue to be cut by smaller organizations, and the faster growing pine will keep a few mills going. The Cummer cypress yard near Immokalee and the cypress poles loaded at Carnestown each winter are more representative of the new era.

Also representative of this new era for Collier County are developments in the continuing search for oil and in real estate.

The only wells now producing oil in commercial quantities in the state of Florida are in the Sunniland Field in northern Collier County. The first producing well was brought in here late in 1943 by the Humble Oil Company, and by 1954 eleven wells with an average depth of 11,575 feet were producing about a half million barrels of oil a year. Other explorations have been made near the extreme southeast corner just across the line in Dade and Monroe counties, and the greater part of the land in the county is under oil drilling lease, but the magic of oil has so far touched the county only lightly.

Real estate changed hands in Collier County in 1956 for a reported twenty-five million dollars, five millions above the previous year's total. This perhaps is the most obvious measure of the somewhat feverish rate at which the county's economy is expanding. And this is rapidly changing the pattern of land ownership. Enough of the county's area is still held in large tracts to provide an occasional spectacular sale, but more and more it is subdivision and development of lands held in smaller parcels that characterize the real estate business. Comparable expansion of streets, water mains, electric service and building construction are apparent in towns and cities, particularly in Naples. New lands are being opened up to farming and ranching, principally in the Immokalee area, and the network of county, state and private roads to serve them grows apace.

INDEX

Addison, Albert, 145-6
Alexander, Ramsay and Kerr, 128, 228
Allen, William, 193-4
Allen, William Smith, 97, 113-5, 116
Allen Place, 193
Allen's River, 113, 234
American Eagle, 86, 221
Andrews, Allen H., 200, 224, 226
Atlantic Coast Line Railway, 53, 130-1, 146, 147, 150, 182-3, 200, 201
Ayers, A. P., 211

Bank of Everglades, 131-2, 211
Banks in Naples, 190
"Barcarmil," 127
Barfield, James Madison, 140, 154, 209
Barfield, Tommie Camilla Stephens (Mrs. J. M.), 154, 157-9, 211
Barron River, 113
Beckner, Lucien, 173-4
Bedell, Deaconess Harriet M., 74-82
Bee keeping, 158
Bertie Lee, 118
Big Cypress, 15, 16, 22, 36, 39, 42, 43, 44, 52, 53, 145, 149, 192, 204
Birds, 23
Bird plume hunting, 240-1
Boat building and maintenance, 142, 143, 145, 244
Boat Landing (also Brown's), 72, 194, 222
Boggess, Charles T., 112, 119-20
Brecht, Dr. and Mrs. J. E., 71, 197
Brown, C. M., 119, 122
Brown, Frank, 195
Brown, William H., 56, 72, 194, 243
Burnham Clam Cannery, 98, 152, 155

Caloosahatchee, 30, 33, 35, 37, 39, 50
Cambier, William, 180, Park, 180, 187
Cane growing, 117
Cape Romano, 19, 47, 140, 142
Cape Sable, 38, 39, 114, 167, 234
Carnestown, 224, 226
Carson, Adolphus, 205, 209, 210
Cat Fish Lake, 52, 53
Cattle, 242-4, 251-2
Cattlemen, 204, 243
Caxambas, 29, 33, 106, 139, moved 161, origin of name 152-3, post office 155,

roads 157-60, schools 156-7, store 160-1
Chakaika, 34-5, 41, 42
Charcoal making, 233
Chatham River, 43, 217, 234
Chokoloskee Bay, 52, 53, 126
Chokoloskee Island, 29, 45, 47, 111, 113
Chokoloskee road, 109-10
Chokoloskee settlement, 96-111, 234, 237, churches, 104, 107-8, post office, 99-100, schools, 106-7
Citrus growing, 237-8
Clam digging, 239
Clam dredge, 143, 240
Clams, 239-240
Cleveland, Rose Elizabeth, 170-174
Collier, Barron G., 83-4, 97, 108, 126-7, 140, 145, 147, 148, 159, 160-1, 207, 208, 228-9, 246
Collier, Barron, Jr., 88, 127
Collier, Chas. H., 211
Collier, C. M., 209, 211
Collier, C. M., Jr., 209
Collier, Miles, 88, 92, 127
Collier, Samuel C., 88
Collier, William D., 29, 140-5, 209, 210
Collier, W. T., 140-1, 147
Collier bus and truck lines, 130
Collier City, 139, 147
Collier County, created 207-8, aerial survey, 215-6, assessed values, 212-3, 214, branch offices, 212, Board of Commissioners, 209-10, 214-5, Board of Public Instruction, 211, Clerk of Court, 210, courthouse, 211-2, exploration, survey, mapping, 13, 14, 36, 215, 216, growth, 218-9, law enforcement, 216-8, population, 212, public debt, 212-3, 214, Superintendent of Public Instruction, 210, 211, tax assessor, 210, tax collector, 211, tax rates, 212-3, 214
Collier County Cattlemen's Association, 251
Collier County News founded, 132
Collier Seminole State Park, 89-90, 223
Comfort, 101
Copeland, David Graham, 33, 42, 53, 61, 87-8, 94, 109, 209, 210, 216, 218
Copeland community, 247, 255-6
Corkscrew, 192, 198-200
Corkscrew Cypress Rookery, 94, 138, 193, 252
Corkscrew Marsh, 18, 192

257

INDEX

INDEX

INDEX